THE GIFT WITHIN THE DARKNESS

HEALING INSIGHTS, HEARTFELT STORIES AND
TECHNIQUES TO RECONNECT AFTER DEATH

BRIAN D. CALHOUN

ANGELS WITHIN PUBLICATIONS

OTTAWA, ONTARIO

The Gift Within the Darkness

HEALING INSIGHTS, HEARTFELT STORIES AND TECHNIQUES TO RECONNECT AFTER DEATH

Brian D. Calhoun

INTERNATIONAL BESTSELLING AUTHOR

Copyright © 2017 Brian D. Calhoun
All rights reserved

Published in Canada
www.angelswithin.ca

No part of this publication may be reproduced in any form or by any electronic or mechanical means. This includes information storage and retrieval systems, without the expressed written permission of the author. The only exception is a reviewer who may quote short excerpts in a published review according to the "fair use" rule of the copyright law.

The scanning, uploading and distribution of this book via the Internet or via any other means without the written expressed permission of the publisher is illegal and punishable by law.

The author of this book does not dispense medical advice nor prescribe the use of any technique as a treatment for your physical or medical problems. You are advised to seek the counsel of a physician as appropriate for your situation. The author intends to offer general information to help you in your quest for general health and well-being. In the event, you use any of the information in this book for yourself, which is your constitutional right, the author and the publisher assume no responsibility for your actions.

Wholesale Orders: Special discounts are available on quantity purchases by corporations, associations, and others. For details, contact the publisher at information@angelswithin.ca

The Gift Within the Darkness: Healing Insights, Heartfelt Stories and Techniques to Reconnect After Death / Brian D. Calhoun
Trade Paperback ISBN-13: 978-1-7752043-0-5
Ebook: ISBN-13: 978-1-7752043-1-2

DEDICATION

To everyone who has experienced a death and the grief that follows this life changing event.

I pray as you read through the following pages you will find the many gifts contained within the darkness and experience your light shining brighter each day. You are never alone; your loved ones are standing by you as you read through this book. They will continue to participate in your lives as you move forward always.

Everyone holds a legacy of treasures to discover. Your loved ones are helping you to open up to yours now with love and light.

Remember death is never an ending; death is the next step within our soul evolution.

Gratitude and Acknowledgements

To the reader and those finding this book at the perfect moments in life: Thank you for the gifts of your support, time and energy. Your love inspires me to share my stories and insights to help you. I hope that you find comfort, healing and the answers you seek within these pages as you reconnect after death. May you feel the enveloping love of your heavenly loved ones with you as you read this book blessing you in divinely perfect ways.

Thank you to the contributors in this book: Thank you for taking the time to share your stories with the readers of this book. Your stories are sure to help someone who has gone through the same pain heal their grieving hearts. Thank you for answering the call to be of service through this book in a way that only someone who has experienced your loss could understand.

Thank you to everyone who are now with us in spirit. The following souls may have left my life but I am truly grateful to have called them my family and friends:

Lincoln Arbuckle-Brown, Eddy Brunet, Elisabeth (Betty) Burns, Brenda Burns, Donald (Don) Burns, "Grandma and Grandpa" Burns, Patrick (Pat) Burns, William (Bill) Joseph Burns, Mable Cadeau, Oliver Cadeau, Donald (Don) Calhoun, Gloria Jean Calhoun, Kenneth (Ken) Calhoun, Millie Ida Esther (Dolly) Burns, Millie Onetta Calhoun, Nancy May Calhoun, Ollie Calhoun, Steven Calhoun, William (Bill) Calhoun, William Reginald (Reg) Calhoun, Andre Chartrand, Pauline Davis, Thomas (Tommy) Dionne, Oli-

ver Flores, Hughie Ironside, Myrtle Ironside, Garry Johnson, Sherman McCall, Mildred Mossop, Edward Murdock, Helene Plante, Terry Recoskie, Helena Savard, Andrew (Andy) Shellswell, Joseph (Joe) Spigarelli, Gordon Spylo, Leonard Webster, Richard (Rick Jr.) Widdifield

Thank you to my animal friends: Blackie, Pepper, Snoopy, Shirlynn, Spicy, Halo, Tiggie and Angel

Without you being a part of my journey in life, soul and death this book would have not been possible. Thank you for your inspiration, guidance, love, light and energy blessing the heart of the reader to awaken them to the many gifts within the darkness.

Thank you to everyone who helped to birth this project into the world from day one. With your support, assistance and teachings along the way this book was made possible. Thank you for your love and all you shared will continue to bless the world.

To everyone in my life and by extension now a part of this book: Thank you for being you, for your time, energy and support with this project. Thank you for the gifts that you have blessed me with along the way as my journey unfolded. Thank you for answering the call of my soul and responding to play the role of a lifetime in my story with a resounding yes.

Thank you to God, Divine, Source, Universe, Spirit, Love and the infinite other names this energy goes by as the Creator & Life force of all creation. Thank you for everything.

From my heart to yours, I love and appreciate you all.

Thank you for being love in action daily.

Brian D. Calhoun

Table of Contents

Introduction 1
The Bereavement Process 9
Types of Grief 21
The Gifts of Mom's Unexpected Passing............................... 29
It is Never Too Late... 47
The Memory of the Light 51
The Gifts Within the Unexpected Loss of the Father 55
Finding Healing and Grace through Grief 71
The Gifts Within Losing One's Parents to Aging or Disease ... 73
The Gifts Within the Loss of Grandparents 85
The Gifts Within Losing a Child 97
Bliss, Heartache, Grief and the Blessings that Come with It.. 117
Rainbow After the Storm 121
The Gifts Within the Loss of a Sibling 125
When it's Dark Search for the Stars 143
A Rude Awakening 147
The Gifts Within Losing Other People in Our Lives 149
The Gifts Within Loss Due to Murder or Suicide 161
Learning to Feel and Heal 177
The Gifts Within the Death of a Relationship......................... 181
Clearing Away the Smoke with Fire... 199
The Gift of Grieving Love 203
Death of a Friendship.. 207

The Gifts Within the Loss of Our Animal Family 211

The Loss of a Pet...221

Minnie's Lessons 223

The Gifts Within Other Types of Loss......................................227

Letting Go..249

Losing a Loved One to Mental Illness.....................................253

We Walk Our Journey Alone..257

Techniques to Heal and Reconnect After Death....................259

The Re-Connection Begins 261

The Gifts of Spiritual Support 263

The Gifts of a Sacred Release Ceremony 289

The Gifts Within Past Experiences...293

The Gifts of Divine Communication 301

The Gifts Within Signs and Symbols......................................341

The Gifts Within Meditation 353

The Gifts Within Mourning Pages 363

The Gifts Within Your Energy Centers....................................367

The Re-Connection Process...387

In Conclusion..393

About the Author 395

CHAPTER 1

Introduction

It was launch week for my latest anthology I had compiled and I was gearing up for the book's release i came across someone offering a 3-month writing and publishing class. The thought of this class made my heart sing and it was beginning within the week. So I followed my heart and took action.

One thing that I have found when something is meant to be and you are listening to the soul guidance, things will naturally fall into place when you take the appropriate action. This was indeed the case with this class when I applied and was accepted within 24 hours. The day before we were to begin, Spirit had inspired me to write a book entitled, *The Gift Within the Darkness*. The rest is history as you now hold that very book in your hands.

When I first started the project I had a faint idea of what the book would be about. The cover had even been shown to me by Spirit. However, I did not have the subtitle or the full details yet.

Over the course of the next 72 hours, I began getting clear on what the subject of the book would be, the purpose, who the reader would be and more. This was attributed to the earlier weekend workshops I had taken part in. I applied that book planning and writing knowledge alongside the wisdom gained from participating in multiple anthologies at this stage of my writing career.

I began writing while continuing to be enlightened throughout the book launch *HALO: Lighting up Heaven on Earth* and the course. This book wasn't written in the usual front-to-back fashion which most people think authors write a book. My intuition inspired and guided me along the way as I started writing the back section of the book.

I knew this section would form a basic course in mediumship which would give techniques to the reader to heal and reconnect with the spiritual realm. With this would also come messages and information that would help improve the quality of the reader's life overall, a theme that would also flow throughout the book.

I felt myself wanting to write a chapter, followed by another and continuing as my spiritual support crew led me along the way. As things developed with the back section, I was gaining further clarity about the front section of the book as it all percolated to the forefront of my conscious mind.

I knew I would draw on my life experiences with death and would invite a few people to write short passages for the book. This would both help empathize what I would write and help the reader heal. They could also share from their own personal experience in areas where my personal experience on the subject is limited to sharing from a spiritual perspective. This first section would help people to understand death from a spiritual point of view and how it impacts our lives in unexpected ways. This would definitely not be your average book on death or the grief we experience after loss touches our lives.

Writing this book was not an easy process for me. I found myself stuck periodically and procrastinating with getting the words downloaded on the page. I would do anything to delay the inevitable of writing what Spirit wanted to share.

At times, the reason was to allow Spirit to prepare me for the next stage and give me further insights.

Other times, mostly it was to avoid going into the darkness so light could heal that part of me. I knew this book would not just be helping others to heal, but myself as well. A part of me was resisting diving into the emotional experiences I would need to in order to let the light shine brighter.

I could not let this go on. I had to find a reason to write which was stronger and bigger than any possible excuse I could come up with.

Spirit was also working with me to keep moving me forward with this book. They figured if I was going to procrastinate my guides and angels would teach me more about writing a book, publishing and marketing it once complete.

With the courses, knowledge and experiences of mine over the last couple years, it became clear Spirit wanted me to self-publish this book. There was clarity that I would help others who wanted to write or publish their own books themselves as well at some point. Everything had a reason for unfolding as it did. Spirit knew what was best to keep me moving forward as we completed this book together.

This book, however, started long before I even knew that I would write such a book. It began the moment my soul incarnated when the divine plan was put into motion on the universal levels. As I began the physical part of my soul evolution, I would begin to experience death in my life. If I was going to be in service to help others along their journeys, my soul physically needed to experience the topics personally.

The first death I experienced within a month of my birth when my Aunt Dolly Burns died. Her death was followed shortly after with the death of my parent's marriage. Death would indeed touch my life in multiple ways and was a catalyst for my life lessons, path and purpose.

The Gift Within the Darkness

Loss would continue to unfold in my life as I would grow up with many of the family members dying. Death was touching my immediate family circle and also those on the outer edges of it. This along with the death in other ways in my life led me to feeling lost in my grief.

Looking back now I can honestly say I was not even aware of this at the time; I just subconsciously embraced it and kept moving forward. In fact, I do not think anyone in my life or I realized the ripple effect death had on our lives. This is also true for many people on the earth.

It was only a few short years into my life and I had already experienced so many deaths. These included family members, leaving a home, my innocence, pet loss, friendships and many others.

As the losses added up, the weight I carried with me took hold as I felt more alone in the world. I retreated into my world of darkness. As a child I didn't want to let others in as in time they would leave and I would feel the pain of loss deeper, so I kept a safe distance between us.

The darkness continued to edge the light out until at the tender age of 9, I would try to commit suicide for the first time. This was something that only my mother would ever truly know about; to the rest that were a part of my life I was just severely sick with the stomach flu. But Spirit had a plan and no matter what I would experience or try, I could not leave this world before my mission was complete.

I was always gifted with a great intuitive sense and many family members used to call me, Mr. Know-it-all. This was partly because I used to pick up or know many things outside the norm. I now realize this was because I was connected to the spiritual realm deeply. Even with this connection I still felt misunderstood and alone (both with family and those in my life). I would put on a mask, gather the strength of a mustard seed and courage of a lion to keep going on; stuffing my feelings down more each day.

It wasn't long before the weight held within my heart made its appearance as body fat. This led me to feeling even more alone. All in a try to protect myself from the outer world's pain that others felt in their own lives. I didn't feel safe to open up about my feelings or what I was picking up around other people. Anytime I tried to be me, others would find a way to make me feel small, insignificant or shut me down. I felt myself dying inside as the world around me was also dying.

I learned that death is a natural part of life and something out of our control, to a degree. But death would continue to knock at my door as I continued to age. It wouldn't just take family members, but also touched our relationships, health, careers, and in many other ways in our lives.

Death is not something one could escape from. It certainly was not a topic people openly speak about around the dinner table or in life. Death was a topic feared by many and only ever talked about when someone dies. It was becoming the silent killer of our soul as people continued to suffer in silence with their grief.

I learned that if we would become more open and talk about what we were experiencing and feeling, we would learn that we were never alone in our pain. Death may touch us with grief in ways that impacted our lives more than we could have imagined but we can allow the gift of healing to take place. Once we recognize our loss and how our choices are influenced by our original experiences, we can allow our hearts to open and shine the light into the world.

I learned everything in my life had a purpose and meaning which was all connected to Spirit's plan to have me help others.

My journey of the traditional and untraditional understanding of death and its impact on our lives would help others to heal and reconnect after death to reclaim their lives. This book was a part of the plan and I thank you for allowing me to be your guide on your journey.

As you read this book, my hope is that you will keep an open mind and heart. Allow the healing energy of the words to flow into, through and to you on all levels. The words shared are just one part of the equation that will help you in your own journey.

As you will discover there is so much more that can't be put into a box and words are restrictive. So as you stay open to the spiritual energy you will learn and experience even more than you could ever imagine at the start of the journey. Spirit is infinite and so is the energy that awaits you within these pages. Sometimes you will only understand one part of the equation at first only to discover with time the other gifts that were awaiting you. So let your heart and soul receive what is yours to accept.

I encourage you to read all the chapters as each has something within them for you from the Spirit world. As you read about the various disguises of death, my hope is that you will feel yourself reclaiming your power to lead a happier and lighter life ahead. Your Spirit friends and family want that for you and even more. They want to help you evolve as a soul having a human experience as you heal your shattered heart.

I hope that as you read this book, you will see how death has touched your lives long after it impacted your life originally. It is my prayer you will receive many healing insights as you read through the heartfelt stories and healing messages from Spirit. My wish is for you to implement the information contained throughout this book. This will allow you to rise out of the ashes and be the powerful light you are.

As you read through this book, you will discover many ways to heal your heart, open up to your soul abilities and reconnect after death. This all will help you live an improved quality of life with your heavenly loved ones by your side.

By the time you finish reading this book and implement the information and techniques into your life you will:

- Feel confident knowing you are never alone;
- Have a deeper understanding into your life;
- Feel lighter and deeply connected to Spirit;
- Received insights, messages and answers to your questions;
- Have had a Spirit communication of your own;
- Feel ready to live and embrace your best life possible;
- See and experience the gift within the darkness;
- No longer fear death;
- And so much more.

I believe by the time you finish reading this book you will have a whole new perspective and appreciation for life, death and the wisdom gained within your experiences. Now let us begin the process of healing and enlightenment.

The Gift Within the Darkness

CHAPTER 2

THE BEREAVEMENT PROCESS

IN ANY DEATH, THERE are various types of grief and five main stages that those left behind will go through. There isn't a set road map to the right or wrong way to go through each. They are as unique as the individual that is going through the bereavement process.

In this chapter, you will find the basics to help you understand where you or family or friends are on the journey with grieving a loss. Please be gentle and non-judgmental of how each may grieve; remember no two people will grieve the same. Allow the mind and heart time to process what has taken place as the soul guides you on how best to serve the needs of the human within us all.

I have included this information as many people have experienced grief but still may need to understand the types and stages involved. This can be particularly helpful for those of us going through it or to in understanding what someone else may be going through.

Please understand not everyone will go through the stages in chronological order and some may not even go through all the stages. Everyone's journey will depend on where they are in their soul evolution, the type of grief one is experiencing and even how deep one is affected. There are so many factors involved that if you were to type "stages and types of grief" into the Google search engine you would get over 12,600,000 results.

In fact, the stages of grief can affect any area of life whenever something traumatic or something ends. This includes the end of a career, a health crisis, relationship ending, the end of your dreams and so much more. The stages involved may unfold in a variety of degrees or intensities. You will go through them somehow and not just after a physical death. Be mindful and allow yourself to process appropriately for your own journey, as needed. Take time to show yourself the love, compassion and gentleness during this processing.

STAGES OF GRIEF

1st Stage: Denial or Shock

This is our first reaction to what just happened after we learn about our loved one's death. We can also experience denial after receiving word about a terminal illness, a health challenge or another type of loss. A part of us may not want to believe what is unfolding and we may react in non-conventional ways after receiving the news. Thoughts like this cannot be happening, this is not real or is this a joke may all cross our minds. These are our normal human reactions trying to make sense out of something that is overwhelming. We are numbed with a disbelief of what has happened.

Denial or shock is our first line of defense that shields us from further pain once that first instinct subsides. During this state, we often go into a spacey state. It is here, we may not know where we are or even what we are saying or doing. We are trying to block out reality and all that comes with it. We want to go into hiding away from the experience as a coping mechanism.

For most people this will be a temporary state, lasting from days to even weeks, but for a select few they can get lost in this state for a longer term. For the vast majority in this stage, life makes no sense or has any real value. A part of us doesn't know how we can go on or why we should. We may question life itself and just go through the motions without really connecting to life. We may even isolate ourselves from the rest of the world as a way to deal with the impact of the first event.

Some older people may even suffer from a form of Alzheimer's disease as they compartmentalize their pain held deep within. I know when my mom died my grandmother began losing herself in her grief over the loss of one of her youngest children.

As a Medium, I have noticed this with a few others who have suffered from this disease as well. I don't have enough information to say this is the root of the vast majority of Alzheimer's patients. But, if we looked into the patient's history before Alzheimer's, I am sure we would discover a connection to a major emotional life event.

Denial or shock is a gift which helps us to process one step at a time. It helps us to cope with as much as we can handle at a time. It is nature's way of helping us accept the reality of loss. This allows us to gain the strength to move forward to deal with what has happened and the pain associated.

2nd Stage: Anger

As our hearts melt from the denial and shock we faced we can now process our pain. It is can be similar to ripping off the Band-Aid to allow what was under the surface to rear its ugly head. This can bring up a flood of emotions to our awareness. Anger is one of the first emotions that will surface in order deal with what has transpired in our world. We begin to take what we are feeling out on those around us and even inanimate objects. We are deflecting our intense emotions from our core pain.

The Gift Within the Darkness

During this stage, we may even take things out on our deceased loved ones. In our minds and hearts, we know that they are not to blame but as the human grieving, a part of us needs to resent them for leaving and causing us pain. A part of us may even feel guilty for feeling angry and this can make us even angrier.

We may even take our pain out on the doctors or nurses who were doing their job and were the bearer of the bad news to us. Remember that despite all outward appearances they too are grieving the loss of their patient. Do your best to be gentle with them; remember you are both going through your own bereavement process.

If you find yourself fueled by anger, walk away for a period and then come back once you calm down. This way you won't be reacting so much and will be better able to process, hear or understand what is actually happening. Anger can often blind us but it is a necessary part of the healing process.

Be willing to allow yourself to feel and go into the emotion. By doing so you will give yourself the gift of healing and then the emotion can begin to dissipate. It is true that what you resist will persist; so let yourself feel your anger. Denying or pushing it down will only make things worse.

If someone comes up to deliver bad news to us, such as finding out someone is terminally ill, a part of us may want to punch the delivery person. Not because we are mad at them, more just because we may be angry over the news. This is normal; this being only one level of what you are experiencing. Walk away and go punch a punching bag or something healthier to help you release your pain. You will feel a little better afterwards. It is only once you peel away the anger that you can then deal with the true emotions underneath. There is no rush here as the gift of time is often the healer.

When we lose someone close to us, feeling abandoned and deserted is normal, and yet anger is the emotion that society fears. There is such strength in anger and in the pain under the surface. The power behind this can scare us because a part of us feels it will suck us deep into the abyss of darkness, leaving us with no way out.

I promise you that you are not alone on this journey and as you process your emotions, your angels, guides and loved ones are right alongside with you. You may even be mad or questioning God and the whole of spirituality. This is okay and normal. Your emotions are valid and so is where you are within your bereavement process. Just take it one step at a time.

Anger can sometimes feel misplaced and like it has no connection to what is going on. You may feel lost in the middle of the sea with no way to reach out for help. However, once you go into the feeling associated with anger, you can then make sense of the nothingness that is loss. You can now begin with a foundation upon which you can build a structure. When you suppress your emotions you will never know the gift that lies within or under the surface of the water.

Let me let you in on a secret: Anger shows us there is truth in something. It also clues us in to how much love lays under the surface.

For me, when someone tells me the truth and I am in denial about it, those saying what they do triggers me into a state of anger. Well not exactly anger perhaps but I am no longer in denial as a part of me has awoken to the truth. I may not even consciously be aware of what the truth is or even want to admit it yet, sometimes not even to myself. In time, there is no denying what was hiding under the surface. Perhaps reflecting on your own life you may find yourself in agreement with this divine truth. This love under the surface fuels us into the next stage of healing.

3rd Stage: Bargaining

When one is processing grief we will go through various thoughts and emotions; this is a part of the normal human reaction to what has happened. However, a part of us will feel helpless and vulnerable with a need to regain a sense of control.

We may find ourselves in a maze of statements including if only we had called for medical help sooner or if we would have recognized the signs, etc... The ego is trying to lead us to find fault in ourselves. We may even try to make a deal with God as a way to delay the inevitable and the pain that comes with it. This last statement can be especially true when someone is experiencing living grief with a loved one.

Often there is an underlying level of guilt at root in this stage. We may believe there was something we could have done to save our loved one. It is here when we may bargain or pray that we will devote our lives being of service for others if God will wake us up from this bad dream; if we can see our loved ones alive again.

We want our life to get back to normal with our loved ones back by our side. We want to find the solution to curing the disease or recognize the illness earlier or stop the accident from happening. Bargaining is just another defense mechanism to help try to protect us from the painful reality of our physical experience with loss.

For each of the stages, no rhyme or reason to how we will process each, exists. There is no set timeframe or order in how the stages will unfold. This can go on for minutes, hours, days, weeks and even months. We can even cycle through each of the stages randomly.

Remember we are responding to something more than just the physical event that unfolded; we are responding to our feelings which can flip like a switch.

4th Stage: Depression

After bargaining comes the darker stage that is an associate of grief: depression. It is a good sign we are now moving into the present. We feel what has been lurking under the surface of our initial stages and emotions; now we are coming into the heart of the loss.

We have removed the rose colored glasses we have worn and which have helped us to get by after the main event. It is here the reality of facing life without our loved one in it hits us. This takes strength and courage to allow oneself to feel all our emotions including sadness, regret, worry and loneliness.

On one side of the coin, we are reacting to the practical implications of loss. On the other a more subtle private part of us needs quiet to process things. Whatever the side we need to know someone is there for us. It could be to give us a hug, say a few kind words, just listen, or lend a helpful hand. That's what any of us wants or needs when we are in this space.

The human in us needs to know we are loved and that whatever we are feeling or experiencing is okay. We are not looking for sympathy, empathy or apologies. Support is all we need.

A part of us worries about not spending enough time with those who depend on us because we have been grieving. There is even a worry about all the things to do after the funeral; such as dealing with the estate of our loved one, wills, payments and so much more. It can become overwhelming for many. We may find ourselves withdrawing from life as we retreat inward and into the darkness.

This depression stage may seem like an unending tunnel where we will never again see the light. As we are processing our emotions we may go to the darkest places in our mind and heart. It can be darker than we could have ever imagined possible. It is important to realize that this stage is not a sign of mental illness.

This is the stage when one could use the support found with bereavement groups or counselors. With the support we can find our way out of being lost in the deep crevices of the abyss. Reaching out is not a weakness; recognizing you need help is a strength. Ask for help to heal your shattered heart; you deserve it.

I know this can be tough or scary even at times. As someone who has suffered many losses in life and found himself lost in the rabbit hole of darkness on multiple occasions, I get it. When someone reaches out to you let them in; they love you and want to be of support. Don't try to be the hero who goes it alone as you came to the earth with a human support crew, let them be of service in your time of need.

If someone you know is suffering in silence and they are not reaching out for the support please don't give up. Keep letting them know you care and that they need not feel alone as many are here for them. Whether you offer a shoulder to cry on or a person to vent to, they need to know someone cares.

Too many people find themselves lost in this stage and unfortunately we end up losing a few to the darkness. If someone is withdrawing and retreating within, keep showing them you love them. This is the time they need you the most. Even though they may not realize it. They may get angry but at least they are processing their emotions and your love will help them in time.

You need not be pushy as you show tough love. Sometimes, we are so far into the dark abyss we do not even realize that is exactly what we need. It is here that gentleness and compassion will go a long way. Small gestures can have a huge impact. Cards, flowers, dropping off a prepared meal or a phone call to let them know you are there for them when they are ready go a long way. And if all else fails one may need to even be picked up and carried to a counsellor or bereavement support group to get the help through this state.

Remember, depression after a loss is normal and natural. We are not broken and need fixing. We don't need you helping us to snap out of it. We need time to process and to know we are loved. Losing someone depresses and therefore depression is a proper response.

Sometimes though situations that one finds themselves in is depressing and they may need help to resolve it. Checking to see where the depression is stemming from is always a good idea as we may be going through something depressing but not depressed. If we find ourselves in the situation long enough, then depression may be an appropriate response.

Depression is one of the necessary steps in healing and processing grief. Much like a fog, depression from loss shall pass in time and the heaviness will lift, revealing a beautiful day ahead.

Like all stages, this too can come in waves. If we don't process, we will find ourselves stuck in a room alone and in the dark without a candle to light. Love yourself to recognize the size of what you are feeling or experiencing with your loss. Allow yourself to process as you focus on the positive memories with your loved ones to help ease the passing storm of emptiness or despair. This way you can reveal the gift in the darkness that is light.

5th Stage: Acceptance

In time, you adjust to life without your loved one physically present. The depression will lift as you reclaim and reconstruct your life, step by step. Each step allows you to continue to process what your new normal will look like without your loved one in the picture.

Remember your foundation was rocked to the core when the death occurred and you need time to reset it. This is what you have been doing on the subconscious level through the various bereavement stages. Now you are ready to rebuild the walls of the house. Building a house takes time; go slow and as far as you can each day with each step. In time, you will have the roof on your new home and it will be ready to move in.

When we reach this stage, we are beginning to accept what has happened. This level of bereavement is a gift that can be a challenge for us to discover. For some people, they never reach this stage as they can never see beyond the denial or anger stage. This is often true when the death was sudden, unexpected or tragic. Examples: murder or loss of a child, or a car accident involving drinking and driving.

In this stage, we make peace with what has happened and withdrawing from the pain of it all. The event no longer holds our power and we are less affected. We will still have our waves of our emotions and grief but have come to terms that our loved one has moved on in their soul journey.

Here is where we accept the news given. We may not be happy but we are in a better place with the situation. There may a level of detachment from the energy behind the grief.

Having said that, it also needs to be said: we may come to terms with what has happened but we can never return to what life was before. This is because of the pain and turmoil we may have experienced in the bereavement process. The damage from the storm and grief has indeed taken a toll on us. All we can do is pick up the pieces and look for a way to move forward. It is here the light begins to appear as we look forward to life a little more each day.

We move slowly towards living a life where we can think about our loved ones without feeling the pain or sadness. We have come to terms that life has good things on the agenda for us and we may even find joy in living life again. This stage allows us to live, laugh and love with our loved ones in heaven by our side.

One Day at a Time

The bereavement process is a profound and deeply personal experience. One has to go through the stages in your own way and time. Often, no one that can understand what we may feel or be experiencing; our journey of grief is unique and never the same as others.

It is a process that can allow us to be comforted, surrounded and supported by others. No one needs to do this alone ever, that is why we have our family, friends and bereavement support groups. This way we can be with others who are also living with their version of grief.

The best gift you can give yourself is the gift of processing it in your own way and time. Rather than resist the storm that often comes with the darkness give yourself the gift of riding the waves and allow the natural healing process to take place.

The journey of processing grief is complex for many and yet it holds many gifts through it. You cannot find the gifts when one is running. You need to stop, breathe and be in the moment to understand or appreciate the gift(s) of each stage that awaits you. When one gives themselves the gift of being present with their experiences and emotions, the world also is gifted. When we are present, we are allowing the gift of processing and healing to take place after a death.

The Gift Within the Darkness

CHAPTER 3

TYPES OF GRIEF

GRIEVING IS IMPORTANT IN the journey after a loss. Everyone grieves in unique and personal ways that may or may not be the same as another. It is important to know there is no right or wrong way. Your way may differ from another person and that is perfectly okay. There is no room for judgment in grief.

> *Grief as defined by Merriam-Webster's Dictionary is "a deep and poignant distress caused by or as if by bereavement; a cause of such suffering; a mishap, misadventure, trouble, annoyance; an unfortunate outcome: disaster."*

We may not even know we are grieving or that the loss experienced deserves to be grieved. Grief is a natural reaction to the death of any type; not just the physical loss of life, However, this includes the death of a relationship, job, career, home and so much more. When something was a part of your life and now is not, a death has occurred and you may be grieving.

There are many types of grief one may experience and may be expressed in physical, behavioral, social and cognitive ways. There are many components to grief and often one will need the help of a bereavement counsellor, therapist or support group to help heal the shattered heart.

There are many books on grief and the various types, not only this, but there are many internet websites for one to research all these in great depth. I am providing you with the basic information to help get you understand a little more about your own grief and the type you may be experiencing.

Absent Grief

When someone does not acknowledge a loss and shows no signs of bereavement in any way. This can be due to being in complete denial or shock related to the death. This is especially relevant when the loss is sudden; one acts as if everything is normal and nothing has happened. This can be of concern if it unfolds for an extended period of time. But remember just because you can't tell someone is grieving doesn't mean they aren't.

Anticipatory Grief

The name gives you a clue what this is about. This is what some may call living grief, as you are beginning the bereavement process before your loved one leaves the physical world. It begins at the onset of deteriorating health or a terminal diagnosis. This type can be difficult for some people to speak about because the person is still alive. The person grieving may feel confused or even guilty about experiencing grief. Let me assure you there is no reason to experience guilt when you are grieving. What you are going through is perfectly normal and healthy.

Chronic Grief

This happens when our stronger grief responses and reactions do not subside. These last over much longer time periods than what may be perceived to be normal. There seems to be an underlying level of distress that does not seem to improve.

This grief can be experienced as hopelessness or even a loss of meaning and value in one's own beliefs. For some it is experienced as an avoidance of anything that reminds us of what we lost. The daily function of the griever is often impaired on a long-term basis due to being incapacitated by grief.

Often the person grieving loses themselves in their mind cycles. One minute they may think about their loss and the next unable to adjust to the fact that their loved one is dead. They may even think about uniting with them.

Support is often needed with this type of grief. If left untreated it can have devastating consequences such as suicidal or clinical depression, substance abuse and more.

Complicated Grief

This can happen when the bereavement process is stretched out severely longer than normal and/or impairs our ability to function. Someone who has lost their loved one suddenly or violently or even multiple people at once often will find themselves in this category.

Complicated grief can sometimes be complex to diagnose due to a variety of factors that include the relationship, personality, life experiences, and other social issues. Grief is often combined with other mental or emotional factors such as post-traumatic stress disorder (PTSD), radical lifestyle changes, self-destructive behaviors and more.

Cumulative Grief

Sometimes, there can be times when we experience a second or third death before we finish processing our first loss. When this happens the effects are amplified for us. It is like pain being piled onto pain, darkness upon darkness or grief upon grief. We call this cumulative grief or bereavement or even grief overload.

For those that suffer from accumulated grief, it can be challenging. They are not only dealing with the most recent loss but the grief associated with every life altering experience before is also triggered. This can sometimes cause them to have an emotional breakdown if they are not ready or equipped to handle such an influx of emotions and memories at once.

Every time we suppress what we are experiencing or feeling we are not helping ourselves or the world. Accumulated grief eats away at us and can be the source of health issues down the line. This is why we encourage you to sit with your emotions, process your grief and get help as required. You will heal and process the many levels of grief and linking experiences with someone by your side. You deserve freedom from the darkness, so give yourself the gift of support by asking for help so you can experience light once again.

Just because you squashed or buried your pain doesn't mean it has gone away. Until you take the time to address it, the energy will wait for processing. Keep adding to the pain and in time something will cause you to blow a gasket. Today, give yourself the gift of processing and you can be free of future eruptions from the past. Give yourself the gift of love, gentleness and compassion as you take it one layer and one day at a time.

Disenfranchised Grief

Often is felt by the griever when others do not acknowledge the importance of the loss which has occurred in the person's life.

People will often minimize the significance of the loss such as when someone's ex-spouse dies, a miscarriage occurs or when pet or even a co-worker dies.

This type often happens when a death is also stigmatized by society. Gang-related deaths, suicide, drug overdose, drunk driving, or disease (HIV/AIDS/cancer/etc) all fit this category. This also includes the non-traditional deaths including dementia, mental illness and traumatic brain injury, amongst others.

Grief is grief; it matters not who it is that we lose in our lives. All losses are felt by people in different degrees and should be acknowledged by our support team. None of us has the right to judge another and if what they are experiencing, going through or feeling is important or not. If they are feeling it, then it is important. That is all that matters. Let's be there to support them in their grief.

Another form of disenfranchised grief experienced by people is when they are caring for someone and this person's health or mental capacities are diminishing. They may not be acknowledging that they are grieving as their loved one is still physically present with us even when they may be absent in meaningful ways.

Distorted Grief

Grief often presenting with extreme guilt or noticeable odd and self-destructive behaviors. There can be anger or hostility directed towards oneself or others when experiencing this type of grief.

Delayed Grief

The regular reactions and emotional responses to loss are delayed until a later date when they can be processed. This is often the griever's way to avoid the reality and pain that comes with loss.

People who had to deal with the funeral arrangements, medical personnel or first responders often push their grief aside until later. They do this to make sure they get through what needs to be dealt with first before allowing themselves to process. This is not limited to any certain group of people; it can happen to us all.

Exaggerated Grief

Often the extreme stress of our grief will cause our normal grief reactions and responses to intensify as time moves on. There are many times that those experiencing this grief will end up with nightmares, suicidal thoughts, abnormal fears, self-destructive behaviors and drug-abuse. They may even have the emergence of psychiatric disorders.

Inhibited Grief

This occurs when one keeps their grief to themselves and doesn't allow themselves to show any typical signs of grieving to the outside world for an extended period. Often problems will arise when one doesn't allow themselves to grieve through physical manifestations and somatic complaints. These can include pain, nausea, dizziness, fainting and other body problems.

This is why so many people who suffer a death of some sort end up sick at some point. It is also an important reason to allow the grieving process to unfold.

Masked Grief

People that are experiencing this form of grief often don't recognize that their physical symptoms or other out of place negative behaviors are related to their loss. Their reactions are impairing normal functioning. This is very much like wearing a mask hiding our scars from grief underneath.

Normal Grief

This is the grief that one may predict or expect to go through after a loss. Let me restate here there are no set rules or regulations to what dictates normal grief as one it is as unique as the individual that is grieving.

Generally, you move through the bereavement process and come to a gradual place of acceptance. The intensive emotions lessoning along the way from what you felt at the onset. Most people can maintain to function with their basic daily activities.

Secondary Losses

Sometimes when a death occurs in our lives, it has a greater ripple effect in our lives creating multiple losses that stem from the original loss. Our grief isn't only about our loved one's death but it also is related to subsequent losses that occur because of the primary loss.

An example would be the death of a spouse. Not only did your spouse die you also lost your best friend and your marriage at the same time. Perhaps you lost the secondary income, leaving you forced to sell your home and now you have another death that is a result. The ripple effect continues with the loss of your neighbors, perhaps even the city you lived in and so forth. I am sure you can see how the ripple can keep expanding.

In Closing

The above list is by all means not complete. It does gives you a good starting point to understand what type of grief you or someone you know may be experiencing. I encourage you to research the types further if you want to understand them deeper.

We all experience various types of grief as we go through life. Reaching out and having support along the way is helpful for everyone. Explore various bereavement support groups to heal and reconnect to life.

You have a choice in how you feel and your loved ones want you to get better. Take one step at a time as you work your way through the darkness and into the light of day once again. It may not always be easy, but it will be worth it.

Love yourself to free yourself and to live with the memory of your loved ones and in their honor. They will be eternally grateful as you do.

The Gift Within the Darkness

CHAPTER 4

THE GIFTS OF MOM'S UNEXPECTED PASSING

ONE THING I HAVE learned over the years is sometimes the best gifts come when you least expect them. The gifts that often show up when someone you love unexpectedly dies can be enlightening in so many ways.

When my Mom died, it was one of those unexpected deaths, as she had just turned 51 years old barely a month before and was fairly healthy. So when my younger sister called to let me know what had happened, it truly was unexpected. Or was it?

A few days before my mom died she made the rounds on the phone calling everyone, unbeknownst to anyone else at the time. Her soul was guiding her to call to touch the hearts of all to share her love and say her final physical goodbyes. Was she conscious of this fact?

Now having read many books and spoken with many people afterwards this seems to be a common theme. Many souls seem to know when their time is drawing near and reach out to those they care about. Many people will say the interactions were out of the ordinary or unusual. There is something about the days leading up to the death that feels off or that we don't make sense of until after they cross. It is then, usually, that we completely understand what it was.

For me, when I received that phone call, I was at work so mom had left a voicemail. I planned to return her call the next day when I had more time to talk. That Saturday evening after my shift at the restaurant was finished, I had other plans. Being a 30 year recently single guy I was trying to get back out into society and create a life of some sort after the death of my romantic relationship. My priorities were out of whack at the time like many young people in the prime of their lives or so they think.

The next day came and went, and before I knew it was Tuesday and once again I was at work. But still, no phone call made as I was just caught up in life. Never once did I think time was running out; though a part of me had picked up something on the voicemail that Mom had left. There was a sense something was seriously off, I could sense something which felt like someone in a health crisis or perhaps even dying. I chalked it up to something going on health wise with my sister, niece or even grandmother. Going through the usual suspects who had health issues going on that might be serious enough to warrant such a call.

So on Tuesday when my 13-year-old sister, Jamie, called me and left a message, I knew I had to get home to return the call. As my boss was driving into the parking lot to take over closing up the restaurant, I was already half out the door. We passed each other on his way in when I let him know something was wrong and left. I got home and returned the call. My sister's father answered and informed me of the news.

I knew it was true and went into the state of shock. At the time I did things that normal humans would not be doing such as getting into the car and driving back to work to inform them I would need time off. Thankfully, my boss's wife was still there as he had already left; I shared the news as we sat and chatted. She then drove me home as she knew I was in shock, even though I didn't at the time.

I didn't want to be at home alone, so I made plans to join the boys and girls at the club for a bit. Now I don't drink but that evening I had a few which went down a little too quickly. It wasn't long before I was feeling the effects of the alcohol on my system. Thankfully I had my marbles still and thought it was best to go home and get ready to drive the 8 hour trip home the following morning.

The next day I went to pick up the vehicle from the work parking lot and away I went to begin the journey north.

Spirit Always has a Plan

I often am reminded that there is a reason for everything and that spirit has a plan; even when we may not fully understand things at the time.

A few weeks before we had hired someone new who had requested a six week holiday for a previously planned trip. That time off started a week before my Mom died. He and his partner left one of their vehicles for me to use while they were away, a gift in itself. This made my travel home much easier and was definitely not a coincidence.

At work, we were dealing with being short-handed already with him gone, and another co-worker also dealing with the loss of her mother. Thankfully, she was returning to work in a day, so when my mom died it was perfect timing on the work front for them.

Looking back, I can truly see that spirit had a plan and was definitely arranging everything. All to make things as easy as possible for me (and for all involved) during this time. Even Jamie calling me was unusual as no one knew she had called me earlier or even that she had my number. Something bigger was in play for sure.

We are Never Alone

I took a few minutes along the way to keep my sisters and everyone in the loop about what time to expect me. This allowed me a moment to relax and breathe.

The trip was flowing until I had to stop on the side of the road to fill up the windshield washer fluid. Nothing unexpected there; as with the mix of wintery road conditions and transport trailers on the road I quickly used it up. It was during this stop that I got out quickly and found myself locked out of the running vehicle. I must have hit the lock button on the way out. Here I was now stranded on the side of the road during mid-January winter conditions and without a coat on.

I soon knew I was being watched over. Everything was set up perfectly for this moment. Where I had pulled over was met by a side road and off in the distance about 300 meters was a shining light.

I ran towards it as there seemed to be a small house beside it, knocked on the door and was met by a family just sitting down for dinner. I apologized for the interruption and explained my dilemma and they graciously agreed to see what we could do about getting me back into the vehicle. As the generous-hearted man got ready, I ran back up to the vehicle at the highway intersection and waited for him.

He drove up, bringing a coat with him for me to put on while we attempted some MacGyver techniques to get the door open. It wasn't rocket science through as we noticed that there was a slight opening in the window. Being an older vehicle we could use a metal coat hanger to unlock the door. Thank God for the older lock system which allowed us entry into the van quickly.

Within minutes I was back on the road and the man at his family table for dinner. Spirit was definitely watching over me and making sure I was supported all along the journey of this trip with the help of this angel.

Having traveled the highway many times throughout my years living up north both as a child and adult, I know the roads and area fairly well. I know exactly where I was as I had literally just passed a local known highway eatery.

To this day there is no sign of this road or the house at the end of it. I have searched high and low for anything that would look familiar along the area in case I may have been mistaken about the location. I remember the man even saying the name of the person who we may have had to call for help if we couldn't open the door ourselves. I remember him saying they lived right by a well-known local highway spot just down the road.

This was a true mystery or was it an angel sent from heaven? Either way, thank you.

The Family Connection

An hour later I was home with the family and surrounded by love. It was weird as here I was sitting on the couch where my mom had fallen asleep the day before never to open her eyes again; sharing plans and conversations with my Aunt Pauline, two of my sisters and my youngest sister's father. Before long we all adjourned for the evening as the next day we had the family coming into town and the wake for mom.

I slept at Mom's apartment that night and my aunt stayed with me. It was truly a heart-wrenching experience to see all mom's stuff and the way she had lived. All without her physical presence. Despite this, it somehow comforted me and allowed me to be closer to her for this time surrounded by her material belongings.

The next morning my aunt and I chatted further, went for breakfast and met up with the family. During breakfast I learned that my aunt used to read tarot cards until she saw a death in the cards and put them aside, never to read again. I have since learned that it was my mom's death and her own that she had read in the cards, which frightened her so. It truly was just another connection that myself and my aunt had in common as it was just a year earlier that I learned to read the cards myself.

The next day was a blur as the many stories were shared, laughs, tears and the unexpected gifts continued. The day of the funeral we discovered my mom had an insurance policy that was taken out when I was a child. It wasn't much, but the proceeds were left to my godmother, who was another of my mom's sisters. This truly caught everyone off guard at the time.

My Aunt Carole, the benefactor, made the choice to split the funds equally between my sisters and me. She didn't feel it was right that mom left it to her. But as a young mother, I believe mom took out this policy in case of her early death. This would make sure my aunt and uncle (my Godparents) had the financial support to help them with the raising of me should a need arise when I was young.

Throughout the week I was definitely in an altered state as I was avoiding letting myself process what was unfolding. Even though I was crying and such in person, much of it was behind closed doors, alone.

I remember going into the bathroom at the funeral home and just feeling out of my body in some way as I hid away from everyone. Heck, I went outside to get away from everyone at one point as well. After the funeral, I wanted to be left to my own devices. The family gathered at my cousin's place and I just wanted to crawl into a hole. A part of me that was dead inside and yet screaming to be heard. I tried to open my mouth and nothing would come out. It was like I was two people and neither was present.

Brian D. Calhoun

A Spirit in Unrest

The funeral went by and it wasn't long before I was back at home trying to live life. You would think that would be it, but for the next 4 months, things got worse as I went down the rabbit hole of darkness. It didn't help that I was being tortured in my sleep with vivid memories of my mom and even seeing her in the coffin; rotting away. I would wake up sobbing, my pillow wet from the tears of the night.

Dreams are expected after the loss of someone close to you. It is during them we can process our life experiences and emotions of the day. For most people they would have a visitation with their loved ones during this time, but, for me, that was not the case. I had nightmares upon nightmares. This went on nightly until that fateful day just before Mother's Day when it happened.

After my mom's death, my sister had unanswered questions. She tried to get the coroner's office to do an autopsy, as one was not done at first. This was due to some misunderstandings after she was pronounced dead. After a lot of back and forth and red tape, my sister finally was able to have one done. I personally didn't need to know the reason for mom's death as I was at peace with it, but she needed answers so I didn't speak up. This was one reason for the nightmares for me, the other being that mom's spirit was not at peace with all this going on.

After months of my sister talking to me about things going on with the city, the coroner and such forth, that fateful day arrived. Just before Mother's Day that year they exhumed my mom's body and performed the autopsy. The results were inconclusive, but it was leaning towards something to do with the heart, confirming what the original report had said. Not surprising seeing that heart disease runs in the family.

It was after this that I finally could sleep better as I wasn't sensing my mom's restless soul further. I could finally process things without my sister constantly updating me, asking for money to help with the costs, or other related stuff.

The darkness continued to take hold as I went through the various stages of grief, getting stuck along the way. I couldn't process this loss in a gentler way. With my guilt over not returning mom's call and everything that led up to and including the autopsy, it all took a toll on me. My mom and I were close in life and so her death was hard on me, perhaps harder than most would think as I internalized everything.

The First Year

The first year after her death was one of the hardest on me because I had all the firsts to go through; the first holiday, the first birthday, the first gatherings, etc… At times, I would cry like a baby having his toys taken when all he wanted to do was play with them. The tears would come at the least expected moments whether it was at work, out walking, socializing or watching television. Heck, I would even wake up in tears crying and not fully even knowing why most times.

While I was processing, I took comfort that mom was with me and watching over us all. I can't say I saw or felt her presence, it was more a knowing at the time. I would reach up to her, talk and ask for help with life's problems. I began having heavenly conversations regularly and also noticed a change happening with me; some of which were for the better and some for the worse perhaps, all depending on one's perspective.

My hair color was one of the first things that shifted as I went from dark to light for a period. This wasn't a major thing as I often changed it throughout life. Though looking back, I can see that it was my grief and wanting to be close to my mom had brought about this change. I was mimicking mom as while most people weren't aware of it, my mom's hair was naturally dark but she dyed it blonde for most of her life. So unless you knew her from her younger days you never would have known her natural hair color unless pictures came into play.

This wasn't the only thing I was beginning to mimic either. My weight shifted as I packed on the pounds of pain. I ate hoping to find peace from the deep pain I was in. I would often find myself eating or craving foods that turned out to be foods that mom would enjoy. The very foods that as a chef I would often make for her. I didn't even realize this for many years at the time until I was searching for the key of my weight gain and saw the connections. I was grief eating and not only that but I was also going down the rabbit hole without turning any lights on.

Darkness set in and I found myself losing myself along the way. The things which I enjoyed often put on the back burner while I sat in front of the television and stuffed down my emotions with food. I stored the pounds of pain on my body as I slowly withdrew from living life to the fullest; the light fading further into the background. I would cry at commercials or at the drop of a hat, never knowing when the wave of emotions would hit me. Life would never be the same again.

I was no longer enjoying going out to listen to the music or dance as I tapped my shoes on the floor for hours at a time. This was a pastime, I normally would have enjoyed doing a couple times a week after the death of my romantic relationship to meet others and get out of the apartment doing something. The acquaintances and friends were dropping like flies dying from the lack of oxygen without my time and energy feeding them any longer.

Work at the restaurant was the only thing that was ever present and often the only thing that would get me doing something outside of home throughout my days. I often worked 7 to 14 day stretches while my health deteriorated. Unbeknownst to me, my body was dying on the inside as my emotions were trying to break through the surface to be healed.

The Gift Within the Darkness

Sure I knew that I was gaining weight but what I didn't realize was I was throwing myself into my work to avoid the deeper issues. I didn't want to face that I was depressed and didn't want to continue on without my mom in life. I just wanted to hear her voice say, I love you, one last time. Even more important, I wanted her forgiveness for the lack of communication during the month before her death and not returning her call. Yes, a mother's nature is to forgive her children naturally, but I needed to hear and feel her releasing me of the burdens held within my heart.

A part of me was angry and acted out like a child who was pissed off with the world. Another part of me knew what I was going through was a natural and normal part of the bereavement process. I honestly didn't know what emotions to feel as I was having a mixed bag of them, either separately or all at the same time, in some instances. I felt like a part of me was going nuts. In the early days after the loss, I had felt that I needed help and reached out, but before I could get the support I so desperately needed I shut the door. In fact, it was more like slamming it closed even before I had fully opened it.

God knows that I wasn't getting the support at home, being single. I sure would not let others know how I truly felt on the inside; about how I felt I was going to explode at times. If I allowed myself to even go within myself it scared me how dark it felt. So, I sure as hell would not put myself into a vulnerable place with a bunch of strangers. Even if it was a group who would understand what I was going through as I spoke about the darkness held within me. Growing up I had tried multiple times to open up and was consistently shut down, so why would this time be any different?

Many years ago, I had shut off the valve, not allowing others the opportunity to be present and give me the gift of support while being true to myself. Something that my mom had often done at times as I reflected on the times we shared. She often learned to process her own emotional states by going within and never revealing her own emotional pain much like I did for most of my life.

The Bonds that Tie Us

My mother's death was one of the greatest challenges of my life. This makes sense when we think about the fact she carried me for nine months and physically gave birth to me. Add to that the whole loving, teaching and guiding part that parents do and the fact she supported me however she was able to. Like any parent, she may have had her faults but the unconditional love was there for us children and she showed it the best she could.

A mother and child bond is unlike any other relationship. It will always be one of the strongest as it comes from sacred space and is nurtured with the blood that runs through their veins. A mother's bond with her child is a gift and one that is hard to sum up in a few words. It is one based in love and light without end. It is something which continues long after the soul exits the body. The soul that plays a mother is often one that will put the child above all others.

Children don't always appreciate how deep this bond with their parents can be, especially the connection between a mother and her child. The bond is often only felt, known or even understood after their loved one crosses to the other side or they have children of their own. This death hurts us deeper than we may want to give credit for. After all, this bond runs deep to our soul.

A mother has felt you long before you were born and knows your energy better than anyone else. This is the reason they have such a deep intuitive sense when it comes to their offspring. When the child becomes a parent, they too understand the power of this bond.

I have known this bond with my mother growing up and understood it better only after her death. Thankfully growing up my mom was there for me unlike no other person was in my life; loving, supporting and protecting me, sometimes from myself. She saw gifts in me I didn't even recognize myself at first and helped to nurture them into the world.

I remember we would play these psychic games at the bus stop or out shopping or whatever we were doing. I didn't appreciate the weirdness of these experiences at the time, but looking back I now can see the reason for them. She would often test me in a variety of ways with my gifts but never truly communicated why she was doing them. Had she shared her reasons, perhaps, I would have been more open minded. If not, at least I would have a better clue what it was all about.

The gift of my mom's unexpected death was opening me back up to my truth, light and natural gifts. Though at the time it seemed as if darkness only existed. In a sense, the present being offered allowed myself to feel, connect and open up to others. But, my fears kept me in the crevices of the shelter I had built many years ago; the very shelter that was beginning to show signs of age and wanting to be nourished with love.

Throughout the years I kept going deeper and deeper into this dark hole, almost as if I was trying to see just how deep it went. But the thing was never ending and eventually I needed to realize that and make a shift. Thankfully, I knew someone else who knew how I felt to a degree.

My sister, Sheri, who I grew up close to as children and I reconnected after mom's death. She became somewhat of a lifeline to other family members; keeping me in the loop of the family drama and such forth to a degree. So anytime someone was going through a health crisis or even found themselves staring into the eye of death themselves, she would give me the details. This was a gift as I didn't need to put myself into the drama of the family as we often didn't see eye to eye on many subjects. This can be the case with most families though.

I often felt like the outsider, something that my sister and my mom often felt as well with many of our family members. This became very clear at my mom's funeral when many family members didn't even make an appearance or reach out to me. We all have our own way to deal with death and a life to lead so whatever their reasons, it was a choice that was theirs to make.

To this day my sister and I stay very close. Almost as close as we were as children who spent time together doing weird and wonderful things. It is a gift we both aim to nurture all the days of our lives together. Death has taught me to appreciate who and what is in our lives each day.

I learned a long time ago that family is what you make of it and who you invite into your space. You may or may not have the same blood running through the veins but the choice always remains ours who we connect to as a family. Family is there for you no matter what is going on in life. While they may not always be present, they maintain a connection of sorts. This is true even when the pathways take you down different highways.

I learned that to be accepted as who I am, I first had to start with accepting myself. For life begins within the heart and soul. We are perfect and whole in every way. We do not need anyone to feel that divine truth as it lies within us always.

Opening to Spirit

The journey continued on for years as I started down the path of reconnecting to spirit as I learned more about my natural spiritual nature, gifts and abilities. The gift of my mom's death allowed me to open up further to the divine plan that was put into place in our spiritual contracts on the soul level. This is something I will discuss in other chapters of the book. It was through this that I understood my reason for being on the earth and part of the reason for my mom's soul leaving the body.

I continued the journey of Reiki, learning more about angels, card readings, and also about my intuitive and psychic gifts. I began being of service to others further as I stepped into the role of teaching, doing healing/energy work and readings. It was along this journey I began to understand the various life lessons and experiences that unfolded in my life which caused a softening of the hardening dark heart. Light was breaking through once again.

About five years after mom's death, I was taken on a life review by my spiritual team to help me understand many of my life experiences. Through this I was able to heal, forgive and find peace with love leading the way.

The weeks leading up to this event I had been getting the intuitive insight on a variety of subjects. This included that I was not the first in my family that had the gift; that I was a fifth generation psychic-medium. I kept passing it off, after all, no one else was a psychic-medium in my family. On one level, this information was false but on a deeper level it was ringing true. The ringing kept getting louder each day.

How could this be so? Yes, there were family members interested in the field but that was about all. My Aunt Pauline even had done readings for a short time before she saw death in the cards and stopped. But no one else went down this path. This information I was intuitively being shown wasn't making sense still.

However, when the life review unfolded, I clearly understood on deeper levels as they showed me the various connections. They also showed me how my mom was gifted, how she meditated and used her gifts; not only her, but my grandmother and past generations as well. They helped me connect the dots and understand each one that much more.

When the review unfolded, my mom made her first appearance since she had died and I had experienced the darkness. Her appearance in my apartment came when I least expected it. Talk about an overwhelming experience, healing and insightful all at the same time; especially so with the life review underway and her presence.

I sat on the couch with tears streaming down my face while I sobbed trying to catch my breath in between wiping my eyes or blowing my nose. This was a blessing I had asked for which spirit answered in the perfect way and time when I was ready on all levels. Spirit always knows what is best for us even if we think we know better.

In the life review, I could see that my leaving my hometown broke my mother's heart again. I was her first born who told her he was moving eight hours away; just days before the actual move took place. She had no warning or anything, the relationship she had with me was ending as we entered into a new phase. A few years before my sister, Sheri had also moved out of town, so me leaving affected mom deeply.

I could also see how her heart was broken many years before. The first time being when her relationship with my biological dad ended. The forced ending of her relationship with my uncle being second and then the other men that followed. Each break up affecting her heart differently.

I understood my mom and could appreciate all she had gone through in life, and I finally understood myself, and my own experiences deeper. A sense of peace was within me despite the initial tears and being overwhelmed through it all. I found forgiveness, compassion and understanding for many, including for myself. I was now ready to reclaim my life.

Over the next while I began opening up to the light of my highest self and embracing it fully, more each day. Sharing my new found zest for living as I began the next phase of living.

Sure, I still get weepy at times and miss my mom, but I know she is always with me as one of my guides.

The darkness has subsided as the light continues to heal and open me up to new levels as I share my gifts with the world. This all now allows me to help those I come in contact along my journey connect with heaven's messages; a path that will continue all the days of life and beyond I am sure.

Spirit continues to both teach me daily and shift my perspectives while I am living life. This happens even as I am in my dream states where I often have out-of-body experiences. I often will visit with Mom spiritually and prepare for the days to come while back at home in heaven. It is then I come back into my body to go through the earthly journey. I feel so blessed and know I am a work in progress like all of us.

I don't claim to know all of life's answers. But I do know whatever I need to know, Spirit will always find a way to get the information to me. It could happen through a book that I am reading, or through a connection on the streets. Spirit knows me well enough to know what way will work best, so I just let go and trust in the process.

I now understand when I meet my soul family members and easily recognize them when I do come in contact with them even if in passing. All this and many more blessings which have opened up since my mom left the physical for the soul journey. This all is a gift in itself and something available to us all when we open to spirit after losing someone close to us.

The unexpected death of my mom truly is a gift that keeps on giving in ways I am constantly discovering.

Brian D. Calhoun

Prayer for those Grieving the Unexpected Loss of the Mother

Dearest Mother-Father God,

We come to you in our hour of need to ask your ever present help. Please heal our broken hearts over the unexpected loss of our first love, our beloved mother.

We ask that you send your angels to be by our side as we go through our bereavement process in our own way and time. We ask that you help us open our hearts to the light of our mother's healing light and love.

Help us forgive ourselves and our mother as required. This will allow us to be at peace within the new relationship we have with our mother, who now rests in heaven.

Where required help us understand and have compassion for our family and those tied to our mother. We know they are too grieving the loss in their own way.

Help us be gentle with our relationships with ourselves and all those that we come in contact with over the days, weeks and months ahead.

Help us be an instrument of your motherly love, God; the love that is eternal, ever present and powerful beyond words. Help us as you open us to our natural gifts, abilities and our soul path now forever more.

For all this even better, we give our thanks and so it is done.

Amen

The Gift Within the Darkness

CHAPTER 5

It is Never Too Late...

Marie-Hélène Fortin

THE DAY MY MOTHER passed away was one of the most unreal days of my life. But the story that followed, years after her passing, is simply magical.

I was 23 years old and scheduled to go out of the country for a few weeks. Before leaving, I made sure I got in touch with my mom's doctor, as she was ill. I asked him, "If it was ok for me to go? How much time did I have?" He let me know that "it was fine and I had time to go away." So I did...

My mother and I did not have the best relationship. She was ill for many years while I was growing up. I was not aware of it until later in my teens. She was suffering from a mental illness. I have never known all the details or the whole story. All I knew is one day she was living with us, and the next she had left. As a teen it left me bitter, sad, in pain, and angry. All I felt was abandoned.

It was a warm June day when I received a call. My mom had passed.

I sat on a chair with the phone in my hand. I remember twirling the phone cord in my fingers anxiously. I could not speak.

The Gift Within the Darkness

This was not real. I had time the doctor said... After a few minutes of listening to the details, my mind unplugged and my heart started to swell and hurt. I was physically in pain; like someone had surgically removed a piece of my being. I cried, and cried, and cried. I hung up the phone and my instinct was to go outside. I laid under a tree and my tears ran down my cheeks, my neck, my shirt, and finally to the ground.

In the last year before her passing, we had begun to get a bit closer. We loved each other, and we were both trying, in our own awkward way, to reconnect. There were many feelings from the past intertwined in those moments for us both. So much sadness and fear of losing her but still so much anger and confusion, from many years before when she left and when I felt abandoned.

After mom crossed over to the other side, I received what we call "visitations" from her. She would come to me in my dreams which were so real. It was truly her and I meeting beyond the veil. With time the dreams dissipated but not all the conflicting feelings inside me.

Now, this not just any ordinary story of loss. What if I told you that, more than 15 years later, my relationship with my mom is thriving and better than it had ever been while she was alive? Let me explain this how this is possible.

As the years passed, after her death, I came to discover and really know my life purpose and be able to use my abilities to help others heal. As a healer and a sensitive soul I feel deeply. Being an Empath, one of my many gifts is to be able to communicate with departed souls. I am very grateful for this gift as it helped my mom and me to heal our relationship. I know that this may be hard for some to grasp. You may wonder how a relationship can heal when someone is not physically any longer with you. It is simple, my mom and I have something in common: we are made of energy. Just like all of you and your loved ones.

It started with me feeling a presence with me, which I just knew intuitively was her. She kept finding was to let me know she was with me, but for a long time, the teenager in me was holding onto the past. I remember often telling people that I missed "having a mom." I would never say that I missed my mom. There was lots of forgiveness work still to be done.

It wasn't until a few years ago, when I went through a major healing crisis, that her presence became stronger than ever. As a healer, I had developed many relationships with like-minded and gifted people. Many of them were mediums. Mom would take these opportunities to come through very strongly to deliver messages through them to me.

Something in me started to shift as I was healing. I was now ready to start a dialogue with my mom. I had so many questions for her. So many "why" questions related to her decisions and actions, and she had all the answers. The more we communicated, the more the heaviness that I held in my heart and body, dissipated. Eventually, a few years later, there came a time when I did not need a third party to help have a two way conversation with my mother.

It was us both being able to take time to truly communicate our feelings. Her being able to tell me how sorry she was for what had unfolded while she was alive and her listening to my side of the story. This all helped to bring closure and relief to her along with me. We don't stop growing and healing just because we have crossed to the other side. It is here we often learn and understand that which has unfolded which helps us to heal further.

I remember the day I thought how amazing our relationship was. How I could feel her love for me and how I could share mine with her. How complete I felt. That piece that had left my body the day her soul left the earthly plane had been filled again with light, love and peace.

Indeed, it is never too late...

Marie-Hélène Fortin is one of the co-authors of HALO: Lighting up Heaven on Earth

CHAPTER 6

THE MEMORY OF THE LIGHT

Robyn Dewar

AT THE VERY CORE of who I am today, I celebrate the journey that has brought me to this moment. It is the memory of the light that reconnects me with my highest self. Being surrounded by love lifters during a time of healing and a change of perception has imprinted on my heart a dedicated commitment to a beautiful state every day.

Starting in my teenage years, I began to experience an unhealthy inner dialogue. This self-talk spiraled into a complex place of self-hatred. I am grateful at that time in my life, I discovered song writing and this musical outlet became a healthy form of emotional release. Writing words on paper was my attempt to make sense of some very dark thoughts. As I moved into adulthood, I did not feel worthy of communicating to my loved ones about this inner turmoil going on. I felt lonely and detached from the outside world. I was suffering in silence.

In the winter of 2009, my emotional world was numb and it was as though I was living in a frozen existence. Due to family challenges, my marriage had been slowly breaking down. My Mom was also very ill and dying. I just would not allow myself to shift my perspective and see how it would be possible to move through life with joy and gratitude. I was stuck and lacked hope. I felt wave after wave of grief and did not have the wellness tools to work through these life challenges. I did not know how to move through the pain. These were truly some of the darkest moments in my life.

When I was going through the process of losing a loved one, a shift happened for me. Perhaps I prayed about it, and perhaps it was upon surrendering that I realized I could not do this on my own. Sometimes the greatest gift comes to us when we least expect it. When my Mom was on her death bed, in the early hours of the morning, I witnessed seeing her room lite with orbs. Angelic support showed up as my Mom was transitioning. This experience was the catalyst for me to move through a very dark time. This angelic experience reconnected me with a knowingness of who I am. I was gifted a greater understanding at a subconscious level. It was a simple and clear message.

Love is all that matters.
We are one.
We are love.

Today, I continue to celebrate this place of healing. I love being guided by the frequency of Mother Nature. When we are in living in the dark it is hard to see what is possible. For me, the love-filled vibration of music is my heart song. I am reminded of the light and the love lift it offers. We are all connected in the memory of the light.

I wrote the following song during one of my darkest moments as a way to heal and work through my inner turmoil. I am grateful that I was able to record it years later with the support of a dear friend. I leave it with love and light and to share it with you, to help guide you in your darkest of times.

The Memory of the Light

Dad, I'm scared.
I don't know what to do.
How will I ever choose?
Do I follow him?
He can lead the way.
He can take me to where I need to go.
I'm so afraid, I can't see in the dark.
How will I ever choose? How will I know?

Darling girl – do you know how much I care?
Do you know I will always be there?
Where ever you go,
Whatever you choose,
It will be the right choice for you.
You'll find your answer,
Listen to your heart,
Live your dreams, And never fear the dark.

If I starred at the sunset long enough,
Until all the colors disappeared,
They'd sink behind the ocean's wall and fade away.
I'd begin to question why I'm here,
There would there be nothing left but darkness and fear,
And the shades of gray in the stillness of the night.
The memory of light guides my way,

A knowingness of who I am today,
The memory of the light is the color to my soul,

The Gift Within the Darkness

It lifts my spirit
Through this darkness I know ...
In the memory of the light ...
In the memory of the light ...

You can find the audio recording for this song at: https://soundcloud.com/robyndewar/with-jody-lee-bigelow

Robyn Dewar is a Singer-Songwriter and co-author in both Goodness Abounds: 365 True Stories of Loving Kindness and HALO: Lighting up Heaven on Earth

CHAPTER 7

THE GIFTS WITHIN THE UNEXPECTED LOSS OF THE FATHER

WHEN THE STORM HITS unexpectedly you need time to catch up with what is happening; this is only natural. But, when the storm is an unexpected death, it can take you through a hurricane of emotions, thoughts and various reactions. It is never truer when it is someone that has been there for you your entire life and gave life to you.

The death of your parents can be especially hard, no matter what your relationship, when or how they die. You need time to process the experience in your own way and time. However, something feels unnatural when it is unexpected to many of us; we expect to see death coming with their aging. When it suddenly occurs, it puts us through a cycle of feelings sometimes we don't even realize. It often even showers us with thoughts and experiences that change how we look at life or even live it.

Our parents were there when we were conceived. They loved us from the moment they had time to process they would be responsible for the life of another. After which, they tried the best to raise us to be wonderful people.

Sure looking back on how their parenting skills affected us, perhaps we may think they could have done better; they themselves may even have this realization. Let us keep in mind that we all can only give our best from where we were in the mind and heart space at any given point. Your parents too had their life experiences which influenced how they were responding while raising you.

Being a parent isn't easy for anyone. It's not like their parents passed down the manual on what to do or not do when raising your children. Heck, often the past generations didn't know what they were doing either; everyone was often figuring things out as they went along. The era they were born in also required them to adjust their parenting skills to the new ways of living at the same time. Let us say considering all the facts and all they went through themselves, they did a pretty good job with raising us. So let's give them a break and perhaps even forgive them for their mistakes. What do you think?

I know you can find it in your heart to forgive and let the past go. If you can let go of what you think or hoped the relationship would have been, you will feel better for it. Forgiveness isn't about saying you were right or even forgetting what transpired. Forgiveness is about saying I deserve to feel better in every way. When one finds and gives forgiveness transformation within the cells can begin, allowing for shifting and healing to take place where required. With forgiveness, a light turns on and reveals itself to all.

Let me now ask you again: *Are you willing to forgive your parents for their mistakes? Are you willing to forgive yourself for your own now?* Remember forgiveness starts with you and you deserve to be set free so that love can expand within all experiences.

For some parents the thought of bringing life into this world is overwhelming and this can trigger their fears and insecurities. They may even have their moments of *I can't do this, I don't want another child,* or even run away from the experience. Many fathers go through these thoughts and more at first. This is especially true when they think of the financial commitment to raising a child.

All this and more could lead them to other reactions such as thinking about abortions or even giving a child up for adoption. It could even lead them to go through with the pregnancy but be detached from their child throughout the upbringing.

Let me tell you that deep down your parents love you more than words can ever share despite all appearances. A part of you on a soul level knows this to be true. This is why when we lose our parents it triggers a whole gamut of emotions to flood forth from the crevices of our being.

This can be especially the case when there has been a parent-child separation or disconnect for a period due for whatever reason. I have seen it time and time again when in service for my clients, let alone in my own life. You can see the sadness and pain in the eyes of another that has gone through darker times, perhaps with loss or grief at the root of it.

There is much truth to this for those whose parents put them up for adoption. They feel deeply the loss from the early days of their life up to and even beyond the physical death of those who they called mom or dad growing up. These children often feel they were not good enough or feel like unwanted trash put out to the curb. This is definitely not the case. Those that were put up for adoption, let me say this to you:

Your parents loved you so much that they put you first and it pained them when they gave you up for adoption. They had your best interests at heart and knew they couldn't give what you needed. Their circumstances played the role in their decision to give you up and it wasn't because they didn't love you.

It was the opposite; they loved you so much it hurt deeply to see you leave.

You can rest assured they thought of you their entire life and prayed you were doing okay. They prayed you were living the best life possible as they sent you love from their heart. One day you will both see each other again.

Losing someone unexpectedly hurts a part of our human nature in ways we cannot even describe fully. However, within the unexpected death is a gift that can bring a sense of peace to your heart especially knowing they left the world having lived their life fully. Knowing they didn't go through the long drawn out process of aging or dying. Our soul knows everything unfolded exactly as it was meant to be. The soul knows there are many blessings through this unexpected journey for all affected by this unexpected passing and time will reveal them all.

I have gone through such loss in my life with the unexpected death of those that played the roles of my stepfather, biological father, my mom and others.

The Loss of a Father Figure

When I was around 22 years old, the person who raised me with mom, my Uncle Bill, died.

Let me give you a better understanding of how he came to be my stepfather without going into the whole sorted details. He was married to my Aunt Dolly on my father's side who had died when I was about a month old. My mom and biological father went through some stuff that led them to separation and eventual divorce around the same time. This is when mom and my uncle moved in together and began their romantic relationship. Through this relationship my sister and their daughter Sheri was born into the world a couple years later.

Uncle Bill instantly became a father figure to me, and in all honesty, he was more a dad then my biological father was. He did all the things that a dad would do with his child. Growing up in Northern Ontario that often meant road trips to see relatives, hunting, fishing, and outdoorsy stuff. He truly stepped up to the plate in more ways than he had to.

The unconditional love was there, despite that I gave him some headaches I am sure. Kids, I tell you; always getting into trouble and testing their boundaries with their parents. I am sure he had a few sleepless nights as he and mom talked about the various children antics we were up to. Not what he needed when he had to get up and go to work hard to provide for his family.

He didn't just have us, but he had four kids from his marriage, my cousins. They lived with my Grandma Calhoun and we often saw them each weekend when we traveled to the Kirkland Lake area to see my other relatives.

The younger of my cousins, Cindy and Billy, were very much like my sisters and brother in many ways, with us being closer in age. During the summer months I would often spend time at Grandma's with them all.

When Uncle Bill and mom were forced to go their separate ways (when I was around 12 years old) it was tough on all of us. It meant an end to multiple close relationships which had been there all my life. A major death of sorts happened at this time, the death of the family unit as we knew it to be.

Suddenly my uncle was gone from my life along with the connection to my cousins, aunts, uncles and grandmothers. My mom thrust into the role of a struggling single parent raising two children. Without transportation we didn't have a way to visit any family unless they came to visit and communication was limited without a house phone. It definitely was difficult trying to pick up the pieces of our broken hearts, live life and try to make the best out of a bad situation. It was tough on everyone involved.

As children, it was hard as we didn't understand everything that was going on, even though I was now approaching being a teenager. Parents tend to keep things to themselves and choose not open up to share fully everything. This often leads to more confusion, acting out and other shenanigans by the children. I know it did for me and I am sure it did my sister as well. A part of us both resented much of what unfolded at that time (whether we were conscious of this fact or not at the time).

For me, there was a part of me that rebelled against those in power at times. I may have respected those in charge but I would push the boundaries still. This often led me to being in trouble with the law throughout my earlier teenage years. Thankfully, I outgrew that but I can still see how certain personality traits were formed to cause me to be a bit of a rebel at times even to this day.

Each of our life experiences impact us more than we realize in the moments. Whether two, five or 20 years later, things will often happen that are connected to an earlier life event. These pivotal moments are often life altering for those deeply affected. This can lead us to take paths that leave us with bumps and bruises along the way. However, everything that unfolds is a part of the divine design and is for the highest good.

The death of the family was a blessing in disguise. It shifted the path for many family members, bringing lessons and things to the surface that was hidden deep below. In fact, the many facets of death in our early years are still bringing forth many gifts to the world over 35 years later. Death can be a gift that keeps on blessing us in amazing ways. All we need to be is open and receptive to the many gifts of heaven showered upon us each day.

For my uncle, the death of the family was a catalyst along the road of his actual physical death which happened roughly nine years later. You see when our family was broken up and everyone ended up on different pathways, his heart was broken at the same time.

His time of playing the life partner, dad, uncle and father figure coming to a screeching halt. His heart torn apart and a part of his soul lost. A perfect mix for the massive heart attack that was looming and would eventually be the cause for his soul to cross into the afterlife.

Life was never the same after that moment for any of us; I don't think anyone truly healed as there wasn't really any closure. It was like everyone picked up from where they were and moved forward along the path never really talking about the situation that unfolded. In fact, some never really speaking or having meaningful conversations with each other again.

Uncle Bill's physical death caused a ripple effect to unfold. It allowed us to re-establish family connections at the funeral so that healing could begin for everyone. The light of love could shine once again bringing with it gifts from the soul.

Death Fragmented Soul

Uncle Bill's unexpected death happened shortly after Sheri had reconnected and began to heal with him as her father. However, that fateful day when Sheri heard the news of his death it caused her soul to shatter as she went into shock and broke down with tears.

During times of great trauma or stress, such as losing a loved one unexpectedly, a fragmentation of our soul can take place. This separation can potentially cause those affected to end up having major health issues unfold. After having communications with spirit on the topic and being taken on a life review, I could now better understand my sister's current health issues.

During, this review I was showed how this experience of Uncle Bill's death impacted her. It was with this trauma that she unconsciously choose to physically die earlier in life. This was the beginning of developing her health issues that would show up later in life. A journey which continues to unfold.

From what spirit has said, we all have multiple exit points along the earth journey. There are many experiences that can cause a choice to unfold to lead us to the fulfillment of an exit plan. With this in mind there will be lessons and experiences that one will need to go through to fulfill the exit strategy.

For my sister, her father's death was one such roadway that could lead her to death. Lots can still happen which could lead to a complete recovery of the soul and complete healing should a different decision firmly be made and soul path taken.

After I had received this exit information, I was teaching a Reiki class and Sheri arrived at the perfect time for one of her Ottawa visits. The students were about to do their practice work and she was open to allowing them to do extra practicing. It was during this time we were able to do some clearing and healing to help her.

Within the year, my sister had a close call with death. Spirit has shared with me that this was the exit point she had chosen and because of the work we did her soul chose to stay until the next one.

This is her path and only she can decide to heal and rise above the experience. This is true for everyone. Hope is always alive and a soul can make a choice right up to the last minute for a miracle of healing to unfold.

There are many stories written and even made into Hollywood movies about the miracles of healing taking place after a Near-Death Experience (NDE). These are stories of when the soul made the last minute choice to come back when they could have easily left when they had their NDE.

During the NDE the soul gets shown the alternative paths they can take. They get to experience a life review to understand, heal and gain a deeper perspective of the bigger picture. Once they go through all this they are given the choice if they wish to go home to spirit or rejoin their loved ones on the earth. If this happens, the life they lead will often completely change as they implement their new perspectives and wisdom of their soul.

Hope truly is a gift, so never give up until that final breath is taken. Love can change life for the better when one opens the heart to allow it to flow. So let's take a moment now to breathe love and let go of what no longer serves you.

Death Affects Everyone Differently

My Uncle Bill's death didn't affect me nearly as deep as it did my sister who lost her father; it also deeply affected my cousins who lost their dad. However, rest assured it did affect me more than I knew at the time. Death affects everyone differently. Even different deaths can affect us uniquely. The way we grieve touches our lives long afterwards and it can often be in ways one doesn't think it will.

We all have our own ways to process what has transpired. There is no right or wrong way; there is no set manual that says, this is the way you should grieve. Many books have been written on the subject with each holding information helping in the bereavement process.

I know people who have lost people in their lives and lived happy healthy lives for years and looked like there were never affected. The thing is these people took time behind the scenes to process their grief. They also sought help when they needed it most; knowing they could not do it alone. They even knew it was okay to be vulnerable and reached out to get the support. Often, it was seeking this help that allowed them to gain the strength to keep moving on.

Others process their grief in various ways but they never fully process it mentally or even emotionally. It is these people that will face something in time to cause them to pause, slowdown or even come to a stop. All to help them process and heal after losing their loved one.

Often the thing that stops us from reaching out to ask for the help is the fear of appearing weak or vulnerable. Let me say to know you need support is a strength; you are courageous to ask for help.

If you are having a rough time processing the death of a loved one, love yourself to give yourself the gift of support. You deserve it and people want to sincerely help you but you have to open the door to let them in. Trying to do it alone will not get you far if help is exactly what you need.

I know perhaps during your early days people may have been asking you: *What do you need?* Or *how can I help you?* They may have even asked one of the many other standard questions people ask the grieving at funerals. Many times they are just saying it to be polite, but most often because they sincerely want to try to help you or your family somehow. It makes them feel useful and even better when they can be of service.

I know during those early days after the death of your loved one you may just want to tell them to bugger off or something else. I have been there. In fact, I remember wanting to scream at the top of my lungs when people would ask me after my Mom's death questions, such as: *How are you doing? Or do you need anything? Let me know if you need anything, okay?*

If I would have found my voice I would have said something like the following and I am sure you probably had your moments of wanting to scream similar thoughts:

Yes, you can help me. You can bring my Mom back to life. She was my best friend. I am torn up over her unexpected death. Please wake me up from this nightmare now. This is just so f---ing wrong. Please fix this error! Tell me she is in the other room alive and well. Can we start this week over? Can everything go back to how it was?

I am sure you have been there in your own story. Unfortunately, no one can help us with that; no one can answer the call to bring the death back to life. Please know their spirit truly does live on and that you can still talk with your loved one daily. There are no words that will heal your hemorrhaging broken heart after touches your life. And any words that could potentially help us feel better we rarely hear. We are in some trance state where our bodies are here but our minds are all over the place with our thoughts and emotions at play.

A Biological Death

I know when my biological dad Ken died, I really didn't expect to feel much of anything as we didn't have a relationship. Anytime, I tried to reach out to him he brushed me off or closed the door on my face. After decades of just wanting a connection with him, I finally gave up. I turned to food as a way to process my emotions of him not owning up and being a father in any way.

When I was young, I remember my Mom and Uncle Bill often having discussions about this person who was biologically my dad who we kids called Uncle Kenny. To a 6-year-old the whole thing was confusing as you can imagine. Everyone was trying to make the best lemonade with the bruised lemons that life handed them on a platter. I understood this on a deeper level as I grew up. Once my own spiritual awakening journey began, I understood even more.

When my father crossed into spirit just a few years ago, it was surprising the emotions that came over me. I remember sitting on the couch and just sobbing over this man that was the reason I was alive. After all, he gave me life through the donation of his DNA. I was grateful, sad, depressed and angry all at once knowing the physical opportunity to establish a relationship of any sort had now concluded.

I remember reaching out to my sister Holly, his other child and feeling out of sorts with it all. Not that she wasn't either, seeing this man had raised her with her mom was now dead and she needed time to process her own grief. We each had our own way of dealing with his death and for different reasons.

For me, his death was unexpected, on one level at the time, as there was no connection with us. However, on another level his death was not totally unexpected seeing he had lost his wife just over a year beforehand. The truth is many soulmates will end up crossing into the light shortly after the other has died when they have a close relationship.

As a medium, I understood this on one level. Yet, here I was now having to process another death in my family and this one made me an orphan at the same time. At my age that would not really be a big factor. After all, the status of the orphan is given to younger people who have lost both parents in their life and definitely not a label given to an early 40s-year-old man, right? However, the word fits no matter what the age. It is something we have to process at whatever age we become an orphan. In my case, it was not just my biological parents that had died but those that played the role of my step parents.

It wasn't long before I was over that fact and the death of my father though. But before I could move forward, I took the time to reflect on the lessons that were taught through him in life. I came to a place where I could forgive him for being who he was and not who I had hoped him to be as a father. Making peace with the experience with him growing up at the same time. I could also come to a place of acceptance that he was just playing a role that I had asked him to play on the soul level.

My father abandoning me after I came into the world and not wanting to have anything to do with me was on his conscience, not mine. I had come to terms with it long ago. As a child growing up in the world, it was a pain held deep within me. It even affects other areas in life as you are learning throughout this book.

I can now take responsibility for my part of the equation. This because I now know we each had a role to play when we created the sacred contracts long before the physical incarnations unfolded. I understood there were lessons that this experience was a catalyst for in my life. Just like there were lessons where I was the catalyst for my father to experience.

I had found the gift within the darkness of the death of the relationship with my father as a child. It was only later that I could see past the burnt out light to find the light which is omnipresent and ever expanding: the light of the soul. I could truly appreciate all the blessings that came forth through the soul which gave me the gift of life. I could take my power back and live life as I continue to process things further.

It's Your Choice, Your Loved Ones Understand

Whether you attended the funeral of your loved one or even the burial at the cemetery that is something you had to decide for yourself. No one else can tell you what right or wrong as they are not in your shoes or processing the death the same way. We all have the right to our choices and opinions. Your loved ones soul understands your reasons and besides the body is only the vehicle for it during the physical journey; it isn't where it lives.

The soul is now free to be with you wherever you are. When you are ready to go to the grave to say your goodbye or scream at them, they will be there with you. They truly understand that you have to take the time to process in your own way. They have been there themselves with loved ones who crossed over.

In fact, the soul is now without a body; therefore now free to be everywhere, including with all those that are left behind grieving. They aren't bound by the physical rules and restrictions anymore. In truth, they never have been as you cannot restrict the soul. They now understand that all which is real and true is the soul love and light.

When you understand who you are, along with your own unique gifts and abilities, you will know that you are a soul first and foremost. The physical is secondary and only temporary. Your departed loved ones know this now.

Your loved ones let go of their past errors, without judgment and found forgiveness in doing so. They own their mistakes. They understand now the past does not matter and that tomorrow isn't assured. All that matters is here and now. So live your life in the gift of the present. They want you to give yourself permission to let go of your past mistakes or errors in judgment so you can start anew. They want you to live life to the fullest knowing they are truly happy now and want the same for you.

Your loved ones want the best for you and only you can take the steps to make it possible. Now, *what will your future look like? What will you create as you move forward with your life?*

Take one step that moves you from where you are to where you want to go. It does not matter the size of the step; what matters is that you are moving forward towards the future of your dreams. Your loved ones will be right by your side as you step into the life of your creation.

Time is the Healer

Take the time you need to process your grief. Remember there is a strength in allowing yourself to feel and sit with your grief. It is when one does this that we allow ourselves to process and move through the dark clouds and the storm that came with them.

Whether it is a father figure or your biological father, you need time and space when their soul leaves the body. You need time to process the many layers of grief you may experience and also to process the physical death of an important relationship in your life. There is no right or wrong way to do so.

During this time use this opportunity for you to further understand your father perhaps by reflecting upon the lessons he taught you by being himself. Perhaps you learned to be independent and rely on yourself because of his inability to be there for you. Or perhaps he taught you what love really meant by showing you acceptance in being yourself and being there no matter which cards you were dealt with in life. Perhaps you have the chance to get to know your father in ways you never thought possible. You are gifted all this and more through the stories that your family shares with you or the questions you ask your relatives.

Take this opportunity to establish a direct connection with your father (or any of your heavenly loved ones) and to talk about everything on your mind and heart. He loves you no matter what even if you push him aside; he will patiently wait for you to be ready. All is that he asks is that you give him a chance. Remember this is both your opportunity to clear the air and really have a heartfelt talk. You may just find answers that help you forgive, find closure or heal your shattered heart. Utilize this time to ask any questions about your family history or other questions that you wish to know from your father. He made be physically dead but he is very much still alive and ready to have those meaningful conversations with you at any time.

With death comes a whole new perspective for our loved ones that pass through the veil to the spiritual dimensions. As they review their own life choices and lessons, they gain a whole new perspective and appreciation for life itself. It is through this that they can heal and return to health, wholeness, love and light. Know they are always watching over and taking part in your life right alongside you. You are never alone for they are never far from their children. They came to earth with the mission to love, honor, teach and support you, and they can know continue to fulfill that soul promise they made to you. Just because they are not physical anymore does not mean that their job is finished. They are still your parent and will continue to assist you from the non-physical world with their new found perspectives for all the days of the rest of your life. You can rest assured on this.

Prayer for those Grieving the Unexpected Loss of the Father

Dearest Mother-Father God,

We come to you today to ask for your divine help with the healing of our grieving heart over the unexpected loss of our father figure.

Please surround us now with your enveloping love and light to lift our hearts and minds to the highest divine energy of our soul. Please send your angels to be by our side as we process the physical death of our father.

Help us recognize that our father did the best he could in life. We know he too had his own lessons and experiences to contend with or make peace with. We ask that you help us forgive our father for his misgivings and that we come to a place of forgiveness for ourselves for our own journey.

Let us know the peace that comes from knowing divine love and light in our hearts now forever more. Help us establish a loving relationship with our father who now rests in heaven.

Assist us to be the instrument of your Divine Love as you take us where you wish us to be. Let us meet who you wish us to meet as you work through us for the betterment of mankind as we honor the father within all creation.

As we process our father's death help us be loving, kind and gentle with ourselves.

God, help us be understanding and compassionate with those that we come in contact with, for they too have their story unfolding.

For all this even better, we give our thanks and so it is done.

Amen

CHAPTER 8

FINDING HEALING AND GRACE THROUGH GRIEF

Tandy Elisala

My parents died almost four months apart. They were married for 45 years. The two and ½ years leading up to their respective deaths was overwhelming, to say the least. I left my corporate career to take care of both parents very unexpectedly after my dad was involved in a massive 20 car pileup. We experienced a lot of touch and go with them both during our caregiving tenure.

My mother died May 3rd, 2012 at 3:15 pm while in the ICU of a local hospital. The hours leading up to her death were beautiful. As she lay unconscious, our family shared stories, played her favorite songs, held hands, prayed and watched her die. The moment she died, I found myself grabbing onto her right arm and leg yelling and crying for her to come back. In that moment, the calm, collective, reserved, and strong woman my family was accustomed to seeing in me turned into a hot inconsolable ball of slobber, tears, and screams. I was heartbroken. The person that brought me into this life was gone and I would never hear her voice or feel her touch again. I thought that if I grabbed onto her hard enough, she would come back. She never did (on a physical level anyhow).

My father died September 5th, 2012 at 10:36 pm in hospice care. I arrived six minutes before he died. I had just enough time to play soothing music and tell him how very much I loved him. After his death, I felt sad that my last parent was gone yet I felt relieved. Then, I felt guilty for feeling relieved.

The biggest lessons I've learned through my grief and healing journey include:

1. Connecting with our loved ones while they are alive is critical to honing their legacy. I believe this head/heart connection helped our entire family heal and reconnect with them in spirit.

2. Grief is a very individual experience. Even my sister and I grieved differently. We had the same parents but our relationship with our parents were different. The one thing I strongly disliked was when well-meaning people would say things like, "I know exactly how you feel." No. They don't. The other thing I hate more than this is when people say, "It's been xxx time, get over it." Grieving happens in layers. The only way through grief is to allow your feelings to come up and out.

The gift discovered within my darkness is two-fold. First, I became wildly passionate about helping others to hone and live their big, bold legacy. And second, I realized that grace comes to us and through us in many forms. It is a quiet whisper, a gentle nudge, a song, a rainbow, a butterfly, pennies, or a meaningful coincidence. Grace is God's way of letting us know we are all connected. I am grateful to feel connected with my parents in spirit and welcome the healing layers as they arise.

Tandy Elisala is the author of Healing Through the Chaos: Practical Care Giving Grief

CHAPTER 9

THE GIFTS WITHIN LOSING ONE'S PARENTS TO AGING OR DISEASE

This chapter can also apply to Grandparents and other members of the Aging Population

WE ALL FEEL CERTAIN a time will come where our guardians will move into the spiritual realm as death becomes them and their soul leaves the body. However did you know your bereavement process for your aging loved ones or those suffering from a terminal disease begins long before they crossover? This is a fact for many people whose loved ones in their lives are aging.

As this happens and you see your elderly loved one's health degrade, a part of you grieves the loss of the healthy, vibrant parent or guardian. A fear takes root that their time on earth is drawing to an end and you soon realize that they are mortal.

Deep down you have knowledge their soul will never die, but the body does and that scares you. This is because you want no one to suffer the pain of losing their memory, having body aches all the time or having other diseases take over. This also stems from a part of you that doesn't want this for yourself, so seeing someone else go through it triggers you. So when a loved one you know and love begins the journey towards the light, a part of you begins the grieving process.

This especially becomes true when the parent ends up suffering a stroke or cancer or even dementia. It sucks to watch, let's face it.

A part of you may get upset or angry that this good person has to suffer; and even more that you have to be a part of watching them go through this. You may reach out and pray, without seeing results, which just fuels the human ego to go into the darkness further. We call this a form of living grief. This can happen to anyone with any loved one (family, friends, or pets) that is suffering a long drawn out terminal illness as you watch them deteriorate and eventually die.

Remember, your parents answered your soul's call to be there for you in the best way they could be in every moment. This all included changing your diapers, cleaning up after you, feeding and bathing you. This is your opportunity to do the same to show them how much you appreciated everything they did for you growing up.

Many people don't see it in this way and it isn't easy on anyone. Do you think your parents want you to be their caregiver or see them at their worst? No, not physically anyways. However, from a soul perspective they have an innate awareness that this was a part of the contracts you all created before incarnating.

Spirit reminds you to be patient with them and just do the best you can. Their bodies may be breaking down as they are aging, but that does not mean to put them out to pasture yet.

Do things together as you enjoy whatever time you have left together. Use this opportunity to get to know your parents again. Your relationship is evolving and will continue to even after they cross into the light. Remember, live life with no regrets from this moment forth.

Your parents want you to be happy and don't want you to suffer either. If this means having the courage to say I need help and reach out to get it, then do so. It is a strength to recognize that you may be in over your head and do something about it. They will love you all the more for it, but, honor them with your presence as often as you can. Make time for them as they made time for you whenever they could.

Remember everyone is always doing the best they can be in every moment. Sometimes, we lose track of this divine truth as we think they could have done better. But their experiences, mind, heart and current life space all plays a role in how they respond or react in every moment. The same is true for you; you are doing the best you can. Understand this while being more compassionate and gentle with yourself; most of all do your best to do the same with your loved ones.

Do you want to be stuck in a nursing home, hospital or hospice and then left alone for the rest of your lives? Neither do your parents. So check in with them to see how you can best love, support and be there for them throughout their final days. The earlier you start this process the better the outcome for all involved.

As your loved one is going through the aging process and their body begins breaking down, they are also having their own feelings about it all. They aren't necessarily happy about it either and maybe even having their own crying moments in private. Love them to talk with them about their future and then respect their desires.

Talk with them before the time comes that they lose their independence and/or mental faculties about what their wishes are for homes, caregivers, etc. This way you are allowing them their power to make the choice while they are still able to and you can respect them in this way.

Spirit says too many are not honored for their lives and their hard work they gave through it. This is just one way you can help them out as well so they feel more comfortable during their later years. Spirit reminds us we never ever forget how people make us feel. This is true just as much after the soul leaves the body as it is on the earth. So always make sure your actions are leaving a good feeling on those you encounter along your life paths.

We are here for temporary periods of time in these vehicles we call our bodies while our soul lives on for eternity. Treat your loved ones how you want to be treated when you reach their age. They will watch over you from heaven once they leave the planet and make sure you receive the same treatment. Just because they may be dying doesn't mean that they are dead yet, and neither are you. Live your lives together making new memories, sharing in loving, living and laughing as much as you can. You will all be better for it.

Take the time to ask your elder questions and learn from their stories. Spirit says many people have lots to teach and share. Unfortunately, the people who would benefit from their knowledge the most aren't asking about their backgrounds or the history tied to the family. You may even find it fascinating to learn or hear the stories for the first time or even the twentieth as you listen with fresh perspectives. Use this time to show an interest in knowing them better as you both ready to say goodbye to the physical part of the relationship.

Our older generation lives should mean something. Learn from them while you can physically. After the soul leaves the body, you then can connect and learn from them from their new perspectives. You can still have the relationship after they leave that you wish you would have had in life. It is never too late to begin anew, have a relationship or heal things with them.

Healing Your Relationships

Let me share about my stepmother, Nancy. She and I never really had a relationship in life other than being my biological father's wife. This stemmed from many issues that went back to my parents personal issues at the end of their marriage. But, I can't ever say I disliked her or anything as I really did not know her.

Over the years there were things that would come up that left a bad taste in my mouth, so to speak, when it came to her. This included the fact she and my dad kept my half-sister a secret for whatever their reasons, from me. Holly had no clue about me and there was no official word from them about this girl who was my sister. But, as life happens, things get around. When she was born I was informed about her almost instantly as my cousins shared the news with my mom who told me; but it didn't come from the horse's mouth directly.

As we grew up and life events unfolded, such as my Grandma Calhoun's funeral, we would come into contact with each other in passing. I remember being at the gathering after the funeral and as I was saying bye to my father, Holly came up to us; but still no official introduction or anything unfolded. It truly was a weird situation. In time, secrets surfaced and were revealed and by the time she hit the early teens she had found out about me as a brother. That is a story for a whole other book, perhaps.

Anyways, as life would have it, the universe always has a plan. My stepmother had taken ill and reached out to me through Facebook. A part of her deep within was holding onto guilt and was trying to make peace for her part of the story; which was her motivation behind contacting me. I didn't question things, I allowed what was to unfold to happen. A relationship of sorts began between us.

We had discussions on spiritual things, keeping things light and airy in our communications as we learned a little about each other. There was more to the story I could sense, but I let it go. During our conversations, I often would guide wisdom or healing energy through the words shared at the same time. It was my way of making her aware that she was loved, accepted and was forgiven by me.

I cannot say if I would have been able to get to that place if I had not been on my spiritual journey. It was through this that I became so much more conscious and aware. But the Divine had a plan and this whole communication with me and Nancy was a part of it.

In time, the day came where her health had deteriorated to the point of no return and her soul left the body. I believe she had found peace with one person she felt perhaps she had wronged and could leave knowing so.

At the hour of her death, without my physical awareness of what was going on with her, I sensed her presence with me here at home. This was her soul making the rounds to say goodbye and make us aware that she was now at peace in spirit. Shortly afterwards, I received a phone call from my sister, Holly, to let me know her mom had indeed died. I shared that Nancy had visited me spiritually a short time before and that she was now happy, healthy and at peace.

Since then I have been blessed to communicate with her and even passed on a heavenly message or two from her to others. We truly did develop a wonderful relationship of respect, acceptance and love once the ego was removed from the equation. This is testament indeed it is never too late to heal, transform or even begin developing a relationship in life. Even if one has crossed over, it is still possible to do so though the processes shared in the second part of the book.

When a parental figure dies it is never easy, no matter what, even when you have a good relationship with them. This is especially true when they are going through a painful experience as they approach the golden gates of eternity. This isn't easy for either of you.

You can help them feel better and help yourself by not asking how they are doing every moment or how they are feeling constantly and things of this nature. Ask them what you can do to support them or do one better and help take their mind off their problems and let them be of service for you. Even if this means just listening to you talk about your own problems and giving advice as they can. It truly does them a world of benefit when they can focus on something or someone else for a change.

Isn't it true when you are going through stuff and you can focus on helping someone else out, and get out of your own head, that you feel better? Spirit often makes my clients and I laugh when they say if they could fix one problem in the world, it would be to get rid of the head. This is because it is the ego mind that is at root of many of life's problems many times.

Sometimes, all that is needed is a little cheer me up. Your regular visits with your loved ones will often do this. You can make it extra special by bringing them something on occasion they could use, flowers or a new outfit or dessert that they miss. It truly is the little things that show people how much they mean to you and love is the most powerful energy in the world. Let your heart open and spread that loving light each day. Your parents will love you for it.

The Day of Crossing Over

When that fateful day comes, you will be glad that you did the best you could for the last moments of your guardian's physical lives. You can move forward with no further regrets and may have even found peace within the relationship or the past experiences somehow.

Know that on their last day, a sense of lightness will begin filling the room and many will sense it. This is because the angels will be ever present, alongside all the heavenly loved ones, friends, animals and other spirit energies. You may even find that your loved one is guided to have you leave the room at the appointed time so their soul can exit the body. This is a gift to you. This way you don't have them taking their last breath as your last memory of them.

Spirit showed me a vision which has helped many of my clients feel better. It is my hope that as I share it now with you that it will help you to understand we are never alone at the time of crossing over, even though it may physically appear to be so.

When the time comes for the soul to leave the physical body, the veil that has kept the physical and spiritual dimensions separated will drop. As this happens divine energy will fill the room with such a bright light and enveloping love which then helps the soul to feel at peace to leave the body.

Many people have a fear of death, due to not knowing what happens after the soul leaves the body. This energy helps them to release their fears so that the soul can separate from the physical body fully. A gift in itself and one of the reasons many who have NDE (near-death experience) talk about how they no longer have the fear of dying.

During this time the heavenly support crew and loved ones fill the room; all dressed in white robes as they move into the physical space around the body. There will be one that will lead the group and usually this will be one of the Soul's Master Guides. Alongside, will be one or two special family members that have sacred contracts to help the soul leave the physical world and be welcomed home to spirit.

Remember the soul is pure love and light. However, because we as humans expect things to show up a certain way, spirit is giving us a physical look at how it would appear to those transitioning. Reality of the matter is as a soul we are pure energy and energy has no physical form.

As this all unfolds, there is an ethereal choir singing beautiful harmonies as the soul exits the body and enters heaven. This allows for further healing to take place to bring them into a peaceful love filled essence; the truth of the soul.

I personally have not heard this Angelic Choir but I believe it to be true. After all, why else would so many people have reported or recorded about the choirs in paintings, music, books and more. There has got to be some truth to this or how else would you explain so many similar reports. Music is truly a testament to love especially when it comes from a place within the heart.

I recommend that if you are going through living grief or have a loved one on their way home to put on some music. It will sooth both of you as the harmonies open and heal your hearts. You will both be better for it, especially as you connect through the communications. Allow yourselves to be present in the gift of this moment together as you share your journey of life, love and laughter.

On the Topic of Hell

In closing this chapter, let me give insight into something else that spirit has shared with me and that is about the subject of hell.

Please know it doesn't exist as most perceive it to be; everyone leaving the physical world goes to heaven. Each soul is met by others of like energy together on the same level much like a floor of the massive apartment building or living in same neighborhood; to use earth terms to describe something that is indescribable. Heaven or divine energy is impossible to sum up in earthly terms as it is a continuous energy ever expanding and words are restrictive.

As the soul continues to evolve, they move up the scale in terms of what soul group they will live and learn with next. Many fear crossing into the light because of their fears of the unknown and because of their life choices they made while living, fearing they will go to hell. But let's be real, why would the Divine ever create anything other than something that is love and light filled? Don't you think the earth can be hell enough at times on the soul?

I know many religious texts and societies out there will disagree with me but I am just sharing what spirit has taught me with you all. You can make your own mind up about this. There is no wrong or right here. It is all just energy, and energy flows where attention goes. I am choosing to expand the energy of love and light by sharing what I have learned along the way. Hopefully, it will empower you to do the same further in your own lives.

Losing anyone is never easy. It is even more challenging when it is a guardian, grandparent and especially our parents who are aging or going through disease processes until death do you part. Thankfully, once they cross over to the light, you will both have a sense of relief.

They are now with their creator and the God of their own understanding; the soul is now perfect, whole, healthy and complete in every way. The soul will now continue to watch over, guide and participate in your lives with their new perspectives of love, light and divinity for they have rejoined the energy they were born out of. Life for their soul has come full circle, and that circle will continue to expand all the days of the universe as will they.

Now you can finally move through the rest of your own bereavement process. You can now do so with peace of mind knowing your loved one is no longer suffering or in physical pain. You can do so knowing they are free in body, mind, heart and spirit fully.

Take this time to reflect on their memory and what they taught you in life by just being themselves, for our greatest teachers lead by example. By doing so, you will love, laugh and cry together as you remember and discover the many gifts contained within their legacy left behind. Keep they spirit alive through your memories of them and sharing the gifts that they left for you with the world.

A Prayer for Those Experiencing Living Grief with their Aging Parents

Mother-Father God, Creator of the Universe

We come to you today to request your ever present assistance, healing and energy for those of us that may be experiencing our versions of living grief.

We ask that you bath us in your enveloping love and light. Lift the hearts of all as you resolve what may be weighing the body, mind, spirit and emotions down doing so forever more. Help us to forgive one another for our human reactions or responses which we may have had throughout life's journey.

Please watch over and aid our aging, dis-eased and departing loved ones through the transformation process. Help us all to have peace of mind and heart knowing all is unfolding according to your will God.

Thank you for sending your angels to be by us and our loved ones side during this time to guide, protect, heal and connect us all. Give us the strength, courage and grace as we say goodbye to the physical body as the soul leaves to embrace spiritual realms fully.

Lift us all out of our darkness so we may see the gifts that lie within the darkness of living grief.

As we say this for ourselves, we say this for all the world, for we are one. For all this and better, we give our thanks and. So it is and it is done.

Amen

CHAPTER 10

THE GIFTS WITHIN THE LOSS OF GRANDPARENTS

WITH AGING WE COME to expect that our family's elders are eventually going to leave and go home into the light. They lived a long life and their soul deserves to rest after all they experienced on earth.

Our grandparents survived things that most of us cannot ever imagine living through. Their stories they passed through the generations to us will continue to live on with their memory. As they shared their experiences they began feeling the ill side effects of the aging process; they job of raising our parents and doing their part in the world slowly coming to an end.

Even knowing all this we still must go through a darkness of grieving the physical loss of our grandparents. Why wouldn't we? They were there at our birth and throughout our lives teaching, supporting and loving us. They watched us as our parents enjoyed a romantic dinner, went gift shopping or just talked about life stuff away from us kids. They spoiled us when our parents weren't around giving us treats and extending us a little more freedom to be kids exploring life.

Watching our loved ones go through the process of death is never easy especially when we had a close connection with them in life. It is one thing when it is a natural aging process that is unfolding. It is another ball game when a disease such as Cancer, Alzheimer's or Dementia takes a hold of them.

Much of what I have shared in the aging parents' chapter would relate to our grandparents, so I won't repeat it here. You will find it beneficial to read all the chapters even if it doesn't relate to the loss you may be experiencing. By doing so you may find valuable information that will help you in your own life and bereavement journey.

Growing up, I remember traveling almost every weekend to visit my Grandmothers on both sides of the family. For a brief period I even remember visiting my Grandfather Murdock, but I was very young so don't remember much about him. I was even lucky enough to be blessed with extended family due to my Uncle Bill's family becoming much like my own after Mom and he connected romantically.

Unfortunately, I was too young to remember my Grandpa Calhoun as he died within the first few years of my life. I do know that he watched over us grandchildren as we grew up though.

Country Living at Grandma Calhoun's

I remember going to Grandma Calhoun's house and spending time with my cousins alongside with her and the family dog, Blackie. We children would often be playing in the other room as the adults played games, smoked and chatted about grown up stuff.

One thing about grandma was that she was definitely a strong woman and set in her ways. You didn't really want to get on her bad side (which rarely happened); if you were family, you understood the rules of the house. Grandma loved her grandchildren and would do whatever she could to protect them or help whenever she could. She even took in my cousins (my Uncle Bill's kids) after the death of my Aunt Dolly, wanting to give them a stable environment and a good home after the death of their mother.

She truly had a good heart but like everyone she had her own secrets and experiences that she lived with and through. You always knew that she loved you; even though she may not have said it directly to you at times.

I remember spending a week or two every summer at her place, having campfires, picking blueberries and just enjoying the serenity of country living. We kids would bike over the lake to swim or walk up to the gas station store a bit down the highway in the summer.

In the winter, we would build snow castles, snowmobile, play games or whatever else that the weather would let us to do. We would run up the driveway to the edge vying for the attention of the transport drivers to get them to honk their horns. It truly was simple living at its finest. It didn't take much to keep us kids entertained or happy. I am sure by the end of my summer vacation my grandmother and cousins were happy that I was out of their hair.

As a child I often just loved spending time with my elders of all ages. I would brush their hair, sit on the floor petting the dog or even just stand around at times, which made some uncomfortable. Even until this day people in the family feel uncomfortable if I choose to stand when there are available places to sit and that is their prerogative. Standing as a kid for extended lengths of time prepared me for when I worked in the restaurant industry or anytime I needed to. It also taught me to be cognizant when my body posture was out of an alignment and to adjust according and even more.

There is a saying that says: If you want to learn pay attention to your environment and people around you. I took this to heart for as a child I was very observant, choosing to watch what was going on rather that partake in the activities at times. I often found it easier for me to communicate through the written word over verbal communication. This was something I learned through life experiences whenever we were told to play and be quiet or whatever the case at the time.

Once I reached the beginning stages of my teens, the regular visits to both grandma's houses would come to an end abruptly. Being a child I just continued on living life, however, part of me didn't understand why we weren't able to go see grandma often. Sure I recognized that it had something to do with the fact that mom and Uncle Bill weren't together anymore. On a deeper level I knew that family should always find a way to stay connected; this however didn't happen. Life just continued to shift.

Eventually, in the later part of my teens, Grandma Calhoun became ill and was diagnosed with cancer. By this time, I was working fulltime and could easily afford my own travel. The ownership now was on me for the lack of connection between us.

I understood deep within that she wasn't going to make it even before I was informed physically and it wasn't something that I could deal with. I even lived 20 minutes away from her at one point when I lived at my Grandma Mossop's house for college temporarily. But I still chose to stay away and remember her as she was as I grew up right until the end.

I could not stand see her in pain, suffering and her body degrade with the disease that had taken over and so I stayed away. But I will tell you this was selfish on my part because I took her joy away from being able to spend time with her grandson; even if it was on her death bed. I would have brought her a little happiness and peace of mind to see me and get to know me a little as an adult. If I would only have had the perspectives on things that I do now back then, I tell you there would be much that I would do differently.

I now understand that cancer is born energetically out of deep resentments, anger and frustrations that are held within us, often since earlier years in life. I can only imagine what would have caused my Grandmother such pain in her life that would breed this disease. Sure her smoking contributed to it, but the root cause was much deeper. I can just imagine what she went through losing her husband and daughter and then raising a second family. She definitely made the best when life handed her lemons. But she held her pain close to her heart.

I can't imagine the pain of watching someone you know suffocating as they face their mortality. But I do know it would be tough on those that have had to endure this loss. To my cousin's she was a second mother and I know the loss was tough on them. In fact, I know this had a life altering effect on their lives in some way.

The things we experience in life can affect us long after the originating experience. My grandmother's death taught me that we can either let go of the past or the past will consume us taking over the body with some form of disease. I truly can appreciate the blessings my grandmother taught while living and continues to from the afterlife. I know she is often around me and keeping an eye on all her children, both living and the ones that are in heaven with her.

My paternal grandmother's death gave the gift of reconnection with my family on my dad's side, and for that I am grateful. Family is family; whether we get along or not. We are born out of love and will die with love by our side. So, why not share it with those family members who we love and love us? Remember, time is precious and one day your loved ones won't be a part of the physical world.

Take the time to get to know your living elders, for they are here for you and ask them the questions that you wish to about your family history. That is one thing that I wish I could have had the opportunity while my grandparents were alive. Thankfully they are still with me and will make sure that I know whatever I need to know at the right moment.

And if your elders have already crossed over, it's never too late to get to know them or experience their teachings. Sometimes it takes losing one that you love to appreciate all that they gifted you in life, love and laughter. Remember love conquers all, heals the heart and connects us all. Let it freely shine.

Grandma Mossop's Deteriorating Health

On the weekends when we would travel from Timmins to Kirkland Lake, after stopping in at my Grandma Calhoun's house we would eventually end up my Grandma Mossop's home. Growing up I remember that we would arrive and be welcomed and made to feel at home every time. Of course, every house has it rules and Grandma's place was not any different. I remember the earlier years of traveling, singing songs in the car or playing I spy along the way.

I even remember going to Grandpa Murdock's work place where he would spoil us with Joe Louis's or whatever sweets he had there awaiting us. I can't say I remember much about him at all as I was very young but I remember that about him. Unfortunately Grandma Mossop never spoke of him and neither did mom or anyone else, really. I am sure because his unexpected death, due to a drunk driver, left an imprint on their heart that would never heal.

Growing up I did not recognize the true meaning of family and the legacy of the stories. So, questions never got asked and no one volunteered any answers without being prompted.

Given what I have learned over the years I would have definitely asked my maternal grandma, mom, aunts and anyone who knew anything questions about grandpa and about their life together. As the saying goes, it's always best to get it straight from the horse's mouth. Otherwise, you just never know what spin the story will get as it is passed on down the line.

I am sure you all are aware of the telephone game that we all have been privy to growing up in school or on the playgrounds. You start with a simple sentence and pass it ear to ear until you get to the last person who then states what they heard out loud. Usually at this point, you are met with a thunderous roar being granted once every one hears what the statement started out as.

Think of your family stories in the same way, every time they are told something about the story changes slightly as people remember or hear different things. Everyone has their own memory of the stories. This is one of the wonderful gifts when we speak to those closest to the original story as we are sure to get closer to the truth of it.

Growing up grandma was good at sharing various stories with us as we grew up, but as kids we just were not really interested in them. Instead choosing to go out to play on the swing set in the backyard or play in our rooms upstairs. It didn't take much for us to keep ourselves entertained.

She would make us healthy snacks and would even stick alfalfa sprouts in our peanut butter sandwiches. A fact that as kids we didn't appreciate. I, for one, would pick them out and leave them behind with the plants. I am sure she had her chuckles once we left and she started to find our hiding places, shaking her head at the same time.

Grandma was ahead of the game when it came to recycling, composting and so much more. Her intuitive sense was leading the way to help the health of the planet by doing her part back in the 70s and probably even earlier. It wasn't abnormal for her to have something growing in her kitchen or in her backyard.

She would wash out any cans and then remove both sides to squash the can down to a pancake to save space in the garbage and use any glass jars along the way. Something that as we grew up, we began to appreciate when everyone started to jump on the band wagon. This elder was a true pioneer when it came to healthy living for the planet and in life.

Ms. Mossop was very wise and always knew when we were up to no good. I can't say if it was because the floors creaked or because of her high trained intuitive awareness, which she developed and fine-tuned when she was at work as a nurse. Whatever the reason, she just knew and loved us still.

I am sure that she and my mom had talks (both good and bad) about us kids. These talks I am sure included my cousins at times, who we got in trouble with on more than one occasion. What can I say we have all been kids who tested our boundaries with our elders at one point or another; I was no different.

I loved my grandmother and whatever I could do to spend time with her growing up I would. She truly was a very kind, patience and caring person, who loved beyond measure.

I would often find myself standing behind her, my mom or even my aunt doing their hair. How is it I never went into hairdressing I have no clue; especially seeing I often found myself in the role of the family hairstylist growing up. Mind you it wasn't anything serious and I am sure that they would never go out after one of my hair styles. They put up with my creativity; out of love, I am sure.

Spending time on the holidays at either grandparents was always a true joy, especially at Christmas where it was like having two Christmas's each year. For a child that was truly heaven. I almost always received double the gifts from each due to my birthday being the week before Christmas.

In time, the teenage years would come along and we would see less of grandma due to various life circumstances. However, grandma's love was ever present. We did however on occasion travel to see her and once I had a vehicle, I would go for a day road trip at times.

When I was in my early twenties, I went to live with grandma for a couple months after I was accepted into college in Kirkland Lake. I got to know her all over again and enjoyed just spending quality time with her. It was a short time until I was able to move back to Timmins to continue my college program there and off.

A few years later and I was moving down south away from my family. The journey would continue with grandma, now in a new way. I wish that I would have kept in touch better with her as time was drawing near. In time, we all learn to appreciate the time we had with our loved ones.

Shortly after moving south, mom would cross over, and grandma was never the same. Losing a child at any age is tough on a parent, and for grandma now being in her late 70s, it was no different. She started to disconnect and lose sight of reality with her memory now beginning to fade.

My mom's unexpected death was hard on her. But watching her youngest daughter, my Aunt Pauline's health deteriorate with the ultimate outcome of death shortly after mom's death was the hardest on her. This was partly because they had lived close together with my aunt making regularly visits and also because my grandmother was also facing her own mortality with her age.

It wasn't long before you could be in the same room as her and she wouldn't even know who you were. She would be talking like you weren't in the room with her, which was hard to experience for those of us that loved her. I remember her speaking to me at my Aunt's funeral about how when my mom died she had wanted my sister to dress her in this blue dress. She continued on about my sisters and me, all the while not realizing she was talking with me.

I may have found it painful but I could pack my bags and come back home and move on with life. The family, who lived up north, had to deal and observe our loved one's health deteriorate on a daily basis. It was indeed a sad state knowing how she cared for so many people in her life. For those left behind watching over her I am sure it was a frightening process at times, never knowing what the next day would bring.

Grandma may have been disconnecting from life but she was connecting to Spirit most of that time as she picked up on the many loved ones around her. This being something that Spirit has shared with me since her death. She would have her lucid moments where she was very much in charge of her capabilities and then there were others where she would need the aid of others.

For grandma, I know it was particularly hard on her. She faced one of life's ultimate fears, the death of the body. Not only that, but losing herself in the process which was something as a nurse she watched so many patients and their family's experience. I am sure this was a nightmare in many respects for her.

Messages for those Living with Grief

For anyone going through this I am deeply sorry for the pain that you are going through. I cannot claim to understand or know what you are going through. But I can say, if you are still lucky enough to have your elder loved ones still alive, spend quality time with them. Life is too short and for them time is of the essence for they may not remember today much longer. They have much to teach and share. As you reflect on their life, you will discover what other lessons they may have taught you by just being themselves.

Treat them like an equal and remind them if need be who you are. The last thing they want to be is treated like a burden or to remember later who you were and feel bad for not remembering you in the moment. Treat them like you would want to be treated (if this was you) with love, kindness, respect and compassion.

Remember that it's just as hard on them; if not harder than on you. After all, they are the ones that are waking up and not remembering who they are. They are the ones that can't remember what day of the week it is, if they had breakfast or even how their body works at times. They have gone from being completely independent and being there for others to having to rely on others for help with their daily tasks.

Know it is okay to feel sad or upset or whatever you may be feeling. You are experiencing and living real grief whether your loved one is alive or the soul has left the body. Take the time to process and know that you will be better for it.

And if your loved one has already crossed into the light, know that they are happy, healthy and alive once again! They are in full health once again, and for that we can be grateful.

Your loved ones want you to remember the happier times and to live life in their honor. Just because they are dead doesn't mean that they aren't living life with you for that is the furthest from the truth. They are with you whenever you think of them or when something reminds you of them. They are participating in life's celebrations and though the journey that you are living each day.

They want you to learn from their mistakes and do better than they could ever wish for. They want you to make them proud and go reach for the stars. Heaven is watching over you always. Follow your heart and do what makes it sing each day.

Do not settle for anything but the best of you and your dreams. Your grandparents want that for you so want it for yourself.

They love and appreciate everything that you did for them when they were alive. Now they are ready to gift you with the gift that keeps on giving, the purest unconditional love and light of the universe.

Prayer for those Grieving the Loss of a Grandparent

Dearest Mother-Father God,

We come to you today asking that you send your Angels to be by our side as we process the loss of our grandparents.

Please surround us with your healing love and light to clear and resolve all that weighs our mind and heart down forever more.

We know that it was their time to return home to Spirit and yet, we are grieving in the darkness of our loss. Please shine your light within us to help us to see past the illusions of death and to reconnect to the energy of the soul now.

Help us to understand the many gifts that our grandparents left as their living legacy and to accept them with love and appreciation in their honor.

Let us be the instrument of your loving light God, and to shine brightly in the memory of our departed loved ones in heaven. Help us to be in service for you each day as you guide us in all that we say, choose and do.

Help us in letting go and surrendering to the power, the will and the love of our divine nature at all times. Help us to relax so that we can be open to the innate wisdom of the soul and our loved ones in heaven now forever more.

For all this and even greater, we give our thanks. Trusting, having faith, letting go, listening and following the guidance of our hearts we know your will be done on earth as it is in heaven forever more.

Amen

CHAPTER 11

THE GIFTS WITHIN LOSING A CHILD

WITHIN THE DARKNESS HOLDS a tragic pain that no one should ever have to experience, let alone a parent or parent in waiting and that is child loss. We have this innate belief that a parent should die before their child so when it happens the other way around it can be excruciating in every way.

Losing a child is never easy and is often suffered by the stronger souls of the planet. Think about it; those experiencing this loss are gifted with a strength unlike any other to move through their grief and pick up the pieces of their shattered heart. Not an easy task to do in any case.

I can't personally imagine the pain or suffering that a parent would go through who has lost a child. But, I have seen many clients who lost children, and it scars them for life. They can get stuck in their grief not allowing themselves to move forward in their life from this experience. They may even be unaware they are still grieving 20 years after the loss. It is okay to feel whatever you are feeling in the moment. What isn't okay is to let yourself wallow in the pain of it forever more. Your loved ones want and need you to process and move forth.

Spirit tells me that those tasked with this loss have an important mission in life which often includes serving others by sharing your pain and grief in some way. This can be done through bereavement support groups, writing, talking or in a vast many other ways.

It is through the connecting and sharing about your personal experience that allows healing to take place. This is one of the many surprising gifts you will find in the darkness of child loss. Not an easy path no matter what way someone loses a child; each is as painful as the next to a parent.

One often finds a strength in child loss they didn't know existed within them as they move through the stages of bereavement. As you read the information below on the various child losses, please keep in mind much of the information can apply to any death. This also is just a small part of insights to start your journey. I recommend that you read the entire book as you will receive many blessings as you do so.

First and foremost, I want to affirm that just because your child may have left the physical world does not mean that you lost your child. They are still with you and thus you are still a parent.

For some parents, knowing this truth helps them to feel more at peace knowing they are not alone. It helps parents to know their child is continuing to experience, learn and grow alongside of them. Know they are still partaking in the functions of the family, and see, hear, feel and know all that is going on with you all still. They are whispering to you to let you know they are okay and are with you all. They want you to be happy and to celebrate living life to the fullest, on their behalf.

Now let's get on with the business of talking about the various forms of child loss that a person can experience in their life.

Remember to read through each type as there is much healing and enlightenment to be received through it all. Much of the information shared throughout is valid and applicable to other aspects of death as well. Of course, child loss can happen at any age and to the parent it is devastating still to have lost a child – whether the child is an infant, fifty or lost through miscarriage or another way.

The Gifts of Miscarriages

Those that have miscarriages often carry a guilt feeling that they must of did something wrong that led to the loss. Whether it was the days or weeks leading up to the actual loss parents often feel they are being punished for something. This could even be related to another part of their life or their past lives.

If you have lost a child due to miscarriage, please know this was all part of a bigger plan that was put into place long before you became pregnant. This often has nothing to do with anything you did or didn't do in this or any lifetime. Many times, the timing wasn't right for the birth or there was something wrong with the child. This may have led you down a road that wasn't a part of the divine plan.

I know this doesn't ease your pain knowing this. Hopefully, it will however bring you a little peace knowing it was not because of anything you did or didn't do.

Let me also tell you, you didn't miss a sign that could have saved your child's life in many of these situations. Their birth simple was not meant to happen. Some people often think if they only went to the doctor something could have been done to save the child. It doesn't matter if you were having cramps, spotting or something else was happening; you did not miss the sign.

You did the best you could at the time. If this child was meant to live something would have made sure you got to the medical help needed in time. Spirit has confirmed this many times when clients come to me after losing a child wondering if they could have saved their child.

Do you really think the Divine wouldn't have inspired and motivated you into action if there was a chance to save your child? Your soul is powerful and if you were to follow a sign, it would have made sure you listened and took action accordingly. You wouldn't have just had one or two opportunities to save your unborn child if it was meant to be.

Let me share a story from my private client sessions; one that is familiar with many clients I have seen who suffered the loss of their child.

Linda and I had been part of an online community group for a while when one day she reached out to me to ask about booking a healing session. I happily agreed to be of service for her in this manner.

The day came for the session and upon her arrival we took a few moments to get comfortable with each other. This would make sure she would feel comfortable laying in a vulnerable state on the massage table for the energy work about to unfold.

Once she was settled on the table, we began the session with an opening prayer. Her angels showed me a hole in her heart and a balloon on the side of her hip. I knew right away she had lost a child and felt it had been through a miscarriage.

Now this is not always how it shows up for everyone. For me, when a client comes to me after child loss Spirit will usually show me the balloon on the side of their left hip. Sometimes it shows up in another way and sometimes the client isn't even aware they had a miscarriage. This particularly can be the case when they suffered a child loss in the early days of a pregnancy.

I sat with the energy for a few minutes allowing the divine spiritual realm to channel the healing light through me for this clients highest good.

When I felt that the client was in a receptive place I opened up the conversation to ask if she had lost a child through miscarriage. Which she confirmed and the conversation continued to flow. It wasn't long before spirit showed me that while she had miscarried that the embryo's energy was still present and that she needed to release it.

I shared with her this information and how it was holding her back with processing her grief. Before long after other information from Spirit was shared she was ready to give birth to her son. This was a highly emotional experience as you can imagine. Thankfully she trusted in spirit and in me to guide her with this process.

We continued on with the session and when we were done, she felt lighter and was glowing. Her heart had been filled with the loving light of her soul and thus she was whole once again. She walked out of the session and it wasn't long before she and her husband found themselves pregnant once again; this time carrying to full term and giving birth to a healthy happy baby boy. The same soul of the child that was stuck in utero came back through them.

I share this particular story with you as many people who suffer from miscarriages have trouble conceiving or carrying a child to full-term afterwards. Spirit has told me that many times it is because they are still energetically pregnant. They need to clear the old energy of the earlier child before they can carry and give birth to a physically healthy child.

In the second part of this book, you will find a sacred ceremony which Spirit has guided to me to help clear the old energy and emotions. This will allows you to make room to carry to full-term and give birth to a healthy child. This sacred ceremony has been highly successful for my clients and I truly pray you receive many blessings as well.

The Gifts of Abortions

There are many beliefs held when it comes to choosing to end an embryo's life. I am not here to sway anyone's opinion either way, I would just like to state what Spirit has shared with me on this subject.

Every soul that chooses to incarnate into human form is doing so knowing the entire main journey they will experience including when and how they will leave the physical world. This is part of the soul contracts made with those that they asked to play the role of the biological parents.

These contracts contain the basics of what each soul wishes to experience, lessons plans and other aspects that will allow the soul to continue to expand; they also include plans to pay off any karmic debt from earlier lifetimes. The pathways on how each aspect may play out are many and are often dictated by the human experience and the choices we make along the way.

The soul may have chosen to be only conceived for a certain period and ultimately be aborted. This choice may have also been made on the spiritual level by the mother and father due to their personal life circumstances. Abortions are often intuitively guided by the soul who has instigated the carrying out of the sacred contract plan for the journey of all concerned.

Sometimes though the soul will step in to cause you to abort the child because there is something wrong with the development of the embryo. When this is the case usually the action step will be after receiving a doctor's recommendation to abort. This can lead to feelings of guilt or the parents thinking they did something wrong or could have prevented it from happening. Many times this is simply not true. Of course, when drugs or something illicit are involved, there may be a component of truth to this. But ultimately the decision was a part of the contracts that were playing out.

Sometimes the abortion is a catalyst for someone's lessons or life mission that will come about after the actual procedure takes place. However, rest assured everything is a part of the divine plan put into place on the spirit level. Life is unfolding as it should be and is always in the highest good of all concerned. This is the case at all times whether we are consciously aware of this fact or not.

The Gift of Stillbirths

I cannot imagine the pain losing a child holds no matter what way the death unfolded having not personally experienced it. I can only imagine that giving birth to a still born would behold great pain for the parents of such a loss. This would be because their hopes and dreams for their unborn child came crashing down around them in an instant as their heart was torn into a million little pieces.

Many times the parents and even the doctors are only finding out at the last minute that the unborn child has died in utero. They may have had regular doctor appointments where everything was normal right up to the week of delivery. The parents go into a shock unlike any experience before when this happens. There is a disbelief that their child is dead. This is quickly demolished when the mother gives birth to her lifeless child after hoping the doctors are wrong. Now instead of celebrating the birth they are left to plan a funeral; a sad occasion for all.

There are many medical reasons which also can play a role in their child's death. Some of the most common problems: Birth defects, problems with the placenta, placenta abruption, umbilical cord problems, preeclampsia or pregnancy induced hypertension.

I won't go into the medical aspects further as that isn't my specialty, so I will leave it to the professionals to speak about that further. However, I will say if you strongly feel the pull to understand all the medical component of stillbirths or child deaths, you are likely awakening to your healing gifts and/or your life purpose. By researching on this topic you are gaining the wisdom and knowledge to further help another on your path ahead.

The Gift Within the Darkness

I would like to share with you the metaphysical components of this death. Like miscarriages and abortions, along with many other deaths, the sacred contracts are a part of the equation. Mostly though stillbirths play a role in the lives of those souls left behind with their life lessons and what they have chosen to experience in this life.

For some people, it leads them to finding their life purpose to be of service to others who have experienced similar life events. Sometimes the purpose is as simple as to bring two people together to work out karma or to be a catalyst for something else.

Death can bring you closer to your partner, family and friends which is one of the gifts of loss. Even with the pain being experienced on this journey the energy that is love is bringing forth healing, helping to shift, connect and awaken all.

We are all more similar and connected than many realize and thus when someone is going through the bereavement process we begin to see the veils of illusions drop. This is why many people often speak of seeing someone's true colors when they are going through something. However, that is only a part of the truth in the case involving death or grief.

The truth of the matter is that many people have a fear of death and the energy that surrounds it. We humans don't want to face that what we see as our bodies or life is not real; that what is real is beyond it which is our soul. We fear that we will be judged or ridiculed or whatever once we transition to the other side.

This is not the case. Yes, we will go through a life review when we cross over so we can see, experience and understand the bigger picture, but we are not judged for it. Everything that transpired was a part of the divine plan. We will feel how our actions, choices, words and everything played out in our lives but also we will experience the ripple effect of it all. The immense love we feel is indescribable and overpowers the lower vibrations of all else.

When you look at any death, including stillbirths, what unfolds is a coming together to share, support and celebrate the life of a soul. It matters not how long the soul was physical; it matters that love is bringing people together. Love truly is all that is real and true; thus love is all that matters. Let the rest go.

It's unfortunate to see that weddings and funerals are often the only time many people will see each other. Spirit wishes to remind you that you were born into a family to learn and grow together, so embrace the part of you that is connected to them. We may not always agree or get along, but love remains to be shared. Look for it and let the light shine.

Often when one suffers a loss is when one awakens to the soul and a higher state of consciousness or spiritual perspectives. This is a part of the reason we have to experience death so we can appreciate or open up to the gifts within that perhaps were ignored along the way.

A Client's Story

Let me share a story with you now about a former client who had lost a child with her husband and the impact of losing this child at birth. Their child's loss was devastating to them both. Unbeknownst, to either of them at the time, they had lost a part of their soul during this highly traumatic experience. It impacted their personal and business relationships which led to the closing of their business and ultimately a divorce.

I met them both 20 years after the loss of their child in a session where they were finally able to reclaim their soul and heal. More importantly in this case was the ability to forgive each other, and themselves for their loss. They each had blamed the other for their child's death, when in truth neither one of them was to blame. This particular soul was not meant to be born physically and it was a catalyst for the life lesson involving forgiveness.

Once they realized what a gift the loss was for them both they found some peace. This led to them moving forward after being stuck in their grief for so long. They came to an understanding which allowed them to process their emotions. With this they stopped blaming each other and could finally heal their shattered hearts.

Having come back to a place of heart they were able to become friends again and could partake in family functions with their other children to live, love and laugh once again. Last I heard they had attended each other's weddings and were genuinely happy for all.

Death does not mean that you have to die along with your child. Death is an opportunity for you to live life in their memory and do something to help another who may have experienced a similar loss. Remember one of the gifts of death is that it can bring people together. So, why not let those that feel alone in their pain know someone understands what they are going through? In this way your child lives on as you are in service for others.

You have the choice to either let their death and the pain you are in cause a separation from those that love you or you can choose to find a way to process your grief together. Remember they are also in pain and need time to process. Take a moment to put yourself in their shoes to find a way to help each other through your emotionally trying time.

Everyone deals with life events in different ways. Each way is just as valid as another to those trying to pick up the pieces after life throws them a curve ball; the same is true for you. So take time each day to look through the eyes of love and let your soul guide you to be there for one another, however you can be.

Ask what would your child say to you and let their soul guide you along the path as need be. After all the soul is connected to the light for it resides within it always. They want you to both heal and be happy once again as you are their parents, and they love you both more than words can say. So love yourselves enough to reach out and comfort each other through your bereavement process.

The Gifts Within the Death of a Young Infant

Like any death, it is always hard to lose and grieve someone that was a part of our lives. This is especially true for parents who lose an infant.

Imagine doing everything to love, protect, guide and support this child to be the best they could be in life. To teach them to do good things in the world, only to have the walls come crashing down upon you in a flash; your heart instantly ripped out. This is definitely not a journey any parent should ever experience.

I have been privileged to be a witness in conversations between a parent and their child after death many times, and every time, my heart feels for them. It truly is an honor to see the healing that takes place throughout and after the session for these souls.

I have found that many times the parents who have suffered this emotionally devastating loss have a higher purpose that involves helping others through their pain. It's therapeutic to share your thoughts and emotions with another that gets what you are going through as you both offer support.

Sometimes it is hard for one to open up to the emotions stuffed behind the door, but that is exactly what needs to be done. The door has to be opened and you need to walk through it to embrace and accept whatever you are feeling. You can't hide from it forever. Like lava heating up in a volcano, the steam will heat will continue to heat it up and it eventually will erupt through the surface. But, you are safe to open the door to feel and experience whatever you need to.

Allow yourself to feel your pain; embrace your anger, your guilt, your grief or whatever else you may be experiencing in the turmoil of the volcano of grief. It is healthy to process as it allows you to eventually move forward into a place of love and acceptance.

Start where you are and take one step forward each day as you can. Sometimes, you will need to push yourself to start to reclaim your life after your loss. I promise you it will be worth it as you keep taking steps; you may not feel that now, but you will someday.

The first step may be to just to get out of bed and looking at your husband to let him know you are there for him as well. Perhaps picking up a pen to journal your thoughts to help you process is your first step. Maybe it is setting up a blog to journal and share your story with others who may be also suffering in silence.

Your child wants you taking loving care of yourself so eat, get out for a walk, exercise and just do something to nurture yourself. Do all this in their honor.

Whatever your step is know you are not alone. Your child is walking alongside you and so if you can't do it for yourself, do it for them. After all you are still a parent, even through your child has left the physical world.

A part of the reason your child has left you is so they can assist with your soul evolution from the other side as per your sacred contracts. I know that this doesn't make your pain go away.

I can't even say I understand what you are going through because it is your personal journey. But as someone who has grieved many I have been close to I can relate in my own way to your loss and I feel for you. I am sorry that you had to experience such pain but I promise you there is a gift in it all, and eventually you will see it.

I hope you are able to start to see the light guiding you along the way through this book in some way. Thus, in time find the gift(s) that have been awaiting you.

Another reason that your child has left the physical world was because their mission was complete on the earth and their sacred contract had ended physically. This also means they can now continue to grow, learn and experience from the soul perspective alongside with you. I know hearing this doesn't make your pain less excruciating. Hopefully, knowing that they are with you still helps.

As a soul, we all are multidimensional and thus can be with many at the same time. When you are thinking or being reminded of your loved one in some way, they are with you, and perhaps other family members at the same time. This is one of the reasons that many who are left behind after someone crosses over have visitations or thoughts about the soul at the time of death. They are basically letting you know they are alive and free of the body; that they are still with you, loving and appreciating you in new ways.

Know they hear your communications with them, not just the verbal ones you have with them, but also those from the mind or heart vibrations. They want you to heal your fragmented heart and find happiness in life again. They want you to pick up the pieces and begin to truly live again. They know it's hard for they are not physically with you any longer.

Know as you walk the path ahead they too walk with you holding your hand as they did in life so many times. You never know what miracles lie ahead unless you take the step to move forward. Your loved one wants you to know you are stronger than you think and you can do this.

Your child will send you signs that they are with you in a variety of manners. It could be rainbows or butterflies to sightings of others who remind you of them. The signs could even come through songs, television shows, or the many things that go bump in the night. Your child knows just how to communicate the sign to you at the right time and moment. Trust that you will recognize it, time and time again; that it will show up when you may need it most. Let me say to let go of the how and the way it comes, just know and expect it to happen. Believe in it!

Your child wants you to move forward and to do so, you must process whatever you are feeling. They want you to get to the point where you can forgive yourself and let the feeling of failing them go. You are not a failure; you did everything you were supposed to according to the divine plan. You loved them. You did your best to protect and keep them safe each day based on where you were in your mind and heart space. You helped to guide them and support them on their earthly mission. Now is the time for them to begin their next phase of their soul evolution.

They ask you to please know by forgiving yourself, and by finding a way to be at peace and accept what has transpired, that you are not going to forget them. You never will; they are a part of you and will always stay a part of your life through your memories, heart and life experiences. Forgiveness just allows you to let the pain go, pick up the pieces and heal your broken heart with time.

They truly love and appreciate everything you did for them in life and continue to each day. Love yourself to free yourself from your emotional or mental prison; love yourself to allow yourself to rise out of the ashes. Please honor your child by reclaiming and living your life to the fullest. Remember you still have a family to live for.

All too often parents lose a child and then they allow themselves to shrivel up in a corner, slowing dying inside. Don't let this be you. Losing a loved one unexpectedly can cause a part of your soul to be lost. But, as you begin to live again, you can reclaim this piece of your soul as I spoke about in previous chapters.

Child Loss is Painful at Any Age

Losing a child is hell, plain and simple; no matter what the age or how the loss unfolded. Whether through natural causes, or murder, suicide, disease, drugs, or another way, each death is just as painful as the next to a parent. Each holds its own special brand of hell for those left behind to deal with what has transpired. Let us try not to compare or judge one death over another, all hold the pain of grief and the darkness that comes with it.

Death changes the way we think and live our lives whether we are conscious or unconscious of this fact. After a death suddenly we are thrust into an experience that leaves us questioning life, God, our decisions and so much more. This is certainly true for parents who have lost their child to a tragedy of any sort.

Parents often may take heat from others which may have questioned their choices in the raising of the child. People always think they know better than those involved in the rearing of one's child. Everyone always has an opinion and let me tell you what spirit says on this.

Mind your own vibrations and energy; don't care what others think. That's their own concern, you have enough of your own. As long as you know within your heart and soul you did the best you could or you try a little better moving forward each day that is what matters!

You are doing the best you can at every moment. It isn't like anyone taught you directly how to raise children. You learned through the on-the-job training you underwent when you were thrown into the fire after your first born came into the world. You learned through watching your mom and dad raise you, and either followed in their footsteps or trying to do better. You may have read books or gotten advice along the way which was beneficial. But, nothing teaches like a little one crying out for your love and attention as they grow up and explore life.

Your soul placed you and your child in an environment where one could learn, grow and experience to the fullest. A place where you felt safe and secure. Do you think it was an accident that you lived where you were living during the time of raising your children? Not at all.

Everything is unfolding by divine design and very calculated for the life lessons and the journey ahead for you all. You all sat at the Divine Counsel table with all the souls that were to play a role in this lifetime's story. Together you set up the sacred contracts and rest of your plans for this life. Your child would play one role in your story, and you would play another.

Sometimes this led your child down a darker road in order for them to find themselves further, to grow or expand as a soul. On the spirit level you understood this and had great love and respect for your child's soul for choosing this path; knowing it would not be an easy journey. But you loving their soul immensely agreed to go through though the journey alongside with them, and to suffer the angst of physically losing them to death.

Losing of a Child through Murder or Suicide

You knew this type of loss would not be easy. There was the possibility you knew that you could end up bitter, old, gray and alone fighting for them after they were murdered until the day you died yourself. A part of you knew if you chose to, you could learn to see the light and find forgiveness for all. You would then experience the gift that would live long after your son or daughter died. You knew it was a choice you could make and either way a gift would be showed along the journey.

You knew there were lessons and experiences along life's roadways for both the victims and the perpetrators. You knew they asked to explore them all in the physical world. You knew the journey wouldn't be easy no matter what, but you agreed to play the role still of a parent and caregiver still.

You knew it would be painful to watch your child abuse themselves with drugs or alcohol until they day the passed from the earth. You knew that this was their path and that you would play a certain role for them, both in life and afterwards. You agreed to support them the best way you could.

You knew the events of their earlier years would play an important role in their life experiences and lessons. You vowed to do the best you could for them. You even knew sometimes the pain they would experience would be caused by you and your choices in life. But, eventually you would have to learn to love, accept and forgive yourself through the bereavement journey.

You knew their pain, struggles and sacrifices would all lead to them taking their life. After all, the darkness of depression and their burdens they carried within the mind and heart would overwhelm them at one point. It is then they sought and found relief to their inner turmoil they were experiencing, through suicide. They felt alone and yet knew there were many that loved and would help them. They just didn't humanly know how to reach out to ask for the support they so desperately needed. Their fears overcame them.

You knew there was a bigger plan in play and that you all were like actors playing a leading role in the movie that was the storybook of your lives. You knew all this and even greater still; in fact, deep within your heart you still do. You just need to reconnect and remember.

The death of a child is horrible in itself, but when it is related to murder or suicide, it weighs on your mind all the more. We shall talk more about this terrible loss in a chapter dedicated to the topic.

The Gift Within the Darkness

Trading Pain for Peace

Meditation is one such way to help you find some inner peace through the process of grieving your loved ones. As you sit in silence their soul will be right by yourself as you discover a part of yourself long forgotten. Though meditation you are able to reconnect and heal as you will discover in part two of this book.

No matter how your child has died, know you have the right to feel as you do. Others may try to put themselves in your shoes or even try to tell you what you should or shouldn't be doing or feeling. But you know what, you are doing exactly what you are meant to be doing in every moment, and no one can tell you otherwise. In time, you will see the light again after you process your emotions and begin moving forward. I promise you that as hard as it may be right now for you to see past the tip of your nose; it will get easier in time.

Remember every action has a consequence in life and those impact us in ways that live long after the initial experience. One may reject relationships later in life because they felt hurt or abandoned earlier in life. This would cause them to protect their heart by pushing away the one thing they wish for and that is LOVE.

I ask you to be mindful of your thoughts, words, choices and actions with your loved ones. Take time each day to show them how much you love and appreciate them. For tomorrow may be too late as you now know through your loss.

You can't change the past but you can sure change the future with simple steps that you take each day. Start today where you are and before you know it, you will be living, loving and laughing once again with your heavenly children by your side in the gift of the present.

Brian D. Calhoun

Prayer for Those Grieving the Loss of a Child

Dearest Mother-Father God,

We come to you today to ask for your heavenly enveloping love and light to surround the hearts of those of us who are grieving the loss of a child.

We know this to be one of the most painful deaths that a parent can experience and thus can hold great darkness within. So, we ask that your omnipresent light shines brightly within the crevices of our being to bless, heal and connect all to the light of the soul.

Help us forgive ourselves for the soul roles we may have played in the death of our child. Let us forgive all others for any role they played in honoring the sacred contracts of our child's soul.

Let us process, understand and find peace within our loss so we can move forward in life, one day at a time.

Help us know our child is now at peace, healthy and whole, and growing up alongside of us living life fully each day.

Please God heal our empty shattered hearts of the grief of the loss of our child and fill it with your highest love and light now. Where it is your will God, please allow our child's soul to be rebirthed into physical reality in your way and time. We ask for this so we can know the soul on the earth as we do in heaven.

We now surrender to your will God our prayer and everything within it for perfect resolution and outcome.

For all this and even better, we give our thanks, and so it is as it is now done.

Amen

The Gift Within the Darkness

CHAPTER 12

Bliss, Heartache, Grief and the Blessings that Come with It

C.C. Charest

My journey through grief starts a couple years ago, it began and ended in the beautiful month of May. My husband and I had started discussing the possibility of bringing children into our lives. We were so blissful that after my birthday on the 23rd of May we started trying. Surprisingly, it didn't take long at all. We were pregnant with our first child; we told all our loved ones and did everything right. We started reading parenting books right away; I ate healthy and took my prenatal vitamin like nobody's business.

This pregnancy was perfect; no morning sickness, no aches or pains, I felt so lucky. Finally, the day came for our first ultrasound. The technician was asking strange questions; it didn't seem at all like the experiences I had read about from other women. We were sent straight away to our doctor's office who was already waiting for us. Our hearts knew. Our little baby was stuck in my right tube and before I could comprehend or understand what was going on I was waking up from an emergency surgery. This pregnancy was "ectopic", we were assured the life wasn't viable and to not worry. Our baby's life was not viable...

The time that passed was difficult, at the time it seemed like my body was the one that wasn't healed. I was truly masked to my own emotions reality. We continued to try and with great fear and hope we became pregnant again. We thought we had passed the storm, and we soon found out that not only were we pregnant but we were pregnant with twins! What a blessing. We had an ultrasound early to unsure everything was where it was supposed to be and got to see two strong hearts fluttering away.

For a moment our hearts felt relief and true peace. It was short lived. Our second ultrasound, which happened to be on my birthday in May, showed they had not progressed; their hearts stopped beating days after our first ultrasound. Everything hit me at once. Every emotion filled my body, and I truly didn't feel an ounce of myself amidst the grief and pain. How could we feel this way for souls that I didn't know in our physical reality? That's the thing about souls, they don't know reality; they only know energy.

Growing up I had felt pain, and I thought I knew what heartbreak was but I had no idea. I didn't know that heartbreak means you can actually feel physical pain in your heart. Everything felt so dark and it seemed the rain outside didn't stop.

My relationship, with my husband, hit a low it had never been to, we didn't understand each other we didn't understand one another's grief. I held on to the loss because I thought if I let go, I was letting them go which was the hardest hurtle. With patience and support I learned how to let go of the pain not the love I had.

I learned to count on my Angels and strengthen my relationship with God.

People deal with loss so differently; some expect you to sweep it under the rug or think saying "next time" will make it better. The best thing to do is to walk into the flame and allow yourself to feel every emotion. The lessons learned through grief become your blessings and your strength that no one not even yourself can take away. I wish I had known how important allowing love into your life is. It is a power that every person holds and it is truly the only thing that can heal a broken heart.

I have finally allowed myself to feel and give the love that is deserved and our blessings have become to many to count.

Update from Author: After using the Sacred Release Ceremony included in part two of this book, C.C. Charest has gone on to successful conceive and deliver a beautiful and healthy baby girl. She cherishes and is grateful every day for this miracle.

The Gift Within the Darkness

CHAPTER 13

Rainbow After the Storm

Angie Carter

A STORM CAN COME through at any moment when you least expect it. It can paralyze you and leave destruction in its wake, forcing you to rebuild your life once it passes. Sometimes the most devastating storms will bring with it a beautiful rainbow and remind you to hold on to hope.

Our storm hit on the morning of June 28, 2014, when my mother carried my limp baby girl down the stairs. Isabella wasn't breathing! I took her from my mother's arms and put her on the floor where I began to perform CPR while I told my mother to call 9-1-1. Strength came over me as I focused on what I needed to do to help my baby girl. Bella was brought to the hospital by ambulance and a short while later, a nurse hugged me and told me that she was so sorry, they did everything they could.

My universe collapsed in that instant and life was forever changed. Bella was only 19-months-old and perfectly healthy; it made no sense! I was a single mother trying to survive when, without warning, every parent's worst nightmare became my reality.

Numbness came over me and I was unable to process what happened. The next day, I began to feel pain as I realized that a piece myself had died. It felt as though my heart was being ripped out of my chest. I felt as though I was suffocating. I began to scream and couldn't stop until I passed out and stopped breathing.

I saw the white light everyone talks about and felt Bella's presence just beyond it. She was just out of my reach and I kept trying to touch her, begging her to take me with her. Bella told she couldn't take me away from my son as he needed me more than she did. She said that my mission in this lifetime wasn't complete; I have a lot more to accomplish and she promised to be with me every step of the way. When I woke up in the hospital, I felt her energy surround me and knew that I had really communicated with her.

The numbness returned despite feeling Bella's energy. I was present in my body but unable to feel a thing. I simply existed and was in denial of my reality. I would close my eyes and pretend everything was fine. In my mind, Bella was visiting her father, or maybe she was at daycare. I was unable to accept that she would never return home again.

Disconnecting from reality allowed me to find the strength needed to get through the first few weeks following her death. My time was spent with family and a few close friends. People surrounded me, yet all I really wanted was to be alone. Slowly, life seemed to be going back to normal for everyone else while I felt stuck and alone. I began packing Bella's belongings into totes I kept in a bedroom I hoped would be hers someday soon. As I did this, I didn't feel a thing. I didn't cry; I didn't feel sad or angry; I just went through the motions. You would expect this to be a difficult thing to do, but it wasn't.

I spent months trying to stop being so strong. I was afraid that if I allowed myself to feel this pain again that I wouldn't survive. Being strong wasn't a choice, it was necessary! Subconsciously, I was protecting myself from the pain, repressing it until I was ready to deal with it. I knew the only way to heal was to feel the pain and release it. I was grateful for the tears when I was able to cry as to me, tears were a reminder of my love for Bella. I was finally able to let go when I was away from everyone I knew. On a beach in Maui, I let my emotions rise to the surface and flow out of me. This was when healing finally began.

The first year was the most difficult as I navigated through many firsts without Bella, but she kept reminding me that I was not alone. Whether it was a rainbow, a song, or a toy playing music, I was reminded every day that she wasn't far away. Bella has confirmed through a medium that she is still very much alive. She is in a beautiful place full of rainbows; she loves to smell flowers and makes sure to kiss me goodnight every night. She led my husband to me, a man she calls her "Dream Daddy." He gave me strength to keep breathing when it felt impossible to go on and continues to give me the unconditional love and support to carry on.

The last year of Bella's life was very challenging and the days I had with her were some of the most difficult of my life. Bella has taught me more in this lifetime than anyone else. She helped me develop patience, taught me to survive with very little sleep and showed me that despite the largest of obstacles, life is beautiful. She taught me to be happy on purpose and to hold on to these happy memories because they are the only thing that can't be taken away from us. In spite of losing Bella, I am grateful for the time we had together. I would choose this unimaginable heartache over and over again because not knowing her would have been much worse.

Three years later, grief continues to come in waves and I have learned to ride them as they come. The storm is finally behind me and I am surrounded by rainbows. Bella is now a big sister and continues to send us signs from heaven. When I look back on the darker days, I can truly see the gifts. I kept saying how life became so complicated when Bella was born. It's amazing how quickly the "worst 19 months of my life" instantly became the BEST and most cherished time I could ever have hoped for. We often have no control over events in life, just as I had no control over losing Bella. The only part of life you can control is your reaction to it, and I will always choose to react with love and hope. If I can have this attitude after losing my baby girl, I think anyone can do this. One day at a time.

Angie Carter is the author of the upcoming book: Rainbows from Heaven: A Grieving Mother's Journey of Love, Loss and Healing and has co-authored a number of other books.

CHAPTER 14

THE GIFTS WITHIN THE LOSS OF A SIBLING

DEATH SUCKS! NO MATTER who leaves the physical world it's hard and it's even harder when they're someone we closely grew up with. When they die a part of us dies with them many a time. If you are lucky through, you will be able to take your time to say your goodbyes.

Brothers and Sisters are our rock when we are growing up. From the moment of birth we are bonded through love. They are often our go to people when Mom or Dad are busy doing something and we want someone to bug, play or just be ourselves with. They are the ones we share our deepest secrets with and can joke about family, life and love. When we are having a bad day, perhaps they will be the ones that will help pick us up or we will help them. We may have our greatest fights with them and in the end all is forgiven most times as we love each other.

Our siblings are often our original best friends and are soul family members here to gift our lives in divinely sacred ways. The sibling relationship can be complex at times and when they leave us, it can be a challenge. When they leave we have lost our friend, our enemy, our teammate, our competitor and a member our intimate circle.

During life we shared life experiences that often only we understand as siblings. We both have been on the two sides of the coin with loving and longing for our parent's time or loving affection. Our sibling rivalry may have continued throughout life and even into our adulthood. But one thing is certain and that is no matter underneath what remains is the true love we have for our brother or sister.

Whatever life may have put you through together or separately the loss is often devastating to those left behind. After all you shared a history together and were intertwined in life for years. When they leave us, to continue with our life, it can be a blow to our hopes and dreams we may have held for the future with them. The pain can be unbearable and felt for years to come.

Losing a loved one is felt by all, on subconscious and conscious levels with every passing holiday, tradition or celebration. A sibling's pain in loss is just as real as their parent's pain who also lost their child. It is as real as the spouse who has lost their partner in life or the child who has lost their parent. There is a profound sense of loss and a hole in the heart left behind no matter who dies.

The simple truth of the matter is the closer the relationship you had with the departed the more difficult their loss will be on you.

The bond of love is strong and can bring great pain with it when a close relationship is lost. With time it will become easier for you especially as you surround yourself with supportive people who can be there during your darker periods of mourning.

Your grief is real and needs to be acknowledged rather than pushed down into the deep crevices of your being. Allow yourself the gift to process in your own way and time. Everyone goes through the bereavement process differently and every time we grieve someone we may experience it uniquely. No two deaths are grieved alike.

Remember you are a part of a family and each family member may have their own way of grieving. Now is the time to recognize and acknowledge the love for one another so you be there for each other. After all, you understand in your own way what they are going through.

Communication is key to healing so have open and honest communications with each other about what you are experiencing. Sometimes, it can be exactly what the doctor ordered to help heal that hole in your heart.

Grief affects us all; no matter what our age.

Experiencing death when we are a child can lead to fears and anxieties taking over and even a lifelong process of grieving and understanding the loss. A child may not fully understand what is going on until later in life, and may end up having a fear of death or dying. It is better to get the proper help to explain and help your child process, heal and understand so they can be free to be a kid once again. It isn't abnormal for a young sibling left behind to end up with anxiety over becoming sick or worse when they lose their older brother or sister.

I know as a child I had my moments and even wished my siblings dead at times (as most of us have at some point). We don't mean this of course, but if a child loses their sibling after having these thoughts or voicing it out, the guilt will eat at them something fierce. They believe they played a role in their death and so they may act out in some way. It is important that we provide them with the support to help them through this. Think about if it was you and how you may feel in their shoes. Use this as an opportunity to open up conversations about death and the doors for healing.

When a child loses their sibling there can be a fallout from other family members also going through grief. Unfortunately the fallout sometimes lands on the remaining children. Children often experience a temporary double or even triple loss. This because their other siblings and parents need time to grieve and process their child's death as well.

Unfortunately too often the parent's loss of a child takes a toll on their other relationships. This can cause them to neglect one or more of their remaining living children only to end up in a grief filled dark hole; leading them to depression or other illnesses.

It is important to get help for the entire family as you are all grieving, each in your own way. Having the proper support for each member can help you all process, heal and find a way to move forward. Don't allow the burdens to fall on the younger generation. They will feel compelled to grow up and become a parent figure for you and other members of the family. Remember it's *a strength to reach out and get help* as appropriate for each person, especially our younger members who lost their brother or sister.

When a profound loss happens in our lives, we can often find ourselves mimicking the deceased at times. This can be especially true for the younger generation left behind. It can be a simple as headaches or stomach aches to digestive systems or more. Grief has a way of manifesting symptoms that many don't understand along the way. This is why it's so important to take time to work through what we are experiencing and feeling and help each other grieve in their own way and time.

Some people will be more emotional or forthcoming in their grief and others like I did will close themselves off. I know for myself when I was in my darker moments with grief I wish that someone would have been there to help allow healing opportunities and conversations. I was blind to my pain and couldn't see it for myself.

Having someone to help guide me through the darkness to uncover the light would have truly been a gift. The important thing is to be a listening ear and not to play the blame game or anything if there was something that happened. We all make mistakes and this isn't the time to bring that old baggage up. It is a time for love and healing.

Your loved ones want you to make peace with what has happened and find a way to move forward without them physically. They will walk and hold your hand each step of the way, spiritually, I promise you. You will never be alone.

To feel and experience their presence you have to move through the darkness of the night to find the light that rises each day with you. When that happens you will feel their heavenly presence. For now, just know it with every fiber of your being they are walking the path with you and with all of you that are grieving them.

Every time you see a picture of them (or something which may have belonged to them) this is their way of letting you know they are with you. The same is true when you think of them, hear their name or a song which reminds you of them. Remember they are now at peace and enjoying life with their new heavenly perspectives alongside of you.

Your siblings don't want you to hoard everything that belonged to them. They would rather you keep one or two special things which bring comfort and good memories to you. This way when you need a reminder or to feel close to them you have something of theirs. They do not want you to make your home a shrine to them or to keep their room the same. Life continues to move on, and your loved ones want you to keep moving forward with it.

Too many people think with time their loved ones memory will fade as well your loved one will always help you remember their happier moments of life. Take time to write your memories of them in a special book. You can then share this at the holidays with your other family members and you can all add your stories of your loved one to this special memory keeper. This way you will have a special heirloom you can pass on to future generations about your sibling and most importantly for you to remember them through.

The Twin Connection

Spirit has shared that twins have a special bond which continues to exist long after the physical death of the other. When one twin leaves the other behind to continue life on earth, it can be a challenge.

Twins often will feel guilty around being the one that survived, or because they felt they weren't able to protect their sibling or there were things left unsaid.

It is especially hard on a twin because you had that special twin connection where you each knew the other from the inside-out. However, perhaps as the surviving twin you feel guilty that you didn't know about their innermost struggles and hardships which may have led to this loss (especially in the case of suicide).

Twins, came into this world together and lived life as one soul split in two. There is a belief held when one goes the other half needs to feel incomplete. This is simply not true as your brother or sister is alive and well; they are now with you in spirit. You need not feel separated or whole as your connection is as strong as ever. You just need to remember this.

When you are grieving, it is hard to connect to the spirit world. Your pain is what keeps you separate. Remember your sibling wants you to be happy and to live life to the fullest. They want you to take life by the balls and show it whose boss.

Moving Forward

Whenever we are going through something difficult in life, it helps to be of service to another. Thus, do something in your loved ones memory: start a journal, create a blog, start a fundraiser, or volunteer with a local charity.

This is a great opportunity to discover something that your brother or sister enjoyed. It is an opportunity to get to know and appreciate what your sibling enjoyed by getting involved in things that brought them joy. Remember just because they have died doesn't mean you have to. Your sibling will be excited to have you join in their passions and will be right by your side through it all. You may or may not enjoy it, either way you got to understand them a little more.

Let losing your brother or sister be the start of something amazing as you continue to learn and grow together in your new relationship. If you have other siblings remember that now is a great opportunity to reach out to them. Get to know who they are and their passions, this will bring you closer together as you peer into their life. You may just discover something you didn't know you would enjoy. Either way, it will be a barrel of laughs as you spend quality time with each other living and loving life fully.

Grief changes our perspectives and our lives as we learn to live with it. But, you have the power to heal and grow through it rather than let it stop you from taking part in all that this world has to offer you. I know it may be hard, but let yourself take one step and then another, and then another. Before you know it you be running marathons partaking in life each day. It is then that the black hole which imploded within you the day you lost your loved one heals and you are once again able to breathe.

The Gift Within the Darkness

You are grieving and grief sucks, plain and simple. Honor yourself and your emotions by allowing yourself time to process everything in your way and time.

Give yourself the gift of love and compassion, for that is the gift your sibling now grants you. They want you to find a way to forgive yourself for your misgivings. Remember it does no one any good to hold on to unforgiveness over anything that has occurred or unfolded in the past. They own their own mistakes and have forgiven themselves. So they want you to give yourself this gift yourself. Forgiveness allows for healing to take place in your heart and soul; it is never about anyone else or the experiences along the way.

The wisdom gained and lessons learned through each part of the journey ultimately in the bigger picture is something that is well worth whatever you went through. Only time allows us to see the gifts contained within it all. When we forgive, we are filing the memory into our memory banks and choosing to start anew today. When this happens the experiences of the past no longer hold power over us and our lives.

Your sibling is now asking for forgiveness for them leaving you behind. It was not an easy task for them to do but it was their time. There are many blessings tied to their death that are in the process of unfolding. In time, you will understand the reasons things unfolded the way they did. Your sibling is apologetic to you and wants to set you free to heal; they ask for the forgiveness as a way to help you both.

Why not choose to just let the unforgiveness and past go, after all as long as they hold your power, you can't! Step into the power of love today so you can experience life as heaven knows it to be true.

Someone once said, "Forgiveness is giving up the hope of a better yesterday and remembering yesterday ended last night." So let's put yesterday to bed in honor of our loved ones and wake up in a refreshed state of beingness. This way you can experience the power of love, health and wealth in heavenly ways.

Grief can affect our lives long after the physical experience happens including affecting our finances, relationships, health and more. So love yourself to process your grief and let the healing effects help you in other ways.

I do not claim to understand the pain of losing a sibling in the traditional sense as mine are all physically alive. But, I do understand loss and having connected with people on the other side for others, I can assure you pain is pain; no matter whose soul leaves your life. Sure we can classify one type as being harder to endure than another, but in the end none of that matters.

Like all death there are gifts contained within each. Once we get past the initial shock of death, we can process and eventually see the blessings in the experience.

A Death Within a Death

Growing up I was close to my sister, Sheri and when life caused our family to be torn apart, it was hard on her and I both. We were suddenly both forced into living in separate homes for a period and didn't have contact with each other during this time; let alone any contact with our mom or family. It was very much a deathlike experience on the grand scale for a child.

While we may have known it was a temporary state of affairs, it was happening so fast we didn't have time to process what was happening. Within a few months we went from a happy family to being a divided family. Our parents separated, we were in foster care, our mother ripped out of our lives and having no contact with any family.

In the meantime, the foster system didn't consider our emotional needs given the circumstances at the time when they separated us without allowing us to have any contact with each other or our family. Children's Aid basically took the last remaining part of any resemblance or connection to our life and shredded it when we felt at our lowest.

I went through the whole gamut of emotions from abandonment, fear, anger, denial, sadness, grief and many others. I may have been coming up to my teens, but I was still a child trying to process the very real adult situations unfolding. I was grieving and yet no one was acknowledging this truth and so I acted up trying to get someone to listen to the emotionally scarred child within me.

No one explained what was going on which didn't help matters. At least when someone dies you can physically understand that, even if emotionally you are still processing and trying to figure out it all. To a child that is separated from the essence of life itself, their family, it takes a toll on them. They are questioning so many things in life, perhaps even questioning themselves. I was entering puberty at the same time as all this other confusing stuff unfolding in life. This led me down a darker path where I would need to process my grief of my hopes and dreams for the future. It may have not been a physical death that unfolded in my life, but grief is grief. It matters not if it is because of physical separation or an actual death one needs time.

One of gifts of this time was that it taught me to appreciate living in the moment and with whoever is in my life. It showed me who was there for me in the end and I need not another soul to make my life complete. It taught me a level of independence and I learned more about myself during that period of my life than the years leading up to them. For better and worse, I was discovering who I was.

In time my sister, mom and I were reunited, but the effects of what transpired those months lived on for years to come. Mom began moving on with life and eventually met someone; not long after we were told that Mom was pregnant. Before she would give birth another loss would transpire in our lives which I speak about in an upcoming chapter the gifts within other types of loss.

Life was changing and it wasn't an easy process as we were both being affected by grief and loss in a variety ways in our lives. For me, I was grieving the loss of my childhood as I moved into the teenage years. We all were grieving the loss our family, our family home, and so much more. For a child it was a lot to process and no one truly understands people who are grieving when changes like this unfold.

Our family had now grown in size and in a few years I would move out to live my own life. The relationship with my sister was changing as we were both becoming more independent which meant another level of loss. During all this we had a new sibling who wanted the love and attention of her siblings but here we were moving out and getting on with our lives.

Jamie is fifteen years younger than I so when I moved out she was young and impressionable. Her oldest brother leaving home and shortly afterwards her older sister following in my footsteps with moving out definitely affected her. How could it not? She was close to her brother and sister growing up.

With us leaving as she approached school age I can only imagine the impact it would have on her. I am sure she felt abandoned, confused and so much more at her young age. Jamie definitely would have been grieving the loss of the relationships with us she had come to know, much like Sheri and I grieved when we were separated from each other and our family. Surely time would allow her to process what was unfolding and heal her broken heart?

In the meantime, we all continued to grow. Soon Jamie would be old enough to make her own choices when our mom would die. This would leave Jamie at thirteen to grieve yet another loss on top of the many losses she experienced already in life. Losses that she never fully recovered from. She would begin down a darker path. She would find herself with addictions and the struggles that came with them. It would be this that would lead her into her own dark hole.

It would only be a few years before she would have her own family and be facing the hardest loss for her: the death of her dad. This was hard for her as she was very close to him from birth and then after my mom's death they would get closer. But like most children growing up she was mimicking him in many ways.

Sherman had his own addictions which he fought for years. After Jamie arrived on the scene within a few years, he was clean and sober for the rest of his life. She gave him a reason bigger than him and any excuse he could find to drink which keep him sober. When he died, unfortunately Jamie went into the first step in the bereavement process, denial. So when he was in the hospital at the end she avoided going to say her goodbyes until it was too late. Guilt would eat away at her for years to come.

Her pain and fear were causing her to react rather than to process and respond. Something all too many times we as humans do when life throws us a curve ball. Rather than take a step back to reflect upon what transpired we jump feet first into the pond; only to realize it was much deeper than we initially thought and that we can't swim.

She would continue further down into the pit of the darkness. Life and her relationships within the experience would continue to change and suffer as she grieved. Having her own addiction problems led her to losing her young child for a time as she complied with the court orders. Once she had custody once again, the darkness, her pain and fears would cause her to go into hiding; away from us all. Leaving her maternal siblings grieving the loss of any relationship with our sister and our niece.

Eventually heaven could reach through the dark clouds and help to reconnect us, little by little. It seemed like one step forward two steps back as we were reconnected with my niece but the damage of Jamie's addiction had taken hold.

It wouldn't be long before my niece was removed from the home and placed into my other sister's custody once again. I am sure this also fueled the anger Jamie already held within. Her life was unraveling with her pain of loss at the root of it. She lost not one but two children now with the youngest now living with her father and her teenage daughter now in family care.

Her fears had come to manifestation as she went on the run because of fear of losing her child and here she was now having to face it two-fold. What you put out into the universe will always come back to you multiplied.

This is just one lesson Jamie's darkness was trying to teach her and now you by extension for your own story. We can run and hide out of fear or we can trust in love to heal, support and bless us in our lives. I have learned this universal life lesson and I know many others are mastering this lesson. It we stop, breathe and take a moment before reacting we are more likely to respond from a place of love rather than fear. It is a choice we always have in all of life's circumstances.

Jamie's story is still unfolding as she is now back in hiding and last I heard expecting another child. Perhaps this will be the one that heals her fragmented heart from all those years ago and helps her comes back into the light of the family who love her. We may not always see eye to eye but love always awaits her. I know the many heavenly lights will continue to shine upon her to bless, heal and help guide her home.

Love Is the Answer

Pain is a powerful motivator but love will always succeed in the bigger picture. Love is the answer many seek. Love is the healer and connector in life. Let the power of the love within your heart bless you and your life.

The Gift Within the Darkness

Our siblings are our flesh and blood; whether we love or hate them at the time. They get us on a level that only they can. When they are alive, we may have wished them dead and when we lose them we want them back. It truly is a catch 22 with nothing more we can do.

However, we can take this time to reflect upon the gifts we learned and experienced along the journey of growing up with them. When we do so we can then master those very lessons in the world each day.

Growing up in a family with a lot of estrogen in it definitely had its curses and gifts for this male, as anyone can imagine. It surely gave me a lot of insight into the general nature of females. This family experience unquestionably helped me to be a more heart opened, sensitive and compassionate person at the same time. I find that I can connect with females quite easily; mostly because of my upbringing and spending so much time with them. After my mom's death one of the gifts which came forth was a reconnection with my sister Sheri who I spent so much time growing up with. With a three year age difference growing up she was my best friend. Sure we had our challenges and fights as we grew up but the love was ever present despite our differences.

Over the years, after moving out, we just lived independent lives so with mom's passing it gave us an opportunity to reconnect; something I now cherish each day. I didn't know how much I missed my sister until I reconnected with her and began to have regular chats just allowing them to flow as it may. Sheri is a gift in my life and every moment we share together is time that we make the most of. As we know life is short and you never know when a life will end.

My sister has many health challenges that are surely leading her to an early death. As much as it pains me to see her suffer and know she will leave us early, this time together is a gift for the both of us. I may have regrets from early in life but I can make sure I have no further regrets when it comes to sharing time and space with Sheri.

Watching someone you love suffer with a disease that is taking a toll on them isn't easy. This is harder when you know what is at the end of the road. You basically live with grief all the days of your life. Watching them try to get through the days with everything on their plate.

Spirit tells me that living grief is one the hardest grief types a person will go through as it basically eats away at you like a moth on clothes. When their life does finally end, you have a sense of relief and joy knowing your loved one is now at peace in spirit. The human part of you will still have to go through the final stages of the bereavement process and this can be a challenge in itself.

We are reminded to take the time required to be with your grief. Know it is okay not to be okay with what is unfolding with your loved one. Remember living grief is a real emotion. You are in your own process when you are watching your loved one go through their own pain, suffering and dying process. Let yourself be angry or sad or in pain or whatever you may be experiencing. You have the right to feel how you feel.

As someone who is deeply connected to the spiritual realm and helps people heal, it pains me to see what is happening with my sister. I will say that it does help me to know everything lies in the hands of the higher self and anything can happen still. It pains me to know there are sacred contracts in play and only so much the human part of me can do unless asked. Free will is a gift but there are moments it sometimes feels like a curse. I am sure many of you will agree on this.

I know that this too shall pass and the light that beckons us all at the end of the tunnel will shine brightly once again. For now, I look past the illusion of the darkness in my heart to see the truth that lies within the light always. This helps me to keep moving forward. I have come to terms that death is a natural part of life and now do my best to accept it as it comes.

The human in me may still have to go through denial, isolate himself, want to bargain with Spirit, get angry or depressed and even have a mix of it all at once and I am okay with that. On another level, I accept that death is not an ending but a step in the evolution of our soul. This is a gift in itself my soul knows.

I have learned so much watching my sister go through her process. Sheri has taught me so much about living life in the now and appreciating what is before me. She has taught me we all have an innate strength within us and that we often don't even realize this until we are in the challenge of our life. My sister has taught me to be okay with whatever I am feeling in the moment and to take time to process my emotions.

Sheri has taught me the importance of staying connected to those we love and working things out if required. She has taught me the importance of self-care, of not allowing the stresses of life to get to us and to be present in the gift of the now. She has taught me the power of forgiveness, love and compassion, and so much more.

I am sure that as we continue this journey and knowing miracles happen every day she will teach me so much more just by being my sister. The greatest teachers in our life lead by example and also sometimes provoke our greatest emotions. My sister is one great teacher for myself and for many others along the path. Sheri is one of the many gifts in my life I hold close to my heart in appreciation for having her in my life.

If you have a sibling still living and yet you are suffering with living grief use this time to get to understand and see life through their eyes. This gift is a wonderful opportunity for you to get to know them in a whole new way. Use this time to heal and make peace with the past while allowing yourself the gift of a closer and deeper relationship.

Sooner or later, the soul will be called home. So make the most of the time together you have as you have the gift of the long goodbye.

The Gift of Reflection

Our loved ones bless our lives each day in ways that are often unacknowledged or unseen. I feel compelled to ask you to take time to reflect on what your siblings have taught you or perhaps continue to teach you as you share in life. By doing so you are both honoring the gift of life and the gift that continues on long after death: LOVE!

Remember whether your brothers or sisters are alive or their soul has left the body, their soul is alive and well. They are forever with you and your earthly family and friends.

They will continue to bless you and your life with lessons and gifts long after their candle light has been blown out. Go out and live in their memory, letting your heart lead the way as it shines brightly and even better than you think you be worthy or deserve. That is the greatest gift you can give to your siblings and one they want to accept from you.

They deeply love and appreciate you for all you did for them in life and continue after their physical death. They want you to be kind, gentle and loving of yourself now. Do all the great things you wish you would have done for them for yourself and those along your path each day; let these be the gifts that keep on giving with love and laughter.

The Gift Within the Darkness

Prayer for those Grieving the Loss of a Sibling

Dearest Mother-Father God,

We come to you this very day to ask that you surround those of us around the world that are grieving the loss of our beloved sibling(s).

We welcome your enveloping love, light and healing energy to bless our lives in meaningful ways.

Lift our hearts of the burdens of heaviness and pain that we are carrying around.

Wherever there is darkness let your heavenly light shine brightly.

Wherever there is anger let peace radiate forth.

Wherever there is fear bless us with love.

God help us to see the gifts of this loss and to help us understand what has transpired in your way and time. Touch us now to awaken us to be the master that you intend us to be.

Please heal our broken and shattered hearts, and return us to the wholeness of our soul. Help us to reclaim our power and our life in honor of our departed loved ones.

Help us be of service in the world as we live the best life possible. Let us do so with our loved ones joining us from the afterlife as we celebrate all the days of our lives.

We now see our loved ones in heaven blessed and in your loving arms, happy, healthy and whole once again.

We look past the illusions to see a life filled with health, happiness, love and abundance. We see this for all the world as we see this now for our heavenly friends and family.

For all this and even better, we give our thanks and so it shall be. It is done.

Amen

CHAPTER 15

When it's Dark Search for the Stars

Annissa Boyce

My dear brother, Alex, was an individual who wrestled with many demons. We were immensely close in childhood–when my parents divorced when I was 12 (he was 10 at the time), my father immigrated overseas to find greener pastures, leaving my mom and us behind. I sobbed for two weeks solid when he left... My mother struggled, suddenly alone with a lot of anger, and my brother and I were united in our support of each other and my mom. I shut my emotions away to get through. My mother's anger towards my father became my own.

At the age of 14, Alex snuck into my grandfather's liquor, For 16 years thereafter, my brother struggled with substance abuse. Alex landed up in a relationship with a woman who also indulged in escapism through both alcoholism and drugs. She introduced him to the latter. By the time my brother passed, they had been in a toxic relationship for over 10 years, because leaving meant he had "wasted his time". Contact was minimal outside of birthdays and Christmas, by their choice, not ours. I missed him dearly.

Many times in his life, my brother had brushes with death. The last, before his passing, was July 2016. He Overdosed. That day triggered an intervention from my and my mother's side, he went to rehab for a year.

When he exited rehab early in January, it was through breaking rules. My mom and I were told: "zero contact till he is clean for a year". When he passed away in July 2017, he was clean. He died of a heart attack, peacefully, at age 30, in his sleep. I hadn't seen him since the intervention... I had so been looking forward to giving him a hug again, after his recovery. The day I got word, I broke down. He had written a letter to me while in rehab, I only received it the day he passed away. "I hope to see you soon" was how it ended. It shattered my heart, realizing that "tomorrow" is never promised.

Standing at his memorial, I was thinking what I could actually say–I desperately searched for good memories amidst the anger and pain of the past. In a moment of clarity, I realized that my brother was one of the most passionate people I had ever known. Whether he loved, laughed, worked, played, fought or escaped... He did it with every ounce of passion he had. It made me yearn for the passion that was absent in my own life.

With my brother passing, my father, who I had not seen since 2001, came back for the memorial. We spent time together, I asked many difficult questions. I found that a lot of my anger was based on misconceived notions and learned the profound value of forgiveness. Reconciliation is underway.

Having a look at how my brother lived with his wife, I also realized how I was doing my partner and myself both an injustice–we had slipped into a space of complacency and codependency. There was love, but we were both numb, indifferent. I realized that I did not want to be in a space, 10 years from now, unhappy. It was an immensely painful decision... But I released her. In doing so, beyond the hurt, there was also empowerment. We have both found a new sense of independence and freedom which neither of us had together.

In the darkness of two losses, I was finding the stars.

Time is short. Cherish the Moment. Live Passionately. Forgive. Love deeply. And never settle for second best.

The Gift Within the Darkness

CHAPTER 16

A Rude Awakening

Mary Rose Chambers

WE WERE BUSY SHOPPING for our return home from the United Kingdom one sunny afternoon in August 1984 and we stopped on the street, checked our watches and said, 'Oh it's 3 here, so it must be 6 at home'. On reaching home, we were then told that there was an accident back home and our eldest brother was killed instantly. The time of his death, 6:00 PM sharp. Was it a coincidence that we stopped to check our watches at the exact time of his death?

My sister and younger brother went into shock and needed immediate help. It was our eldest brother; the one who paid for our trip to the UK to attend our cousin's wedding. It just wasn't fair. I accompanied my uncle to my Grandmother's house to break the news to her.

The ride on the bus was pathetic. As I sat there, tears burning a trail down my cheeks, my 14-year old mind kept trying to accept this dreadful news. We prayed for a call back saying he was still alive, that never came. I tried to imagine our parents' grief.

I heard other passengers talking, giggling, listening to music on their Walkman's and I wondered how they could be so normal when my world just fell apart? My world would never be the same.

The scene at home was calm but it was obvious that death had caused a huge sink-hole in our lives. The finality of death was unfathomable. I couldn't understand why life had to come to an end that way. It was unimaginable that we would not have the joy of his company ever again. The loss of one out of five brothers was no less. None of them could replace him. He was unique. The church was over-flowing with friends, family and work colleagues who came to bid farewell to a beautiful soul. Every time someone said they were sorry for my loss I wanted to scream back, "You know nothing of my loss!" Every time someone told me to be strong, I wanted to yell 'I am strong but this is not about my strength'. The priest prayed for his soul to rest in peace but all I wanted was for him to come back home and let us know he's ok and that he's with us. And then one person in the line said, 'he will always be with you, even if you can't see him'. That one statement made me wonder at that possibility.

Since then, I've felt his presence at many family celebrations and he's usually come through whenever I've asked him for help in my darkest moments. He even came to Mum's bedside as I bid farewell to her recently. His death marked a turning point in my life, I learned then that life is so much more than what we see around us. Life continues in different dimensions and with such depth if only we use every experience as a training-ground for growth.

CHAPTER 17

THE GIFTS WITHIN LOSING OTHER PEOPLE IN OUR LIVES

This chapter is dedicated to the over thirty souls of my family, friends, co-workers and others who have left the physical world to move home. I love each and every one of you. Thank you for teaching us so much about life and death while sharing the many gifts along the journey.

IT IS NEVER AN easy task as a human to have death enter our lives, whether it is our family, friends, co-workers or another relationship. Every time we experience loss a part of us will be triggered by the previous deaths we may have experienced. This is because our soul is looking for a similar emotion that we can relate with to help us understand what is happening on a human level.

As a soul we understand from a divine perspective what is unfolding. However, when someone goes through a physical loss, they often will disconnect temporary from a part of their soul through their grief.

Our family is our family; it matters not if they are a part of our immediate family, our extended family (including in-laws) or a distant relative. It is normal we will grieve, in various intensities, the loss of a soul family member who played a role on earth in our lives. It is a part of the natural order and cycle in life. Our soul family often will extend to include others in our daily circles.

One could go through the bereavement process after the death of anyone. This could include the clerk at the local supermarket, former landlords, neighbors, former in-laws, a celebrity or the librarian that checked out our books. Anytime someone has someone leave their routine after having a relationship of any type, grief may be felt. *Who are we to say who may grieve or not? We are here to support others on their journey and that includes if they are experiencing a loss. Judgment has no place in loss and bereavement in any shape or form.*

Remember there are gifts within every situation and experience in our lives waiting to be acknowledged. Upon reflecting on the personal characteristics, traits and conversations we have with those in our lives we can see the gifts that each soul has blessed us with. Having experienced many deaths in life, including those that are untraditional losses, I can assure you there are plenty of gifts in each as you are learning.

Growing up, I had many people who were part of my extended family by the extension of my mom's relationship with my Uncle Bill. These included my uncle's parents, sisters, brothers and their offspring and all of them were like family. My uncle had his own circle of friends, co-workers and more who we all got to know as we grew up. So the death of my mom's relationship also meant to the death many other relationships which we would grieve.

Brian D. Calhoun

The Gift of Conversations Never Had

Before this happened there were physical losses that affected the immediate family unit my mom and uncle had formed with us kids.

I remember being young when Uncle Bill's parents died and us going to his dad's funeral. I remember us seeing his cold, lifeless body in the coffin and never really understanding at the time that there would be no stopping at his home on the weekend travels again.

There was a part of us who were just happy to be with many people but we felt alone at the same time. I don't really recall any other kids being at the funeral, though it's possible. It was also one of the first funerals we would go to and we were somewhat detached in our grief as kids. Looking back, I can definitely say we kids grieved in our own way, and I know that the adults processed as well.

I don't ever remember being told what death meant or having any conversations including the subjects surrounding it. On one level, I was very much aware that Spirit was very much present still even though a part of me couldn't visually connect with them. I knew within my heart and soul this spiritual truth.

I remember other losses that were felt by our family as well, each affecting us in different ways. As we grew up so did our understanding about death. Though there was still no conversation on death or grief or about how the ripple effects in our lives could unfold. If there was I cannot honestly remember for the life of me now.

Life just went on with the adults holding the meaningful conversations and letting the emotions be expressed behind closed doors. I can now say that I wish this was different at the time as it would have helped us all process and understand things better. In fact, if our parents would have opened up on a variety of subjects it would help us to experience life in a more open and communicative way overall.

This lack of communication is a two-fold gift. On one side of the coin: it taught me to be more open and forth coming in my later years around speaking my truth. On the other side: it brought the adventure of my life which gave blessings and opportunities to grow. Without these life lessons and experiences, the relationship I formed with the pen and paper in the earlier years (and later when computers were a thing) wouldn't exist.

Through, the gift of loss, another gift was revealed. The gift of divine communication and a connection with spirit.

With so many people leaving the physical world it lead us talking with those on the other side. For me, it was a more sporadic connection until later in life when I took it more seriously after losing my mother. But throughout life at least I was aware of people who we loved watching over us. This was a gift in itself.

Awakening to My Abilities

There would be times when I would be in my bedroom and hide in the closet just to get away from life itself. It would be there I would close my eyes, pray and talk with my imaginary friends, who were my loved ones.

I already felt like the black sheep of the family, different and alone many times, so I choose to keep my secret to myself. This choice was made out of fear of being made fun by those closest to me. After all, I had already been thrown to the curb by many people, both at home and school. Why would I give them another opportunity to do so?

There were only a couple family members I felt comfortable being myself with knowing they would love and accept me, quirks and all. My Mom, Aunt Pauline and two or three cousins were a few such people. The rest had their own nicknames for me, suspicions and criticisms about who I was or what I had done.

Now I recognize that I may have given them reason to but many times they were reacting or responding to something from the past. This all caused me to retreat into my own world as a way to deal with the views of others. There was a part of me that knew my family was joking or playing with me. But, being a child I felt ridiculed, put down and ashamed just to be me.

As I grew up, I could see how death and the roles and views of each person I came into contact with affected me on so many levels. This would become a gift which allowed me an opportunity to come to a place within my heart. A place filled with love, acceptance and gratitude for the many lessons they taught me just by being themselves.

As I spiritually woke up, I realized each person in my life was asked by my soul to play a certain role. Each helping to bring about key lessons and life experiences so that my soul could continue to evolve.

I like to think about it in this way. Each person is an actor or actress who has won a specialized part in the lifetime movie of me. These souls were given basic concepts to incorporate into the human script and then granted freewill to improvise the rest of the story. The same is true from the opposite side of the coin, I was also granted a role in their stories.

It was through this realization I could make peace with the way things unfolded and find forgiveness for those who caused me pain along the way. This included with both those that left the physical world and those that were my family, friends and people in my life growing up.

While I have many family members alive, the ones that I am closest to mostly are the ones in heaven. I learned long ago that family is there for you and not just blood. Over time, I have come to the conclusion even in families there may be cliques, like in

The Gift Within the Darkness

high school. I can either choose to take part as a member of the "cool kids" while accepting all that means. Or I could choose to hang out with those that love, support, respect and accept me as I am. Either way, I will always love, accept and appreciate the gifts that everyone brings into my life.

I no longer chase after people to be a part of my life. This was something I did long enough as a child who just wanted to be loved, acknowledged and accepted. I tried multiple times and ways to reach out to have relationships with many only to be pushed aside or trampled on throughout my life. I now know my worth and I deserve so much better. I always have a choice to manage my own vibrations and energy fields so I choose loving experiences.

As Spirit reminds us, everyone will understand how their choices, words and actions affect others when we cross over. Each of us will know and understand deeply how we made others feel. We will all experience the many ripple effects of our life choices on the world for generations to come.

Today is a new day and your loved ones ask you to be the best you can be. Not only this, but to be mindful of how your choices will affect others long after you are gone. Start today to shift your perspectives and you will live to see changes unfold.

Losing many people in life and connecting after death has taught me this and more. It is a true gift which allows me to make better choices in my life moving forth so I have an impact of love on others. People may forgive our actions but the feeling we gave them is something that never goes away.

The transitioning of many souls in my life has taught me to rely on myself and be open to the many gifts that spirit blesses my life with each day.

I may have been disowned in life by many but I will never disown another for they are my soul family and I know how it feels. The statement rings true that which you give out will guaranteed come back to you in the divine way and time. So I choose to respond with love and let love lead the way as best I can. Through death I have awakened to the divine truth and continue to be blessed with gifts each day. For this, I am grateful for the many who have been a part of my life and now are in Spirit.

The Discoveries Within Death

It is often through loss we will discover just how strong we are, not believing or knowing so beforehand. The death of anyone in our lives can be a very painful and exceptional loss to us. But, it is often only after this loss that we discover the gifts that lie within ourselves, such as strength, courage or faith. I am sorry it took you losing someone in your life to reawaken to your divine nature and potential. However, your sacred contract you had with your loved one had this written into it.

For me, I can honestly say the passing of many people brought forth a bereavement process that was intense and challenging at times. It was through these crossing overs that a great depth of freedom and light came to be experienced by me. This was especially true once I was reconnected to my own spiritual gifts and abilities.

Death also allowed me to shift my perspectives about life itself and to live from the heart more. It gave me the gift to see the beauty within all experiences; even when I may be having a human reaction to them.

I always know who I am and that I am spirit having a human experience and not the other way around. When I am remembering (and living from this perspective) life runs smoothly and I am connected to the divine abundance that is my true nature in every way. Therefore, abundance naturally radiates through me, into the world and comes back to me in the infinite number of ways in which I'm open to receive. For I am abundance; I am love; I am health; I am life; I AM all I AM. This is my true na-

The Gift Within the Darkness

ture. And within me is the spirit of everything. All this and even greater is also true for you.

With so many people crossing over in my life, death taught me to appreciate being in the gift of the present moment with each person in my life. Too many times we are with someone but we aren't truly with them. We may run through (in our heads) our list of tasks to finish, or checking our phones or the time or worrying about something else. Spirit has taught me to be more present in the moment so I can truly hear, feel and appreciate the here and now with those I am with. After all, one never knows when anyone's time is up.

Through the experience of death I now understand faith and synchronicity better. I now get there is a divine order to everything. When I am trusting, having faith, letting go, listening and following the guidance of my soul everything just falls into place with ease. There is an ebb and flow in my life. This is also all true for you at all times.

There is a simplicity, beauty and grace in it all; the human mind is the one that will complicate things. Death teaches us to come back into the heart. This is why we grieve and feel so intensely after a loss; it is here we can begin tuning within to the soul on a deeper level. Many of us miss this gift.

Through loss I was able to understand and see the similarities with others in my own way. The light of compassion was able to shine brightly each day. By putting myself in the shoes of another it allowed me to find something similar in my journey so I can relate to what others are experiencing. It may not be the exact same situation but it allows us to find common ground.

When one travels through the darkness we may be blind, feel alone and lost. When we start shifting to look for the light in the dark, we are sure to become immersed in it. For me when this happened I was able to start to see the immense potential that lies within all of us. Once I realized that I was the light the whole time I could shine the gift of my potential in the world each day. I could be love in action.

Through death I found the place where I could meet with the divine and the souls that are awaiting to connect to others through me. This in itself is a gift that keeps on giving. I liken this to a classroom where I can go to learn, expand, support and teach; somewhere where I go to plan and set things up for the days to come. It is here that death made me a better version of myself and allows me to help others channel their true nature forth into the physical reality.

Remember just because your loved ones have left the physical body and are now non-physical in nature does not mean that you are ever alone. Your heavenly loved ones are always by your side ready to meet and open up a conversation with you in a sacred meeting space of your own. The tools in the second part of this book will help you do this.

The Gift Of Divine Connection

It is crazy the number of people that have moved from physical to spirit that have been directly connected to me throughout my journey on earth. And I am sure there are many more that I am not even remembering or even aware of, perhaps. Each of them have brought their own gifts into my life as do each of your heavenly loved ones.

Not all the gifts were ones I wanted or even could appreciate in the moment. But with time and space I can see each was something I needed and valuable in even greater ways. The greatest gifts often come with the greatest challenges through your greatest teachers. If they were delivered in any other way, we may have missed receiving or appreciating the gift in time. I am sure you may agree on this by looking back on some of your own hair raising experiences. It takes you getting out of your own way to be able to see life from a higher perspective.

Death has taught me we are the ones who are at root of many things in our lives. This is true; whether we are consciously aware of this or not. We are the source, substance, supply and energy of all of creation. Therefore, we have the power to re-create the life of our choosing with our heavenly loved ones with us by our side. When we give ourselves the gift of awakening and remembering our divine nature and truth, something magical unfolds in our lives. The energy takes on a life of its own.

We all have the power to connect with spirit through our psychic and intuitive gifts. But, if we are still fiercely processing our grief we have to concentrate on healing and moving forward in our lives first. Once we can do that, then the door to the many possibilities to connect, see, hear, feel and know our spiritual friends and family in heaven will begin opening to us. This is just one reason that our loved ones want us living, loving and laughing more in our lives. It helps to brings us in alignment with the energy of our true nature and by extension them.

Prayer for Those Grieving the Loss of Someone They Knew

Dearest Mother-Father God, Creator of the Universe

We come to you requesting your ever present help with the healing of our grieving heart.

We know that you created this world out of love and that every soul has a mission including our beloved departed loved one. We ask as they continue their soul journey you guide and watch over them.

We ask for you to fill the hole of our broken heart with your ever expanding love. As you do so, guide us to share your divine love with the world in the best way we can each day.

Help us be at peace with what has transpired with the death of (name of person). Envelop us with your loving angels to shift us to a higher vibration of love as we process our grief in a way that is gentle and blesses the world.

God, we ask that you watch over those that knew (name) best as they adjust to the physical world without them in it.

Let us feel the love of our departed loved ones. In this way, we can know they are now at peace in heaven as they watch over us and take part in our life from their new perspectives.

Shine your bright light in the deep crevices of our being to eradicate the darkness held within. This way we can be a messenger of love and light on the earth for the blessing of those we meet each day.

Let us see, feel, hear and know all that you wish us to. Doing so as you we walk the path before us living life to the fullest with our loved one by our side.

Let us shine our true nature on the earth as it is in heaven now and forever more

For all this and even better, we give our thanks and so it is.

Amen

The Gift Within the Darkness

CHAPTER 18

THE GIFTS WITHIN LOSS DUE TO MURDER OR SUICIDE

LOSING SOMEONE YOU KNOW hurts. When you lose them unexpectedly or in a violent it may feel like someone turned your world upside down. It may seem like someone unleashed the destructive storm and you will never see the sun shine again. Life has indeed forever changed for you and the depth of the wound penetrating your heart will never completely go away.

You may have known them your entire life or perhaps for a short time before their death. Either way, time really is irrelevant. You had a connection, and that connection is has now been severed brutally when you were looking the other way.

The horrible news of the sudden unexpected death of your loved one is bad enough. You will get through this, you think as the movie of your life comes to a pause. You go into shock as your breath is taken away. Your heart beats and you hear the slightest of words off in the distant. Murdered. You deny what is heard as your mind must be playing tricks on you. The world pauses and then nothing.

Next, you hear the distant voice saying, "Ma'am? Ma'am?" You realize that you are laying on the floor as an officer is next to you. You come to and he asks you if you are okay before repeating what has happened. Leading with his apologies and then saying that your child was murdered. You fade into the distance once again as he explains what happened and asks if there is someone he can call to be with you.

The next days you move through the fog and deal with the after effects of what has transpired. You are going through the motions but you aren't fully here. This cannot be happening; this is a bad dream you will wake up from, you think. Denial sets in.

You reflect upon the last days of their life. Recognizing that you were losing them, piece by piece, until the glass completely shattered with the devastating news of their death. You question if there was something you could have done or a sign you missed. You even feel guilty for perhaps not reaching out to them or being there for them during their darker hours. Anger sets in.

Know it's perfectly okay to wonder about things and to feel whatever you feel. It is natural. You need time to process. You are overwhelmed with emotions all over the map. One minute you are up, then next you are down.

Your heart has been ripped out of your body. The numbness you once experienced now replaced by pain twenty-four hours a day. Tears leaving permanent marks on your face. The reflection in the mirror shows a bare shell of a person who hasn't slept in days, let alone be able to do anything to make themselves look presentable. You couldn't care less. You just want your loved one back. You feel depressed.

You find yourself wanting to pray and bargain; in hopes that you can wake up from the nightmare and your loved one will be physically present once again. You just want your life back. You will even settle for five more minutes. But, nothing you say or do works.

Someone needs to pay, you think, as the anger returns once again. You become motivated to seek justice. You talk regularly with the police and the prosecutors to see what is being done in your son's case. Upset that they have not progressed further.

You become more vocal and begin speaking to media and anyone who will listen to you. All to try to ease your conscience of the guilt you may hold. You unconsciously hope that this will ease the deep pain of your heart and help your child find peace in the afterlife.

As the process continues you begin to uncover more about your loved one's life; much of the information being delivered through the media and court system. You go into the denial that your son played the role in his death and all these things being said are true. Your anger is fueled as you continue to grieve the loss of your child along with the hopes and dreams you held for them.

Eventually the rose colored glasses are removed and you realize the truth. Your child wasn't as innocent as you once thought. The secret life they lived now exposed to the world. With time and space you begin to find yourself making a little peace with what has happened. You still think of him as your baby and know him as the good child; but, you also now see he had his own darkness he lived. You find yourself getting angry with him; only to feel guilty for yelling at his spirit.

You decide that you will take this tragedy and turn it into something positive. You begin the journey of becoming an activist for those without voices in honor of your son. You want the world to know your boy as the good son and leave his mark in a positive way on the world. You are unsure what that looks like still but you vow to figure it out. No other parent should have to feel the pain you went through. You vow if you can shine a light on the darkness, perhaps one life will be saved. Your child's death will no longer be held in vain.

Finding yourself in a place of acceptance and making the best of a bad situation; a light is now beginning to shine once again. You still miss your child, but you are getting through the bereavement process with the help of your memories of your child and your new found mission in life. You are well supported and can feel your child standing by your side as you journey forward in service sharing life, love and laughter along the way.

You may have found yourself at the edge of a cliff ready to jump along the way; perhaps more than once. This can be especially true when everything may have gone the way you had expected or hoped for in the justice system. Your faith and new found awareness that life continues on after death gives you hope that one day you will be reunited with your child in the non-physical. Until then you will just do the best you can in life.

A Gift Within the Dark

You realize that losing your loved one was a gift as you found a path that was greater than you and that is your mission to serve others. This slowly fills the hole in your heart. It may have come with a cost but you now can appreciate there is a divine order and plan to everything unfolding in life.

Both your souls had a plan to work together and one was meant to be heaven. The love your souls had for each other decided your strength and wisdom would be best served on the earth. This meant that your child would walk the path from the afterlife.

You recognize you each asked the other to play the roles for the mission on earth. This despite how painful it would be for you as the parent to a child who died in this way. You now recognize there is a gift in it all and that in death you have been brought closer together in a strange twisted manner. You realize this is the relationship you both longed for all this time.

It is never easy for anyone to suffer the pain of losing someone they love. This same story could be told of someone finding out that someone else they knew had been murdered or even died at their own hands. It could be your brother, your sister, mother, father, neighbor or anyone who has been killed by a drunk driver or another tragic unexpected way.

There truly is a gift within the darkness. One only needs to feel around to discover the switch that turns on the light once again. It is then that the gift is revealed. Your loved ones never want you to stay stuck in your pain of loss. They want you to move forward moment by moment, step by step, breath by breath.

I assure you that the sun will continue to shine long after the storm passes; for the sun has always been behind the clouds. One only needs to look past the illusions of the clouds to discover the gift of the light. Once you do, you will feel lighter and better each day. The grief won't have a death grip on your heart any further; you will still cycle through your grief but with each passing day the pain will be a little less.

Your loved one will always be by yourself cheering you on; loving you as you so dearly love them. They be helping you the best they can with their new found perspectives to go on. Know what you feel is completely valid and a necessary part of the journey. It will empower you as a human that much more and thus you are encouraged to take all the time you need to process what has happened. It is vital to the success of your mission as a human in service.

Remember, no one expects you to be happy all the time for they understand that you have had a life altering experience; one that took you to the edge of the darkness and back again. Let yourself be vulnerable as you share your story and are in service for another. You child wants you to be real with both yourself and the world at large. They don't want you to hold back their secrets or even your own. Shine the light on the darkness as it will help to eradicate the dark and expose the truth to the world.

A gift that can be found in the loss of someone to murder can be the gift of living and appreciating the present with those that are alive in your life. Let this be a gift that brings you closer together in honor of those that have left the physical world.

One often will find the gift of revealing ones darkest secrets sometimes during these times with those closest to them. Let this be an opportunity to begin anew with those in your life presently as you get to know them better. Your departed loved one would appreciate you using this gift to talk openly with those closest to you. Allow them to open up about what is going on in their lives without judgment.

A Path to Healing

We all have the choice to forgive as a way to heal our hearts of the pain of losing someone in such a tragic way. Forgiveness sets us free to love those that are in our lives even more. We all have made mistakes and we would hope someone would be a little compassionate or understanding enough to forgive us of our past errors. The soul which played your departed loved one's murderer made a mistake.

Perhaps it was out of fear, or they were incapacitated in their mind, or out of a moment of rampage or for another reason but it was a mistake. This error in judgment will cost them the rest of their lives. They will have to live with what unfolded as they will relive it over and over in their mind. Forgiving helps you to heal. That is enough of a reason in my books to forgive.

If I had lost someone in this way, I would want to find a little peace and a way to move forward. Forgiveness is one way to do that; it may not bring our loved one back from death but it can help us heal.

Furthermore, the person who murdered our loved one is also someone's son, daughter, mother, father, brother, sister, or friend. Remember, these people are now also grieving the loss of this relationship. They know their loved one will end up paying for their error in judgment for their rest of their lives in some way.

We have the choice to forgive as a way to move forth and not cause further pain in their lives. This doesn't mean we forget the horrible act that has unfolded. Give the gift of forgiveness to yourself, to your departed loved one and to everyone else that has played a role somehow in this tragic story.

If you can't forgive fully today that is okay; just be willing to one day be willing to free all with your forgiveness. Your loved one wants you to all be free and filled with the peace and love that forgiveness brings after the storm of darkness.

The Power of Love

I once had a client whose brother had been murdered and when I connected with him on the other side, he showed me his death scene. It looked like something out of a horror movie with the blood splattered walls and a dead body on the floor. As I explained what he was sharing with me with his sister, she had tears moving down her face; expected for sure.

I continued to pass on the message as her brother shared about how he played a role in his death with the choices and path he lived in life.

He explained how the experiences of this lifetime and past lives lived have a role to play in the making of our lives. He went on that as a soul he had asked a very strong soul to play his murderer. This soul agreed knowing it would not be an easy path at all. The soul only agreed out of the love they had for their soul family member who brought this assignment to them.

Her brother explained there were many people's lives and lessons that were a part of this transaction between souls. These lessons would continue on long after the physical violent act originated and there would be many positive things that would unfold as part a ripple effect.

He told her she had an important role to play as his sister as she spoke up on his behalf and lived her life. He showed her how it helped shape her into the more positive person she had become; a task that came about because of the sacred contract. She would go on to do good things in the world.

He continued to state that many other things would unfold to make the world a better place with his death. This was all tied to the sacred contract continuing to unfold after his death. He let us know much would happen that would go unrecognized for a variety of purposes. Most being because this would not directly affect her or their family but it would affect others in the family & circle of friends of the perpetrator. He told her that his death was something bigger than any of them.

The session was very powerful and healing for her. She had long moved forward in her life having found forgiveness in her heart for all involved, including for her brother who had walked a very dark path. The person who had killed him was also forgiven as a part of her moving forward to find inner peace of mind and heart. She said it was the toughest thing she did but was the best thing that happened as she felt so much happier and lighter for it.

Her brother's encouragement throughout the session to let the remaining pain of the experience go and move forward helped her to realize it wasn't hurting anyone but herself. The weight she had carried around had been released after our session.

When I last saw her, she informed me she no longer revisits the night her brother died or plays the scene in her mind. This was something she used to do many times over. She was so grateful to her brother for that short visitation and for helping her to understand and let go of what no longer served her. She regularly speaks to her brother and has a wonderful relationship with him. She sometimes forgets that he has left the earth as she knows he is with her always.

She still has human moments where she misses him but then she opens her journal and communicates with him and it passes. When she allowed the power of love to heal her traumatized heart through forgiveness, her life got even better; something she never thought would be possible. She now feels whole again. She realizes that we always have a choice in how to conduct ourselves and if we want to let the pain of the past hold us back.

No matter where you are in your journey today, please choose to keep moving forward, one step at a time. Let love lead the way all the days of your life.

A Death Unexpected or Was it?

I remember being in service for a client who had a fear of death immensely. When she came to me she didn't want to hear any bad news or anything on the topic. Of course, Spirit always knows where people are at in their journey even if they aren't conscious of this themselves.

When clients first arrive for their sessions, I will often take a few minutes to just share about my process to help them be more comfortable; sometimes I am even guided to share particular stories from my life. I have learned there is a reason for this; just like there is a reason for everything even if we don't always understand things in the moment.

On this particular day, one story which I shared was about a client of mine who I picked up would die on a particular day.

Here, the former client had cancer, and I was doing healing work on her when I was given this information. At the time it felt relevant for the client sitting before me even though I didn't understand the reason at the time. It was through this that I found out she didn't want to know anything dealing with death.

I get it, death scares people. It can be particularly scary if the death someone may be picking up on involves them or someone they are close to. It was the same with this client. She was fearful I was picking up she was going to die and I would tell her the exact date. Which is why she didn't want to hear about death. Understandable for sure.

A few moments later we were in our session with the angels with her asking questions and me responding with the information I was receiving from Spirit. She had been asking about her then husband and if they would stay together. I was clearly being told no and shown the person she would end up with.

Now sometimes when I pick up stuff, sometimes the information is not always clear how it fits in the moment. This is because the information often can come in symbol form which can have many different meanings that only time may answer. In her case, I was picking up a different person in her future who she would be end up spending her life with.

This information that Spirit shared with me could have easily been a sign that her husband's energy would completely change and he would be a whole different person down the line. Sometimes only with time we understand the meaning of the words that come forth; this is especially true when the words have multiple meanings.

We continued on with the session where she continued to ask about things related to her husband and their marriage. Throughout our time together, I would pause to ask and receive information on her questions from Spirit; only to receive nothing further. I found it strange but let it go as it can sometimes happen that the information isn't meant to be revealed then or through me even.

A short time later after other questions were answered by spirit, we concluded the session. She found many answers she sought and left feeling lighter, ready to continue on with her day.

She called me the following Wednesday morning and left me a message as I was busy with other commitments. Later in the day I was returning the calls of those that had left messages and reached out to one particular number.

When the person answered I realized that I had the wrong number when they said the person didn't live there. By now I had realized that I dialed a number of someone that was on my return call list, even though I didn't exactly know who yet.

But all unfolded as it was meant to as Spirit had a plan as it always does. At this time, the plan included me talking with this particular woman at this moment as it was her number I had called in error. Thankfully the person who answered recognized my voice or phone number on their call display and passed me to the correct person.

A moment later my client gets on the phone and still without me knowing who I was speaking with she immediately asked if I had anything to say to her. Taken aback I told her no.

She filled me in that she had come to see me the previous weekend. I could now place her but her energy was totally unrecognizable at the time and even though it had only been a few days I would have thought months had gone by, it had changed so much.

She told me the story of the reading and how she was listening to the cassette tape in her car. She told me how every time I would talk with Spirit about her husband that there was a huge heart beat that would come through very loudly on the recording. She also shared that there was music in the background of the tape which wasn't playing in the room where the reading had taken place.

She continued on her journey home. Shortly after she got home she was greeted by a police officer who told her that her husband had committed suicide earlier in the day.

She went into shock as is normal and a few days later when she had called me she had just attended her husband's funeral. By now she realized she had blocked Spirit from preparing her for what was about to happen in her session. She had called hoping to receive a message to help her through this emotional time. We spoke for a period and that was the end of that. A month later I would be back in the area where she lived where I would learn further details from someone who knew her.

A year later I was preparing for a session when a friend of this client came for a reading. She gave me an update on how this client of mine was doing since that fateful day. She said she had met the man I told her she would meet in her session. He had all the qualities I gave her but one thing was missing. The name didn't start with a V as in Victor which I referred to.

She continued with the update to share that she had received the final piece of the puzzle in an email. It wasn't about the message contained within the email and was more about the name on the account. In the middle of his name was in quotes "Victory" and she knew this was indeed the man. She learned that Victory or Victor was a nickname that many of his running friends called him.

Until this day she has not come to see me. I think she is a little still freaked out by the experience and afraid I will share with her bad news or worse yet something about death. She has referred others and I know when the time is right, she will find herself in front of me once again.

Spirit knew she wouldn't be open to hearing about death and to clue her in on what was to come. It did so in the only way they could; by me sharing a story on the subject.

The Gift of a Second Chance

One of the gifts of suicide is often the relief from the pain and suffering that those leaving the physical feel upon their return to the spirit form. Depending on their life lessons, karma and sacred contracts, the soul leaving the planet may need to return to the earth to complete their journey. Or if they completed what they needed before leaving they can continue to evolve soulfully.

Suicide often will play a role in helping those left behind after death develop a closer relationship once they can move through their grief. It also often helps to reveal the pain those that took their life lived with each day they were alive. Such as a client of mine's brother when he had me feel his physical pain before he died.

His pain was shared with me so I could help his sister and family understand one of the major reasons he took his life. He also let her know the decision was not made lightly. He loved his family so much but couldn't stand watching them suffer in silence over his health and choices in life.

Tears streamed down her face as her brother communicated the message but deep within she knew it was true and could forgive him for what he did. She was able to put her anger aside after this revelation from her brother.

He also said his brother's wife would become pregnant and the soul she was bringing into the world was his. It was through this new life he would find peace, love and happiness in health and wellness. Last I was in communication with them a birth had indeed been welcomed into the family and everyone was doing well. The baby had many of her brother's characteristics and everyone often comments about these. A true blessing for all.

Sometimes the greatest gift in suicide is a second chance. So when the opportunity presents itself to reunite with your loved ones be sure to use it wisely to share in love, life and laughter for all of time. Everyone will be better for it.

Gifts of Love

In grieving the gift of love is forever present. Tears that swell up and run freely out of the corners of your eyes are one way you know you loved someone so much more than you knew. This pain is your soul letting you know you will miss them because they have died and returned to the afterlife.

When your heart lingers in agony, it is the love under the surface that is trying to burst through your layers of pain. The hole left behind after your loved one's soul left the physical can only be filled with the remembrance of your love for them.

The lump in your in your throat every time you go to speak about your loved one is love bubbling up to the surface to be expressed into the world.

Love is the emotion under the surface of everything; for love is the core of the universe and who we are. Love is the answer to all of life's questions and the healer in all matters. Love is the connector and what is the basis of all blessings in creation. Love is all that matters for love is what we are here to expand in the universe.

Your loved one has discovered this divine truth and remind you to always let your heart guide you along the roadway of life. Let love be the gift that keeps on giving all the days of your life in all ways. You deserve it and so it shall be granted.

Your loved ones may not have always remembered who they were while living their earthly life but in death they now remember. They know love is who they are. They want the same for you now. Your loved one wants this even more than they could have ever wanted it for themselves. They want you to know just how much you are worthy of such great loving blessings in all areas of your life.

Now the question remains: Will you let yourself experience the gift of heaven on earth? The choice is always yours. Whatever your answer heaven supports you always. For they love, respect and appreciate you for the creator that you are.

Prayers for Those Grieving a Loss Due to Murder or Suicide

Dearest Mother-Father God,

We come to you now to ask for your even present help, healing energy and love. We request your blessing on those of us grieving the loss of our loved ones whose lives cut short unexpectedly. Please envelop our body, mind, spirit and emotions as we process our grief in lovely and gentle ways.

Help ease our anger and rage at the situation that played out that led to our loved one departing the earth.

Help us with releasing the unforgiveness we may hold against another including our loved ones. Release the pain in our hearts as we now know everyone were just honoring the sacred contracts in the events leading up to the death of our loved one.

God, we soulfully know everything happens for a reason and there is a divine order to the universe, but the human part of us is processing. Please take us on a life review to understand, heal and release these situations so we can be find peace, forgive all and move forward with love filling our hearts. Clear from us the burdens weighing on our mind and heart, resolving them in blessed ways.

Release our regrets, choices and actions of the past so we can begin anew here and now.

Reveal to us what our life purpose and mission is so we can now fulfill it in memory of our departed love one. Help us live a life that is on path and purpose with divine love and light all the days of our lives.

For all this and even better, we give our thanks in advance, knowing our prayers have been heard and now answered. And so it is. So it shall be. It is done. Amen

The Gift Within the Darkness

CHAPTER 19

Learning to Feel and Heal

Fiona Louise

It should have been a time in my teenage life for fun, new experiences, relationships and self-discovery as I navigated campus life in my first year of tertiary study. My older brother was attending the same campus. I would see him every day for the first few weeks either bumping into him on the way to class, or in the library, or at one of the cafes. But this all ended, on the day he decided to end his life. I was beyond devastated; I was broken, and I felt like my life ended that day too. Despite the world continuing to turn, everything seemed so unimportant, frivolous, and meaningless in the face of this huge loss.

I am forever grateful to my friend Monique, who having only befriended me at the start of the year, never faulted in her willingness to be by my side. Though it must have been difficult for her to spend time with someone so consumed by this devastating situation. The campus was a constant reminder and every place in which I had seen him over the previous weeks was tinged by my loss. I got through that year, somehow, with her friendship, and with the constant deadlines to adhere to, and the following year started my first job. It was a welcome distraction. Because I had so much to learn, it was easy to put all my focus into this job, and over the subsequent years building a career and identity. This conveniently ensured I blocked out any thoughts of my brother, and as such, prevented me from actually grieving. One day a group of students came through our business for a tour and I recognised a couple of the students and realised it was my brother's class. Had he not died, he would have been standing there with them. So even my job wasn't free of reminders. I still tried as hard as I could to block it all out; it was just too painful, too raw, to deal with at the time.

Soon after, the once enjoyable job changed drastically as the business was sold three times in as many years. It ceased to be ours. The stress that came with the uncertainty, re-branding and loss of valuable staff and clients took a serious toll on the once cohesive team. One staff member got cancer, another had a heart-attack, yet another had a stroke. We were all bitterly unhappy at the poor decisions made by each owner, and today the business is no longer in operation.

Losing my career and identity was another blow I faced without the maturity and life experience to handle it well. I moved overseas, travelled, and met new people but the cracks appeared quickly as although I wasn't aware of it at the time, I was experiencing burn-out. Four years later in a stressful job with a lot of responsibility, my body started failing. Little by little, my energy declined and pain increased until every inch of me was screaming. Completely depleted, I was bedridden for six months.

It turns out that my body was essentially killing me slowly in response to the mental anguish that consumed me. Besides my brother and my career, several friends, family members, and my boyfriend also died over a fifteen year period. By working long hours, without proper nutrition, and by not grieving, I kept all of that misery, heartache, disappointment, anger, betrayal, loss, blame, and pain inside of me, in every cell until my body could no longer function. It is difficult to talk about just how dark my thoughts were for so long and how I too often thought about ending it all. My sister had made me promise that I would never take my own life. But I had no real will to live and so my body responded by turning on itself and attacking cells.

Losing my health was a consequence of holding onto the pain and not grieving properly. I now live with those consequences daily with irreparable damage to my body, and I only wish I had seen it sooner and sought help. Living with these consequences and adjusting to a 'new normal' of what my body is capable of now has meant I've had to mourn a future that is no longer possible.

However being ill afforded me time to rest, recuperate, and finally acknowledge all those dark thoughts and all those losses so that I could truly grieve, and release all those pent-up emotions I had pushed down for so long. Letting go enabled me to feel lighter and freer, and positive emotions could fill the space they left. It was the wake-up-call I needed to grieve everything and over time rediscover passion for life. I am grateful for all the experiences that have led to this point, and I hope that by sharing I can demonstrate just how important it is to your wellbeing to acknowledge every loss in the moment. It is vital that we give ourselves the time needed to process the grief in whatever form it appears in, deal with the emotions and ourselves compassionately, and learn how to not only release all the pain, but also to heal.

Fiona Louise is among the co-authors of 365 Moments of Grace, HALO: Lighting up Heaven on Earth and multiple other anthologies.

The Gift Within the Darkness

CHAPTER 20

THE GIFTS WITHIN THE DEATH OF A RELATIONSHIP

This chapter applies to both Romantic and Platonic Relationships

LOSING SOMEONE, NO MATTER how, is tough on the human in us all. We need time to process what has transpired, both grieving and afterwards. Either way, the hopes and dreams we may have been held for the relationship have been squashed and stomped upon leaving a crushed heart in its wake.

Life is built upon relationships of all sorts, we come to earth with the sole purpose and intention of experiencing relationships.

Our first relationship came to be when we developed the overall plan for our soul journey to earth with other soul family members. These relationships can often be the most challenging when we experience them on the earth. This because of the deep soulful love and passion held within them for all to express.

Soul relationships are not confined to soulmate romantic relationships; they can be in any area of your life. One can be almost certain when they meet a soul family member because of the instant recognition on the energy level by the souls. There is a familiarity about these people, like you have met them before; even though you may have never physically come in contact with them. These are the people that when you have a conversation with them you feel so comfortable or at home and can talk about anything. With them you can chat for hours or days at a time like you are catching up with an old friend or long lost a family member. This is most certainly the case with these souls. Sometimes these relationships pass through your human experience simply to exchange a soul gift on another level of being. Other times they can enter your life to support, experience or teach a lesson requested in the divine contracts. These are the soul relationships which sometimes are the most challenging but the most soul fulfilling. Soulmate relationships will often fall into this last category.

Soul relationships are not positive or negative in nature, for they encompass both the upper and lower part of the totem pole and also all points in between. Understanding that sacred contracts are playing out is key to more harmonious and loving relationship with your soul family member.

When one seeks to understand and learn the lessons involved it often will help improve the journey for all; resistance will often just cause further friction in life. You will also sense when the time is to move forward and end the relationship before it reaches the battle ground. This creates a loving closure for the parties involved with good wishes for all flowing forth.

The ending of a relationship of this status never truly ends as you are always connected energetically on the soul level. The contract may even bring you back into contact with each other later in life; should another part of the contract need to be fulfilled. But, it doesn't mean it there is no pain when the death of the relationship initially occurs. Egos will get in the way often on both sides and will edge out the divine energy of love. Death is death, no matter what shape or form it may take. It profoundly influences the human psyche and leaves long lasting effects unfolding and rippling throughout our lives.

Think about this: How often does a relationship end and it affects our future relationships in some way and time? It happens more than most realize, I assure you. However, when one sees the relationship as a soul contract that is being fulfilled and listens to the mind, but follows the heart, blessings will be shared. Spirit has said when this happens love, support and respect will be experienced at all times, even when one may not always be in agreement on something.

Spirit also says many times the basis of many disagreements is a lack of clarity in what is said or expected which often leads to further miscommunications further down the line. Spirit says when both souls enter the relationship living presently and the heart does the speaking, success is almost most certainly ensured.

This is especially true when both sides take the time to truly listen, hear and understand what each other is communicating. Take time each day in your relationships moving forward to make sure you are both on the same page. You can do this by repeating what you heard and understood back to each other. This way you can clear up any miscommunications right away and make sure you are both on the same page.

Another thing that Spirit has shown me is that many people don't know how to open and share what is on their heart. This is because fear often gets in the way. Spirit says paying attention to the body language and communicating how something feels to each other will help with this equation.

Words are powerful, so be conscious of how something is communicated. If someone says: I feel you are holding out on me; take a moment to check in. You may find truth to this statement. Perhaps, a part of you is holding out on sharing something within your heart you have not been conscious of. This also could be a sign they have something they wish to open up and share to you; though not always the case.

If someone says: I feel misunderstood or invisible with you. This is their truth in every way. Honor this but ask questions to help you understand what the basis for their statement is. By doing so, you will learn a lot about each other.

The Gift of the Mirroring Effect

Soul relationships often mirror one another. When you see something in other you perhaps don't like, chances are this energy is active within you, though sometimes showing up differently. The energy most active and needs to be acknowledged will always be reflected in our relationships and life experiences. Become conscious and appreciative of the gift of this energy.

If you see a pattern appearing in your relationships with people, take ownership of it. This is the universes way of showing something within you that is active and at play on the unconscious level. That is why this pattern is showing up in your relationships. Once you get this and you learn or understand what the repeating cycle is about, this shall dissolve in your relationships as well. This is one gift in the universe of relationships.

This mirroring effect can also happen in other areas of your life. So be aware when something is repeating in your life so you can be aware when the universe is trying to show you something active within you. This will allow you to potentially heal and clear the issue up right away when you get the bottom of the lesson you are to understand.

To help you further understand the mirrors within your relationship. Take time to make a list of all your relationships, past and present. Writing the positives and negatives to each on two separate pages. As you do, this you may begin to see a pattern emerge. Meditate about the lessons of each of the experiences and what this pattern is trying to show or teach you about yourself. Once you understand this, you can then begin to master the lesson moving forward.

But why stop there? You can now take the time to change up the negative energy to positive by getting clear on what it is you wish and write it down. Many times we enter relationships without a clear plan. By getting clear, you are allowing the universe to bring you into harmony with your wish. Dream big here for you deserve to have quality relationships.

For example: If you have been in multiple relationships which have been unbalanced, unhealthy, disrespectful or perhaps even felt like you were their therapist. Your wish may be for a balanced and healthy relationship with each other. You want a relationship where it is very supportive and respective on all fronts.

Now that you are clear about what you wish, you can now get clear about why you wish this type of relationship. A few of the other reasons may be listed here: You wish to feel happy, respected and supported each day. You wish to be able to go out knowing your relationship with this person is in a good place. You wish to be listened to, understood and heard.

Your relationships have been a mirror for you. Take time to look in the mirror to see where it is you have been unbalanced, unhealthy and disrespectful in your life. It could be with yourself, in your relationships at work, home, health, or somewhere else. Remember, the relationships patterns will always reflect what it is you need to heal and improve in your life.

Once you understand where you need to work on clearing up, you will begin to see the relationships of all types shifting. Start today by mastering being the person you wish to have more of in your life. As you do this, you will start attracting more of these qualities in all your relationships in life. You can't have something you are not, so become what you wish. Your true nature is all this and more, so be the highest energy you can be.

In the meantime, look for five to ten things you can love and appreciate about the relationships now in your life each day. As you acknowledge these gifts, the divine energy will bless you with even greater blessings within them. Remember life is about living in the moment with love and appreciation. Life in its entirety is a gift; the more you see the experience as such, the more you will be blessed.

This is a great opportunity to let the past stay in in the past and start anew with your relationships each day. After all, every moment before now is a past life lived and you are given the opportunity to be reborn in the gift of the present.

Look further than just the physical relationships, look to the skies and beyond for you have relationships within the entire universe and beyond! Use this opportunity to re-establish relationships with your non-physical friends and family who have left the earth for they are a part of your soul family

The End of an Era with a Soulmate

I know for me the death of my romantic relationship with my ex was one of the greatest times and worst of times. I was the one that ended it, but it was still hard as love was present. But from the day we met I knew there would be issues and it would not last. I knew it was a short-term relationship, but I stuck it out longer than I should have because of the love energy.

In fact, the cracks appeared shortly after we moved in together but wanting to deeply to have something meaningful I stuck it out. The honeymoon phase was definitely over after a few months and the cracks deepened along the journey forth. I am grateful for this relationship as it was a gift. It helped me get grounded when I first moved to the area as I became familiar with the city. But, it was never a balanced or healthy relationship in truth.

In fact, I felt I was the husband going to work to pay the bills and provide for the family as I worked 6 days a week. The person who was to be my life partner often quit jobs, got laid off or fired, leaving the burdens on my shoulders. Yes, there were wonderful aspects of the relationship, but, there was an air of insecurity and jealousy from day one that would appear with him.

It only got worse as I formed work relationships, got involved in the community, was getting healthier and trying to live life to the fullest. I was evolving and it was time to leave the relationship which became clear after a family wedding when the last straw hit the fan. After just over three years, the end was in sight.

In the interim, I prepared for the coming day and grief was being felt along the way. In my case I was feeling good with the new direction as I took my power back and reclaimed my life. I was exploring my holistic, new age interests and spiritualty. Light was shining on the dark as I was connecting to my soul pathways and my ex was feeling the shift. Deep within, he knew the death of the relationship was on the way as there were signs. By the end of the third month after my cousin's wedding the end unfolded and the next phase of grief began.

Like all deaths you need time to process the gifts, lessons and closing experiences. For me, I grieved the loss of this relationship as I discovered there was a soul family connection unfolding here. It was a blessing and a curse for the both of us. He was in pain over the loss of the relationship and was reacting from the pain rather than responding from the soul.

We all do this at times. If we would take time to process before we react, when something unfolds, we would allow the energy to dissipate; this then allows for a more authentic heart response to come forth. Like a fine wine, we need to breathe before experiencing the gift.

The Gift Within the Darkness

Death and grief, go hand-in-hand and we need time to go through the bereavement process before we can see the gift within.

In time, we both could move forward. It was about a year later when I was seeing someone when it ended when I realized that I was now ready for a relationship, should I choose one.

Having begun on the path of awakening to my soul further I choose to wait it out and work on bettering myself first. After all, everyone deserves the best of us, and first we have to be the best version of ourselves for us then we can open the door to others. I am still bettering myself every day as Spirit teaches me and I am in service. But, I am now ready to open the door to whatever gifts await on the other side for me. I am excited for the infinite possibilities.

Spirit brought our souls back together after quality time apart so both apologies and forgiveness could be exchanged between the two of us. This was a part of the divine plan to allow for an energy exchange to take place. One which would show me he learned he was the source of many issues in our relationship. Though it wasn't all on him, I had my fair share of the responsibility which I owned.

Spirit's plan also included an opportunity for me to be of service for the souls of his brother and father, who had both passed since our parting of ways. During the short Spirit communication he also could heal and move forward on his own path having found peace within himself. We were both now free to move forward having completed the contract.

Looking back, I can see my patterns of dysfunctional relationships started back in the womb with my mom and dad's own relationship struggles and eventual death of their marriage. My own insecurities and abandonment issues surfacing in this soulmate relationship like a mirror showing the worst of us. This was a gift showing up to be healed and addressed once and for all.

The death of the relationship allowed me to find my truth, step into my power, experience and explore who I was in the bigger picture. It is the gift that keeps on giving as I continue to evolve as a soul. It allowed me to open up and connect to the Spirit within me, discover my intuitive and the sacred nature of us all.

Spirit has shared that we never come to the planet alone with only one soulmate who we to be in a romantic relationship with. We come with many soulmates scattered around the globe for us to connect with in a variety of manners. Many are potential lifelong romantic soulmate relationships for us.

If you are in a relationship that is no longer serving you, you are safe to walk away, should you choose to. It is assured you will meet someone who meets and exceeds your hopes and dreams. You can have your fairy tale ending. This is a guarantee if you are following the heart and soul guidance. It is just one of many gifts that your soul has blessed your life with. Take time to discover the many more blessings along your journey forth.

The Womb Effect

Our parents are some of our greatest soul relationships. We asked them to play the roles of villain, hero, guide, protector, teacher, friend, and supportive character in the movie of our lives.

At the time of our conception, we begin fulfilling the sacred contracts we wrote with each other on the soul level. It is then that our deepest relationship was formed with the soul who would play our mother. This was because she would carry and protect us in the womb. She would open us up to the infinite possibilities of life on earth through her emotional and physical experiences.

During our time in the womb everything that our mother experiences we embrace. This then forms a file in our subconscious mind from which we will use to create our beginning human beliefs, fears and experiences.

When I underwent my life review I was taken back into the womb to understand certain parts of my experiences. I can honestly say there was so much that was shared during this review; it was impossible to go into all the information here. But it was very clear what our mothers experience and felt during our time within the womb affects us profoundly.

With this knowledge it came as no surprise how the events leading up to the death of my parent's relationships affected me. This underlying subconscious programing is still being uncovered as I live and breathe long after the first events.

One way these beliefs affected me is by causing me to fear accepting healthy relationships and even partly my good in life. This, in part, caused me to unconsciously worry that something negative would happen if I did. It also caused me to create a need to self-sabotage my relationships or push away my good throughout my life. All stemming from the energy of fear and its influence I felt deep as I was in the womb of my mother.

My inner child still at times feels the need to rebel out of fear of being put out to the curb once again like a piece of garbage. I now understand that much is connected to the demise of my parent's relationship, the many other deaths and other experiences stemming from the earlier years of life.

I know I deserve and am worthy of the gift of accepting my good. This includes having healthy and balanced relationships; something I strive to master daily. I am conscious that I am the source of everything in my life. Thus, if I want more healthy and balanced relationships, I need to start with having this with myself. Only then can I attract to me that which I wish to experience more of.

After all, the energy within radiates out into the world and comes back to us as that which we are in truth. The soul will never lie to us. It will always show us what our energy is radiating most actively into the world (both in known and unknown ways). Therefore, relationships are just one way it can mirror the energy to us.

As humans growing up, we tend to mimic those that are the closest to us; or we may choose to go the complete opposite of them. There often is no middle ground. For me, I tend to mimic many things of both my parents, even though the models themselves were not perfect humans. Many of the attributes I choose to mimic unconsciously.

Once we meditate to see the root cause of situations or behaviors, we can then take responsibility for our own healing. We can also forgive where required and step back into our soul power. You cannot turn back once you begin. Life will continue to gift you with opportunities to heal and improve your life for the better. Only you can make the choice whether you take the action step or not.

Thankfully, the universe will always support us if we are following the heart along the path of the soul. We are imprinted within our being to connect with the Spirit within at any time along the journey. At any turn of the road or crossroad we have the choice to do just that, connect. Unfortunately too many times, it takes a life alternating event, health challenge or a crisis to awaken us to our true nature.

This is why we often have to go through or experience a spiritual awakening of sorts. It is this experience where we are re-connecting to the wholeness and remembering who we are. When this happens the imprints of our time in the womb can begin to be cleared and dissolve. We essentially are being reborn as the gift we are, Love and Light!

Friendships by Divine Design

Relationships take all forms in our lives from family relationships, friendships, acquaintances, co-workers, and our spouse. We have relationships with our bodies, our money, our homes, and so much more. The list of relationships we form in life is endless.

Many of these relationships will change or even end in time and you can rest assured that you will go through the bereavement process for each one. Many times the process will be mild in nature and you may not even recognize it as grief. This being because we tend to think of grief as something we go through with a physical death, not a death of relationship in whatever form it may take.

I am sure when you take a moment to think about when something ends, you'll agree you have a period of adjustment you have to go through. The closer the relationship the harder it can be to process what has happened, you may even go into shock or denial around it all. You may go through stages that involve getting angry or depressed over the loss. You may even try to bargain your way back into the relationship. But eventually you will come to terms with what has unfolded and begin to move on.

There is no set way someone will grieve the ending of something; you could go through multiple stages at once or in reverse order. Everyone grieves how they grieve. One way is not better than the next. Your way is the perfect way for you; allow yourself to go through the process and get support if you need it.

You may as well come to terms that all relationships come to an end, one way or another. It will happen all in the divine way and time and as humans we need to accept it as a part of life. Our divine nature is in charge here.

I know growing up as kids we are much more resilient to relationships that end as people are often coming and going at school. We may even hang around different people in each grade or school as we grow up. It is natural for us and our soul is much more at peace as it transpires.

However, sometimes we connect with souls which seems much more than just a passing school chum. There is something special with these souls we bond and form a friendship with. These souls are often part of our soulmate family. To a child these friendships mean more than anything much of the time and an ending can sometimes tear apart their heart with the loss. Being quick to get over things, the child's heart mends and they move on to form a new friendship in time.

However, eventually children have many scars on their heart. This because as every friendship dies their heart breaks leaving them a womb to mend. This can cause a delay in healing or them being able to move on at times. I know for me as a child I had many friendships that would come and go, and I never gave them a second thought as it happened.

I was choosy or picky about who I allowed into my inner circle. I never had more than a handful of people who I would call a close personal friend, at any given time. With these people I could be myself and allow my spirit to be free. They loved, supported and accepted me as I was without judgment as I did the same with them.

We would go to each other's parties and houses to just live, laugh and play, sometimes getting carried away leading to one of us being hurt along the way. For me, I often took things to heart and it would pain me; a few people may even have called me moody as a child. Not understanding that my gift of sensitivity was one of my greatest allies, I often found myself alone in my own little world. It seemed like the circle was getting smaller partly because I was being pushed out of the equation as the weird moody kid.

I found that in elementary school my social circle before grade five was much bigger. Once grade six came, it came to a screeching halt. Not feeling comfortable in my own skin at times led me to developing skin irritations. This all led me to scratching the scabs profusely to the point of bleeding in class. It wasn't long before what seemed like the whole school turned against me and the nickname Scab took root. I had the plague and no one wanted to catch whatever disease it was, it seemed. Even after Mom took me to get ointments to help heal the arm, the damage had already been done.

I socialized more with a different crew which ended up putting me into a different class of individuals; which I mainly didn't want to hang out with. I found myself soon afterwards down in the dumps, depressed and ready to leave this world. I even tried to end my life at this point by taking a bottle of over-the-counter pain pills that were in the medicine cabinet. It wasn't like anyone would miss me as I felt judged by family members, by the school and last straw, those that I called friends.

The universe had a plan and it didn't include me leaving the planet just yet. I ended up being sick and threw the pills up, and no one was the wiser. I am sure that Mom wondered what had happened to the bottle but I know she clued in when I was sick that I had gotten into them. She left me a sign saying as much.

I closed myself off further and became more independent; why let people get close if they will turn on me or throw me away, like used tissues. I had my own family members doing that after all and felt like the black sheep of both sides of my family. I just wanted to be loved, acknowledged and accepted for who I was. Something we all wish for in life.

The universe had a plan for me though which included me loving, accept and acknowledge myself. This being something

I learned later in life as I came out and owned my truth in my early twenties and through my spiritual awakening. I began feeling lighter.

It was here where I began processing my grief and understanding all the connected experiences. I also learned about my life mission and how I was to be of service in the world helping people through their grief. Who better to do so than someone who has gone through the darkness himself and uncovered the light within?

Many times we go through experiences involving pain and hardship so we can use it through our life mission somehow. But, instead of embracing it, we resist what we are to experience; something that we should never do. After all, if we keep pushing something away or denying it, the energy of it will keep pushing back at us. Once we learn to allow ourselves to embrace the experience, we can process it quicker and move past it.

Through the ending of friendships and experiences I learned I didn't really need anyone outside of myself to be happy. I knew as a soul I already had everything that could ever be required. However, as souls we come here in groups and our friendships are a part of our family. Due to this, our nature wants to be around others; this because love connects us.

This is partly why we feel sad or down when we are rejected or a death of a friendship happens. Another reason we feel sad, down or depressed is because a part of the human consciousness is jealous the soul is moving on and leaving us behind. It is one thing when it involves the soul leaving the body. It is another when the soul family member is still living and has moved forward without us. The human part of us can feel abandoned and alone.

There is a gift in every death and we need to remember to look for it. After all, once we look past the illusion of death we can begin seeing shadows form. When this happens the gift will soon be discovered. If we let our fear of the dark (the unknown, death, being hurt, etc...) hold us back, we can never experience the freedom of the light.

I have lost a few close childhood friends to physical death in the more recent years. Each time it was unexpected and caused those of us left behind to question life or our mortality.

Whenever I hear of someone that leaves the physical world as a Medium I can appreciate the gifts within the loss. The human part of me still feels his heart triggered with grief and knows the heart needs time to process what has transpired. Thankfully time is just what the doctor ordered in our healing journey with grief.

Please allow yourself the time to breathe and process in your own way; there is no rush. Be gentle with yourself. There is no expiration date on when one will no longer be grieving or how it will unfold. It will get easier, little by little, I promise you.

In the meantime, take time to reflect on the lessons that your friendships have taught you as you honor the blessings of yesteryear. As you do, you will make room for new memories to be made with new and old friendships coming alive all the days of your life.

Remember we always have a choice in how we respond to life and what unfolds. So make the best of the lemons you are handed and go out and enjoy life. Your loved ones in heaven want to celebrate you living life fully. Let's give them a reason to party.

Prayer for the Death of a Friendship

Dearest Mother-Father God,

We come to you this day to ask for your ever present help with the loss of dear friend.

We know that life continues on after death and the soul will continue to evolve, but our human heart grieves. Please help us find peace within this transition as we process and move forward on our soul journey.

Surround those of us that grieve with your enveloping loving light to lift us up and transform our pain back to love.

Please help us take time to nurture ourselves through this process in ways which are filled with your heavenly blessings here on earth, God.

Let us understand the many gifts contained within the darkness of losing our friend so we can once again see and experience heaven's light on the earth.

With every ending comes a new beginning. With this we trust and welcome the new soul family members with open arms who come into our life to fulfill the hole left behind by our dear friend.

We know you have a divine order and plan for the universe. It is with this we are willing to trust, have faith, let go, listen and follow the guidance of the divine heart always.

For all this and even better, we give our thanks and so shall it be.

Amen

Prayer for the Death of a Soulmate Relationship

Dearest Mother-Father God,

We come to you today, to ask for your divine help and healing. We ask for your enveloping presence to be with us and those that are now grieving a physical loss of a soul family member.

We ask that you help us process and find peace within the heart and mind, knowing our soulmate continues to evolve in the spiritual dimension.

Please help us recognize the signs and symbols they may leave for us along the earth journey. We know these signs are letting us know they are now healthy, that all is well and they are taking part in our lives each day.

God, we know our soul family member played a role in the many life lessons and experiences on the earth. So, we thank you for bringing to our conscious awareness the gifts our soulmates blessed our lives with.

We ask that where we may hold unforgiveness that your divine love melts the resistance to letting it go. We ask for this so we may be free to forgive ourselves and those who have been a part of our lives. We ask do so from a place within the heart with love and light.

Help us remember our soul family and to live life to the fullest in their memory each day.

We know that our reunion with our Soulmate will one day unfold at the perfect time and way according to your will, God. In the meantime, please watch over us all and guide us to live from your perspective of love and light God.

For all this and even better, we give our thanks. Trusting and having faith that our prayers have been heard and answered, we now surrender.

Amen

CHAPTER 21

CLEARING AWAY THE SMOKE WITH FIRE

Jamieson Wolf

MY MIND WAS A sea of fog.

Through the thick cloud I could hear nothing, see nothing, and feel nothing. My entire world was numb. Within that numbness appeared three words: *"You're a failure."*

As I tried to go on with my life and attempted to find something good left within it, I walked through the fog that followed me everywhere. From within that fog came three words: *"You're a failure."*

I lay within my fog. The last three words he had spoken to me repeated again and again inside my head.

"You're a failure."

I replayed every moment, everything that had been said, as my marriage crashed to pieces around me. I saw myself trying to catch the pieces in the air, but they were jagged crystal from a broken chalice that sliced through my hands until they erupted in blood. My palms looked as if they were covered with liquid rose petals.

I was like this for a few weeks. Until the papers came.

When they arrived, I didn't know what they were. I felt a sense of unease as I stared at the official envelope. The plain rectangle screamed not to be opened, but I had to know. When I slid the envelope open and withdrew the papers, I saw Robert's name.

Then I read through them, one sheet at a time.

They were divorce papers, the ones he didn't even have the courage to hand me himself. I sat down, gutted, the walls moving around me as if the world itself was shaking. He had asked for the separation and I had given that to him. I had given him everything: my heart, my comfort, and my sanity.

I had given him everything and he had given me nothing in return.

I sat there, shaking, the papers trembling in my grasp. Then I looked at them again. He had not signed them. Both spots for the signatures remained empty. He had mailed me the papers to goad me into coming back to him, or just to upset me. It had the desired effect, but not the way that Robert hoped it would.

"You're a coward," I said out loud. My voice boomed in my small apartment. "You're a coward, Robert. You're a coward."

I felt furious. A fire burned in me, bright and strong, and it cleared away the fog. It cleared away the fear. My sense of self returned to me, an awareness of me that hadn't been there for years. I had sacrificed a lot of myself to my marriage and had let Robert cut away until I was but a shell of who I had been.

He had taken away my friends, who had stopped calling to talk to me. He had driven a wedge in between my parents and me. He had left me alone on an island within a marriage. At that moment, when I was at my lowest, I decided that I would never be alone again.

I would come to know myself once more, and I would start living my life, not just merely existing or wading through the fog. I wanted to engage with life, celebrate life, and truly live it. I would not let Robert's last words be my own.

I began a journey that day, sitting in my dark apartment. I searched for the light in my life. Where there was none, I created light so that there would be no more darkness or mist. There would be no more shadows. I would finally take control of my own life, rather than let someone else control me.

I reconnected with friends, forged ahead in my writing career, and strengthened my relationship with my parents. I also stayed open to love and the possibility that there was love out there in the world for me—real, true love.

The separation had taken over my life, but now I could focus again on living. In the end, what had seemed like the most horrible thing to me at the time turned into a gift. I was no longer under someone else's control, no longer in the dark.

What Robert had unknowingly given me has continued to give back. The death of my marriage had brought me a new life, a new existence. I was able to mend my chalice.

For that, I am eternally thankful.

Jamieson Wolf is the author of multiple books including Lust & Lemonaide and his latest Life and Lemonaide

The Gift Within the Darkness

CHAPTER 22

THE GIFT OF GRIEVING LOVE

Roni Campbell

LIFE AFTER DEATH. COPING with losing a loved one. You don't, not really, in my opinion.

My life partner of 43 years, my Johnnie, suffered from Vascular Dementia and took 7 years to finally find relief by transitioning aka going home. Hard as the journey was and however much I thought I was prepared, I can honestly say, you are never prepared.

With his passing, numb was the best way to describe how I felt. Another biggie was guilt – could I have done things differently? The normal things like eating and sleeping didn't really matter to me. Normal—what on earth was that and would I ever be normal again? I was devastated, confused and terrified. My heart hurt with a pain that I cannot describe. Sharp like glass and black like night. Totally overwhelmed. Anger. Crying didn't make it better, it just hurt more.

Auto-pilot took over to do the things that had to be done. People said, "I was brave." Not a word I would associate with what I was at that time.

One of the phrases that stick out in my mind, that people often say to those grieving is, "I am so sorry for your loss." It should not be used. Believe me, it hurts and sorry does not help. What did help was when people shared their memories of this man I loved with all my heart. Some funny, so I could laugh; some sad, so I could cry.

Another phrase that is often said, "He is in a better place." Believe me, when one has watched their loved ones suffer on the way to dying, we know that. We don't need the reminder. It only causes us to feel the loss further, despite the well-meaning intentions at the time.

Words that do help are: "I am here for you. We don't have to talk; we can just sit together. But I am here. You don't have to do this alone." Coming from special people, who you know mean exactly that, is the greatest comfort to the grieving. The thing is to let them know that they are not alone and that you are there for them.

I have found that grief does not end over time. It has been 3 years since my partner passed, and I see signs from him every day. But the tears can fall at the sudden playing of a song, or a memory of a place, or when hearing a British accent out of the blue. It is okay to give these emotions the space you need to give them to help you process them. When you have lost someone close to you, you feel left behind. But you are never alone. They are with you all the time, and you can feel them, talk to them and they will be there.

On the way home after learning that he was gone, I suddenly saw hawks on every other post on the highway. I learned over time, that this was Johnnie's way of saying, "I am here." He is around me all the time, and if I am down, there will be a hawk come to assure me, "It is alright, my love. I am here."

Although I have not heard him speak to me personally, he speaks to others who can pass on his message to me. One friend asked if he had a message for me to which replied, "No, she knows." When she questioned him about what I knew, he said "I AM HERE!" Dreams bring him close to me, and when I wake up I feel comforted.

I recently went through a cancer scare, resulting in surgery and other treatments, and when I came out of the hospital, I went to get in the car and saw a coin on the ground. When I opened the door, I picked it up and discovered it was a 20pence coin. Johnnie, who was British, was once again making sure that I knew he still had my back.

Before Johnnie passed, I had made up my mind that I would spend the rest of my life alone. But God and the angels had a different plan and wasn't going to put up with my stubbornness. They had set a plan into motion and Johnnie was making sure that I was going to be well taken care of before he "crossed over to the other side."

I met a man who was going to save me in more ways than one. He helped me through my tougher times as Johnnie progressed into the later stages of the disease and eventually passing away. Tom was there helping me along the way through my grief and gave me permission to take my time to process it. He was kind, loving and comforted me. I knew that Johnnie had blessed this relationship and eventually after his passing, we were married.

I wish to share with all, don't make assumptions that what you decide will actually happen. Grieving is okay, but you still have a life to life. The greatest gift you can give the ones you have lost is to live life to the fullest. Never lose sight of the fact that you still have a life, and it can be as wonderful as anything that has gone before. Grab it with both hands and hold on.

You deserve to life a life that is filled with happiness and love. Know that your departed loved ones want you to be happy and to find love again, no matter what age they may have transitioned.

Today, I feel so blessed, happy and surrounded by love. I thank God and my Angels for the divine intervention; the gift filled with their love, support and guidance that helped me to open my heart to the possibility of love while I grieved the passing of my partner. I believe that Johnnie was a part of this divine plan who gave us his blessing which allowed him to leave the world in peace knowing that I was now being taken care of.

Roni Campbell is one of the co-authors of Guided by the Light: Following Your Angelic Messagers

CHAPTER 23

Death of a Friendship

Georgie Deyn

SITTING ON THE FLOOR of my healing room, knees hugged to my chest, gently rocking backwards and forwards, tears rolling down my eyes. Something in me had died, what was it? A major part of me was missing, I could no longer sing, or connect to my angels and guides. I felt totally bereft and alone. If it were not for my two boys life would not have been worth living.

"So what happened to you Georgie", I hear you ask.

It was 2009 and I was living my life on auto-pilot! I now know, looking back that I was living from fear, in fear and emotionally wounded. I never thought I would return to my 'normal' bubbly, happy, carefree, positive self. She seemed as though she had deserted me in total disgust at how I had allowed this to happen. How on earth did I let this happen? How?

I had managed to get myself entangled in a web of fear and false perception. The spider at the centre of the web had drawn my dearest friend and me into her world of dangerous deception. We had both been pulled into her universe which revolved around control and manipulation. Looking back at the situation now I can see I was allowing my ego to respond to the black widow and my spirit had been totally locked out of my life.

I wish to share with you how the entanglement temporarily kidnapped my spirit, stole my friend, killed our friendship and threw me into a cell of grief, misery and self-loathing. Pseudo psychic people can be very cunning; they reel you in with words that comfort your ego and somehow they can manage to hook you into their way of being. My friend and I had both received soul clearings with the therapist (spider) in question. We later became her disciples; we wanted to learn all she had to share, we allowed ourselves to be brainwashed with her demented take on life, past-lives and manipulating the future.

Looking back with love (and believe me I have sent the lady so much love and healing in the years that followed my fall from her grace), I can now see that she may have been suffering from a mental health problem.

I can also see how my friend and I may have been sucked into her spiral web, we had both been recently divorced, single mums and vulnerable. I had a desire to be the best version of myself; I had goals and aspirations and honestly believed that continuing to work with this therapist and performing the soul clearing, would give me a better chance of fulfilling my life's purpose.

Together, for two years my friend and I continued to use the soul clearing charts and pendulum, clearing the past, present and future, contacting our "guru' when we got stuck or hit a block.

During this time we became quite insular, as friends our friendship revolved around the soul clearing and our guru. We did most things together, socialised, travelled on holiday and were so close, we could not explain our secret work to others; they would not understand and would think we were mad. So it was easy to just keep oneself entwined in the web together. My ego told me that not many people were ready for this work and would not understand the importance of my role. How many times had my guru put me on a pedal stall, as she told me how wonderful I was and how I had come to the Earth to help the planet.

However, alarm bells started ringing incredibly loudly in my ears. Our guru began to say extremely negative things about my friend. Behind her back, to me, she would comment, "She is trying to control you!" "Her vibration is low and toxic, she will pull you off track" "She is jealous of you"

I had trouble believing these lies and unbeknown to me, my friend had the same lies being told to her about me. Unfortunately, she did believe the lies and the manipulation worked.

Over the next few weeks whenever I saw my friend she looked at me in a different way; as though she was scared of me and what I was capable of. The fear in her eyes broke my heart. My best friend whom I was so close to no longer could be in my presence.

When she shared with me the allegations that had been told to her, I tried desperately to stand up for myself and help her to see past the illusions and how we had both been manipulated. But she was so drawn in and trusted the guru implicitly that the fear won over our friendship. She dropped me from her life like a hot coal from her hands.

My world fell apart. How could she believe these lies about me? At the time I even started to believe them myself, maybe it was true. Maybe I was a bad, evil person.

It took me a year to heal and grieve the loss of my friendship. The biggest healer for me was connecting to my Spirit, living my life from love and singing every day. Finding my spirit through my voice and music released me from the prison of grief.

Out of the grief, I arose like a phoenix from the ashes of a hellish existence. Now I am pleased to say that I help others overcome grief, depression and sadness through music and sound.

The Gift Within the Darkness

I would like to say to those reading these words that you are stronger than you may realize. When life gets you down and you are in pain from the grief, your soul will help you rise from the ashes of death and heal to sing your life's song once again. You are always supported and never alone. Love is always with you.

Georgie Deyn is one of the co-authors of HALO: Lighting up Heaven on Earth and one half of the musical duo, Seraphisa

CHAPTER 24

THE GIFTS WITHIN THE LOSS OF OUR ANIMAL FAMILY

LOSING A PET IS like losing a child; after all, you love, care and protect them all the days of their lives with you. They look to you like a parent for they can only care for themselves so much. They need you as their human to nourish their needs with food and water, give them shelter (of some kind), love and playtime attention, and a little spoiling occasionally. In return, they offer you with unconditional love, company and healing as needed.

This darkness is a double-edged sword many times. One side holds a pet that lives a long and healthy life; where in time their body fails them and they naturally fall asleep. On the other side is a pet whose health eventually fails and a choice to put them to sleep is made by their human caregiver. Each has its own burdens and often leave the human feeling grief for their animal family.

Unfortunately, those of you that had to decide to put your beloved pet to sleep have the hardest time. After all, you have been playing nurse to your beloved pet before it came to this.

You question: Is it the right choice; even you know you made the right choice. You may have had medical guidance saying that the time has come. Your human mind needs to question, and the heart has to go through the bereavement process; both of which can take time.

You have had a routine with your loved one, getting up in the mornings to feed, walk and have your special moments with your animal confidant. You told them all your secrets and your thoughts regularly as they looked at you in wonder. They made you laugh; they irritated you, and they made you feel in other ways. That my dears was one of their jobs, to help open and heal your hearts which perhaps was hurt along your human journey.

They came into your life to help, guide, heal and teach those that were their humans about oneself and the world around us all; often doing so in ways that are unexpected. Think the about gifts your animals brought into your life and you will begin to expand your perspective when it comes how they blessed your life.

Unfortunately, many times our animals are undervalued or under appreciated. It is only after they are gone from our lives we can see how we could have been there more and the gifts they brought into our lives.

You will learn more about Animal Guides later in the book. For now let's continue to discuss the darkness of losing our pets.

The Gift of Blackie

As a child, I can remember having a very close connection with animals of all sorts, including those that I was blessed to have under the same roof. I am talking cats, dogs, mice, hamsters, fish and I know a bug or two was in the mix.

I remember going to my Grandma Calhoun's home on the weekends and connecting with the family dog, Blackie. He was always such a sweet and loving dog. I personally didn't like the fact he was limited to such a small area. For his size, age and for a variety of reasons I totally understand it now. As a child I wanted to run, play and have fun with him. When he into the afterlife and I found out, it hurt my heart; as it would any child.

Blackie taught me much with his gentle smile, patience and love. He didn't seem to lack any love that's for sure and seemed happy enough with his surroundings. I know when it came time for him to cross the rainbow bridge into heaven he did so knowing he was loved and appreciated by all of us children. I often think of him and feel his presence with me, and I would hope that others in the family know he is still with them.

That is one of the many gifts that unfolds once our four legged friends leave this world, is that they can be free to visit with us all. I have received this confirmation many times for my clients when their animal friends stop in for a visit while we are in session.

One of the main messages the animals share:

Thank you for all the love you gave us. You blessed us with a great life and for this, we will forever be grateful. Please know we are happy, healthy and enjoying life right alongside you. Please know that you are not imagining that we are with you when you feel our presence with you. We truly are with you at all times.

We appreciate the fact you were there for us in good times and bad, and that you loved us enough to set us free when our soul was longing to be. You honored the soul contracts we made long ago in spirit. We understand that it was not an easy decision or one that you took lightly. Thank you for being brave, courageous and taking action as needed. You helped us to find relief. In return, you can rest assured we will be will you all the days of your life watching over you from the other side of the rainbow bridge.

Our animal friends are limited in their time on earth as are we physically. Eventually the body will break down or something will transition in life to bring their presence in our lives to an end. This is all part of the divine plan. When something happens unexpectedly, it can leave a hole in the heart of those left behind. This also happened when both my cat Spicy and my cousin's dog, Snoopy came to live with us for a temporary period.

The Gift of Snoopy

Snoopy was an Irish Settler and Cocker Spaniel mix who lived with us for a temporary stay. He was a loving and smart dog. He had found his way to Timmins after he was let out one evening when my Aunt Sandra let him out for his nightly nature visit and he ran away. He travelled his way the 132kms from their place to our home where his human (my cousin) was living with us at the time. But, after she left, Snoopy remained with us for a short period. He was a great dog; I love spending time with him.

From the day we moved into this particular house I had an unsettling feeling about the dog that lived and protected the scrap yard kiddie corner from our house. This feeling was amplified whenever I had to pass by the yard to go to school.

One day when we were playing outside Snoopy and that particular dog had gotten loose. Before I knew it, the two dogs met in our driveway; I immediately understood why I felt the way I did all those days in great depth. It was a feeling of dread of what was to come.

The scrap yards dog was like: Who is this dog that has moved into my neighborhood?

Where Snoopy was like: What is up with this dog in my yard?

Together their personalities clashed and a fight broke out. Being a young child it was frightening to see this dog I loved so deeply with his fangs out and ready for anything. It wasn't long before blood was drawn and before Snoopy had ran away. Within a short period the city's Animal Control Unit had retrieved him from the streets and took him to the pound.

Now you would think that would have been good news as we would reclaim him and bring him home. However, with my mom being a single parent and us not having the money, it wasn't in the cards to bail him out of the pound. And my cousin couldn't afford to rescue him from the pound either.

As a child I didn't understand the linguistics of what was going on, all I knew is my dog was not at home. I would visit him daily and he would cheer up. But, it wasn't long before his time came to cross the rainbow bridge with the pound putting him to sleep. My heart ached and I remember crying deeply at this loss; Snoopy taught us to play and to stand up for what you believe in. Something I had trouble doing for many years.

Snoopy was the second animal I had lost due to getting outside and roaming free. First, was my kitten Spicy that I got when I was in first grade, who I found shortly afterwards under the haunted house of the neighborhood. The children that lived there decided that because they found her under their stairs, she was now theirs; a fact being a child found cruel and saddened me. And then Snoopy when I was a few years older.

This all took a toll on me as a child and I acted out towards the animals I would come across in life. A part of me in a sense hated others who had animals. This caused me to become aggressive when people were not looking with the animals, who I so dearly loved. Looking back, I can clearly see that the pain I was in was causing me to take it on those that I was closest to, my animal friends. Deep down, I knew they understood and got me; they loved me beyond measure and would forgive me.

I also started down a darker road, one that led to me stealing as a child and getting into trouble with family, friends and well the law. I am not proud of this period of my life, but knowing what I know now, I can understand where it was all coming from. I figured if people could take from me, well then I could take from them. After all, we learned at school the golden rule:

Do unto others as you would have done unto you. Or put another way, what you put out in the universe will ultimately find its way back to you. So, be mindful of what you think, say and do.

I was mad at Mom for not bringing home Snoopy. I took out what I was feeling on her in a multiple of ways, all which led to me getting the wooden stick many times. I lost a part of my soul throughout this journey through the multiple animal losses in a variety of ways and acted like a totally different person at times. I felt like Doctor Jekyll and Mister Hyde in some ways, one hiding behind the mask of the other.

This went on for many years until I grew up and out of the pattern. But by then the damage was done on a subconscious level. I found that many of my actions when it came to animals in life could be traced back to these earlier losses in my life.

The Gift of Transitions

For now, let me close this chapter with another personal story of loss. Madeleine had lived across the way from me for many years and whenever she would go away, I would care for her cat, Tiggie. Over the years of being a good neighbor and animal lover, I had this love and respect for this gentle but protective feline.

Now Tiggie was not like any normal cat, this cat had an attitude and a fierceness about her. When you walked into her home, you knew who was in charge and it wasn't Madeleine. She was a very spoiled cat but loving towards the feminine visitors. When it came to men, it was a whole other ball game. You could be even sitting in the same room with Madeleine and if you made a slight move you had better be prepared as the cat would come at you.

On more than one occasion I would walk into the apt to check in, feed and clean her litter, and she would rush the door and come after me. I can only assume that I had caught her off guard as she moved amongst the rooms of her home. It wouldn't have mattered who had opened up the door. But if you were a man, you better have strong ankles or boots on as she would attack and bite them.

Thankfully, she never bit me. I think she recognized where I was coming from and that I had a level of love and respect for her. I respected her limits and didn't try to show further affection; it was her house so therefore her rules. I would talk with her as I fed her and just let her know how much she was missed by Madeleine and when she would be home, etc... Then off I would go.

One day it was midnight and Madeleine had come knocking at my door and needed my help with her loving cat. She was frantic and before we knew it we were whisking her feline confidant into the cage and off to the emergency veterinary clinic we went. Shortly afterwards, Tiggie was put to sleep. A decision that for Madeleine was heartbreaking. After all, she had raised, loved and nurtured her child from the kitten stage until her end of life, playing nurse on occasion over the last several months.

Over the next couple weeks Madeleine was lost and alone, as she sat in the apartment, reminded of her furry companion everywhere she looked and went. A scene all too familiar with many people who live alone and have lost a four-legged friend, or any loved one for that matter.

She would talk with me about this often on our visits and I could see the heartache in her eyes as she spoke of it. She had that last memory of Tiggie going to the vet and looking at her from inside the cage, scared, sad and in pain. This is certainly not an easy memory for anyone to have as a last memory and not one that our loved ones want us to have after crossing the bridge. They want us to remember the happy times, the love or laughter they gave us and not the sad memories or how they died.

She spoke about getting another cat, but she wasn't sure at her age, being 73 years old, if she wanted to go through it all over again.

One day I came across someone who had found kittens on the side of the road. There was this little angel looking up in the pictures who I knew belonged with Madeleine. I brought it to her attention as soon as I could. Within the hour we were going across town to pick up this little bundle of fur for her, who we called Angel.

Angel was the complete opposite of Tiggie, friendly with everyone and even made friends with my cat, Indigo. They had their nightly meetings in the hallway of the building to start and moving inside the apartment once they were more comfortable with each other. Life got back to normal for Madeleine with me watching over Angel often and playing with her. She was the belle of the party in every respect, soft, gentle and love filled. She had more energy than anyone knew what to do with but it was all good for Madeleine who now had a purpose in life again.

However, within two years of Angel coming into her life, Madeleine once again found herself on an emotional roller coaster. The vet visits became a regular thing as they tried to figure out what was going on with Angel.

Angel was clearly in pain, was bleeding and having other issues that just never made sense to anyone. The point of no return came, and a decision was made to put her to sleep. We were all heartbroken over the loss of this special angel cat. An autopsy was performed and cancer had been discovered, which answered everyone's questions.

Just a few weeks before this, I had been at Madeleine's talking about something she was going through. She had been scared about having cancer again and many of the symptoms she was having were the same. I had done a scan of her body energetically and didn't pick up anything at the time.

Knowing cancer has roots tied to our emotions it wouldn't have surprised me if she had it. Her personality traits leaned towards expressing the underlying energy behind this disease, at times. The emotions of anger, resentments and other strong emotions from our childhood are often playing a role in our words, reactions or responses in life.

When Angel was diagnosed as having cancer we realized that she had been Madeleine's savior. Often our animal friends will absorb energies or health issues from their owners. In this case, Angel had taken on Madeleine's old emotions and potentially even her disease. I believe the disease which Madeleine was sensing wasn't so much her own but Angel's, as they had a very close connection. A part of her knew something was coming and this was why she reacted when she was scared of her own cancer resurfacing.

Knowing all this and knowing Angel's mission was to help heal Madeleine's broken heart after putting Tiggie to sleep; we now understood where her zest for life and play came from. It was because she knew her time on earth was limited and acted as such. A lesson that many of our animal friends come into our lives to remind us all to do more of. To do more living, loving and laughing in your daily life experiences.

Angel has not been replaced, since her passing in the summer of 2017, despite Madeleine attempting to find a new feline friend. Like anyone who has or is experiencing grief, it takes time to heal the heart and open back up. I know that when her heart is ready, she will attract a new animal friend into her life for the two hearts will be ready and become one.

I encourage each of you to spend quality time with your animal friends for life is short. Let them help heal and open your hearts as you learn from them by observing what they are teaching you. After all, just like anyone else that enters your life, your animals have come onto your path for a reason. Discover that and you will find a greater appreciation for them.

Prayer for those Grieving a Pet

Mother-Father God, Creator of the Universe

Here this day our earnest prayer as we come to you now to ask your ever present help for those of us grieving the loss of our beloved animal family.

We ask that you envelop us with your love and light to heal our grieving hearts. Aid us to come to a place of peace, love and acceptance with the loss of our beloved animal companion. We know they are now in the light with you God watching over us.

Help us be at peace with our decisions when it came to the care, feeding and nurturing of our animals, in life and at their time of death. Help us forgive ourselves as required as we forgive those leaving us physically and answering the call to spirit.

Aid us in moving forward with their loving memories in our heart and mind. We are comforted with the knowledge our heavenly animals are now with us as we live and embrace life fully with your help.

If it is your will for us God, help us open up our hearts and homes to another animal companion. Let this precious soul fill our heart with the divine love, light and laughter once again in your way and time.

Heal the hearts of all those around the world giving the loss of their animal friends and family now, and forever more. For all this and even better, we give our love and gratitude, blessing all in the process and so it is.

Amen

CHAPTER 25

The Loss of a Pet

Sue Charbonneau

Most pets become part of the family. They interact with everyone differently and create relationships with every member. So their death can be emotionally painful. When you have to make the decision to have a beloved pet euthanized, a plethora of emotions wash over you. It is difficult to watch a pet get old or sick. Wanting to prevent them from experiencing too much pain & suffering, this decision is made out of love & kindness.

Nevertheless, your heart feels heavy, broken, you feel the loss of this small personality that filled your days & nights with such joy & laughter. These pets teach us unconditional love, the joy of playing, the pleasure of eating a treat and the peace found in rest and a good night's sleep.

Our pets feel our sadness, our joy, our excitement. So their loss leaves an empty space inside of us. We see their favourite blanket, favourite stuffy toy or ball, and we feel the loss. We miss them.

Personally, I found that losing a pet made me reflect inwardly. I wanted to stay in contact with my pets so I talked to them anyway; I talked about them with others and looked at pictures. Sharing memories with others is always helpful.

During my life, I have had a number of pets. My first loss was our cat Star. She was almost 20yrs old and was part of my whole family for this whole time. We were all very sad but when Midnight got so depressed after losing her Alpha partner, having to euthanize her only 6 months later, was even harder. It left an emptiness, a hollow in our life. Having to put away all their toys, blankets, give away their food made it very difficult. But the memories and story sharing always made it better.

In the year 2001, we found Rosie. She became my sidekick, my partner for walks, my devoted sleep partner and my confident. I told her everything! We would take her to our store and there she became a healer for many. Her loss at the age of 13yrs was very hard. Not only for us but for the many people that she had touched through her time as "store dog."

I felt empty, lost. I had no one to talk to about how I was feeling since she was the one who would always be there listening. But one year later I saw a picture of Rocky posted by a friend who runs a shelter outside of Timmins. I looked at that picture and knew instantly that Rosie was sending him to us. He is her opposite in so many ways, male, black, loves balls (Rosie hated balls) but I sensed Rosie saying: "You took care of me when I was lost now you can take care of him too."

So even though we have lost many pets, I know that they are still with us in some way. I believe they have a "Heaven" and we will be able to reunite again someday. I cheer myself up by picturing all my pets playing together and sharing memories about our family!

CHAPTER 26

Minnie's Lessons

Marianne Soucy

To those of us who consider pets to be members of our family, losing a beloved pet feels like losing part of ourselves. The unconditional love, joy and presence they give us create a bond like no other.

Unfortunately, the death of a pet is rarely a peaceful, natural death, but is often sudden or tragic due to accident or illness, or their life may be ended by a vet's assistance because of the seriousness of their condition. Very rarely do pets die a peaceful death on their own terms at home with their loved ones.

I have been through all those scenarios with my own animal friends, but when my beloved cat Minnie was close to dying, everything changed.

Minnie was an abandoned cat who wandered into our home, our lives and our hearts. She showered us with love and gratitude from the moment she met us. She was such a joy and blessing in our lives. After only a couple of years, she started losing her eyesight and her health began to fail. The vets couldn't find or do anything.

The Gift Within the Darkness

From previous experience with pets dying, I knew that making decisions out of fear would only lead to decisions which are deeply regretted and a guilt that is devastating.

I often use shamanic journeys to connect with pets and spirit guides, so I used the journeys to connect with Minnie to ask for her wishes and how we could best help and support her.

Right from when I first connected with Minnie in my journeys about her imminent death, she was very firm that she wanted to pass naturally, in her own way on her own terms, and when she was ready.

She wanted to stay at home with us and not have the assistance of a vet to help her transition. This was her choice, and obviously, each animal is unique, so what was right for her might not necessarily be right for others.

In the months that followed, we went through one of the most challenging times in our lives; supporting Minnie the best we could in all ways, making her comfortable and being there for her night and day.

It was during this period that I discovered what an amazing teacher Minnie was. As I connected with her spirit, I found that the spirit was well and oh so wise, and through many journeys, she guided us through this long goodbye in a way that no one had done before. Her words of wisdom brought me the comfort, strength and guidance to honor her specific request to "Let the light be unbroken" as she put it.

When I grew up, death was a topic to be avoided, and the result was no closure and no proper goodbyes when my parents or other family members died. There was always much fear around death and the dying.

My beloved cat Minnie changed all that and taught me to see beyond the failing body of a loved one. She taught me to see the shining light that is within each being—human or animal. She taught me to put my own fear aside so that I can truly be there for and honor the wishes of the one who is dying instead of reacting from a place of fear.

When Minnie passed quietly during the night of December 6th, 2016, it was the peaceful passing she had wished for. She came into our lives with gratitude, and her light continues to live on within our hearts and fills our life with gratitude.

Minnie shows up sometimes in my journeys and brings her light and guidance to others who need it. When my cat Sam died suddenly, she came and guided him into the light. When one of my oldest cats, Freedom, passed, not only did the lessons Minnie taught me enable me to provide him with the passing he wanted, but Minnie showed up with her light and love to make his passing a beautiful and peaceful one.

Pets are not only wonderful companions but can also be wise teachers.

Difficult lessons like patience, surrender, presence in all circumstances, returning to gratitude in the darkest moments, seeing and holding the light—those and many other lessons I owe to Minnie and my other animal friends. Teachers in life and beyond; loved always and remembered with gratitude.

Marrianne Soucy is the author of Healing Pet Loss: Practical Steps for Coping and Comforting Messages from Animals and Spirit Guides

The Gift Within the Darkness

CHAPTER 27

THE GIFTS WITHIN OTHER TYPES OF LOSS

This chapter applies to Loss of Home, Job/Career or Health

LOSS AND THE GRIEF that one goes through can happen in any experience or area of life. There is no limitation when it comes to the extent of its reach on one's body, mind, spirit, emotions or our lives. The grip that death has is far beyond what anyone could ever imagine. As you have discovered through the proceeding chapters, grief impacts your life in so many ways; often long after death touched your life.

In this chapter, I will talk about the gifts within a loss of our home, job or career and even our health.

Please take note, we are only touching the surface of the many ways loss and the grief accompanying it reaches into your life. If you were to think about it, I am sure you could think of another 10 ways or even more it has already touched you or will at one point in your life. Death is the end of a cycle in the life of a living organism or human.

All of life is living and breathing, as energy is flowing through everything, whether or not we are conscious of this divine truth.

When a chapter in one's story ends, whether abruptly or gently, we have to process what has happened. This journey of coming to terms with closure can be felt and experienced in a variety of intensities and speeds. Like all grief, there is no right or wrong way or time limit for it as each soul is unique. It is, therefore, possible for two souls to experience the same loss and each be affected differently. It is one of the gifts of life where we all get to choose and have our reactions or responses to something.

Ripple effects are often experienced outside the main area that the loss has transpired in, with aftershocks felt many times after the initial earthquake of death. When one is going through the bereavement process a simple shift of locations for their favorite chair or losing their shoes after a move, for many, can be traumatic. For others, these small life shifts won't have an effect at all. You never know completely how far the ripples will reach, especially the more subtle ones.

It is always best to try to be compassionate with others by putting yourself in their place for a moment; this allows us to gain a better understanding what they are going through. By remembering this, we may respond to the experience differently. Knowing grief may be playing a role in our reactions, we often will find common ground and support. Each of us are more alike than one may ever realize or want to even admit.

Having experienced many losses, throughout my life, I find it easier to find something in my own life to relate to my client's journey. I believe this helps me to connect with each one on a deeper level as I can usually transcribe the information from Spirit in a way they can understand.

The Foundations of Life – Home

After our birth, we are brought into the family home where we would spend our first days, weeks, months or years. This is where we dig out holes to place our roots and get grounded on the earth. Sometimes these early days are filled with chaos and experiences that rock our world, and other times they go smoothly. I like to think of this period of our life as building the foundation of our home on earth.

We often use this time to get accustomed to the surrounding earth experiences and inhabitants with us. Like a building crew preparing to lay the footings and foundation of a building, we encounter many types of soil (personalities). Some soils can be heavier and denser; just like there are some which are more light and airy. In the end, they all work together to aid us in building a solid foundation on which we can build our home. Our foundation in life (childhood) is where our beliefs, catalysts for our life lessons and our reactions to life are often created.

As we grow up we continue to build upon the foundation and as life dictates we may even expand upon the original plan to build something bigger. Life is running smooth and then something happens: a move. This can be a challenge for many people as the foundations built had a reach wider than the actual home. Friendships, neighbors, schools, work, routines, shopping and so much more can all be affected when we move. This also all depends on many factors associated with the move including location, memories associated, our age and more.

As a soul, we trusted those souls who would play our parents to do their part to raise us in a safe and secure environment. This would be where we would solidify our earth foundations and begin to build our home. So when a move happens when we are a young child or of youth age, it can be especially hard and traumatic for us. We may kick, scream and hit things, all trying to voice our unhappiness with our parent's decision to move. It matters not if they are forced into the decision or made it willingly, all we know is an earthquake just shook our foundation.

Our safety net has been pulled out from under us and we begin the grieving of our security blanket, our home, if you will.

The Gift Within the Darkness

We can't yet see the gift that this offers us. All we see is the dark gloomy sky as we leave behind all we came to know and love. In time, the clouds shall clear revealing the bright blue skies and bring the knowledge of the gifts to the forefront of our conscious mind.

When I was a child, I remember we lived at 400 Pine Street in an apartment upstairs for the first few years of my life. I remember certain life events happening in this location for me, both negative and positive. The foundation had been poured and it was now time to begin to build the home. We were now ready for the next steps on our journey, so when we moved from Pine to Knox Avenue, it was a neutral experience for me.

I am sure like anyone that moves forward from something that may not have been positive, we are happy to start anew. In my own child way, I was as well. Now bear in mind this move was over forty years ago now and the stories in the memory banks may have been altered over the years. The mind is a powerful thing and sometimes we will imagine things to be one way, only to discover that the truth is something else. This is one gift I have learned over time.

For the next several years we built the walls of the home on Knox, which is where we grew our roots. This is the home where I have the most memories for sure; both the good and the bad; each a gift in their own right. Some gifts keep on giving for many years others where others were temporary. Many important life lessons were uncovered and the process of mastery began here.

It was here I learned to ride a bike, be responsible to take care of things and explored my sense of adventure or even creativity. Here, all this and more happened, both as a family unit and independently. I finished my primary elementary school and started senior public school when the earth shook again. My perfect vision of life shattered into a million pieces and the cracks in the foundation were exposed with the death of the parental unit.

My hopes, dreams and imagined future killed in an instant. Life turned upside down, never to be the same again.

The fall out began as my sister and I grieved our losses and tried to move forward. Before our hearts could heal the walls came crashing down once again, just as I entered high school. This time we were being forced to move.

Within weeks we went from living in a three bedroom house to a 2 bedroom apartment and a newborn welcomed into our lives a couple months later; spurring another move. During this time, we discovered the losses of many precious items with each move; adding to the other deaths and accompanying grief we were experiencing.

Life was changing so fast that looking back our heads were spinning, I am sure; in the process making us look like something from some horror movie. In time, I would learn that this was the root of my fear or dislike of change. Once this gift was revealed, I could start to take my power back and heal the root cause. I have discovered for me, home is central part of my foundation in life. When I am rooted, in one location, changes can unfold in my life and I am much more comfortable with them.

During my formative years as a teenager, I didn't really have any roots and was all over the map with the various moves. It would take me years to get over this as from my later teen years until I hit thirty I was constantly in flux moving every year or two. Without my conscious awareness, my soul was looking for that same feeling I had growing up in the Pine and Knox locations. This was all shown in my life review. Once it found the feeling I had sought, I poured the foundation and dug my roots in deep.

My current apartment may not be luxurious, but love and light fills it, and is located in the heart of the city of Ottawa. Indeed, a perfect location for this small town boy that grew up in the city with the literal Heart of Gold—Timmins, Ontario. I love my apartment and I am sure when I move from here I will grieve as well as this all is a normal part of when we move or change locations.

This time I will be better prepared to handle and process the experience with the tools in my treasure chest. I will start with being gentle and giving myself permission to allow the bereavement process time to unfold in its own way. Time and love is the healer and answer, always.

I hope you can do the same for yourself. Give yourself the gift of allowing yourself to grieve, as you move forward living, laughing and loving each day. You and your loved ones will be better for it.

Prayer for those Grieving the Loss of their Home

Mother-Father God, Creator of the Universe,

We come to you today to ask for your ever present assistance as we grieve the loss of our old house and make the transition into our new place.

As we move forward please help us in letting the past go with ease and to be relaxed, calm and at peace as we make this transition. We bless the home we are leaving with love, light, appreciation and blessings for the new occupants of our former residence.

We know that change is a natural process and we are willing to go with the flow knowing everything is unfolding according to your divine will.

Guide us to meet new friends and neighbors who we will connect with on all levels of body, mind, spirit and emotions. In this way, we know everyone wins with this change of residence.

We now fill our new home with lots of love, light, appreciation and blessings for everyone that passes through the doors. May everyone live a happy, prosperous, healthy and love filled life for all the days of our lives.

For all this and even better, we give our thanks, knowing our prayers have been heard and now answered and so it is.

Amen

The Helping Hand — Career or Job Losses

When one finds themselves at a crossroads in life we are presented with different opportunities to continue to build and grow as a spiritual being having a human experience. Each pathway is a part of the bigger picture and yields many gifts along the way. However, in order for us to walk forward, a door must close behind us.

Many people have the fear of the unknown because of the uncertainty of what comes next after something ends. It makes no difference if it was a door we intentionally closed or one we were giving a helping hand in closing. Either path involves a grieving and processing period for us to reflect, heal and an opportunity to shift onto the path of our soul.

As humans, we like to stay in our comfort zone and not rock the boat with changes too often, especially when it comes to our work life. We can find ourselves not feeling fulfilled, appreciated or just bored out of our minds when this happens. This is especially true when our soul is attempting to guide us in a new direction or for us to take the next step in our evolution. But, instead of embracing the guidance we resist it. This is when the universe will step in to put our secondary plan into action to help us move forward.

It may be at this time you find the job security that was present in your life come to the end. This could unfold with the location shutting down, laying you off or you getting fired or something else happens to assist you in moving along. Whatever the way the transition unfolds it truly is a gift within the grand scheme of the universe. You may not see this as the case at the time, but, I assure you it is.

I, myself have been on both sides of this coin; with one side finding myself being fired and the other side quitting the job. Both sides had blessings and lessons in the experience, through and after the moment of action; all of which could be seen as positive or negative.

Let us remember that our mindset and feelings play a huge role in the creation of our lives for a moment. With this information Spirit recommends we do our best to see everything working out positively in the end. This doesn't mean ignore the way you feel in the moments along the journey, for part of the gift is being in the now. Let yourself feel whatever you are feeling in the gift of the present for this is a blessing you sent to yourself to receive when you were ready. This is why we call the now the PRE-Sent.

Bear in mind we set this all up on a soul level with our sacred contracts, lessons and experiences we wished for this life. Through this we are soulfully evolving and must take responsibility for everything in our life. Or at a least the part that is ours in the universe. Doing so allows us to stand in our power without putting the blame on others. When we are serving the world through our jobs this is an opportunity for us to listen to our innate wisdom and take action accordingly along the path.

For me, back in the mid-nineties I was being guided to quit the job I was in. I was finding myself drained, not feeling happy and stressed whenever I was at work along with having conflicts with people. I was aligned and doing the best to stand in my power but didn't follow this intuitive guidance to quit the particular job.

I took on side jobs working at the local paper or other jobs along the way. I enjoyed each of them for different reasons. But, my main job was stable and secure and I didn't feel comfortable leaving it yet, despite already giving my notice twice. Each time the ego would get in the way as I would get a raise or something else that was in my favor. So I would retract the notice and stay in what was my comfort zone. After all, I had climbed the ladder here from the ground up to management and there was much about the job I enjoyed.

My inner voice would be subdued for a period but only to come back louder in time. Eventually, it became so loud that this one particular day ended up being extremely stressful at the restaurant. Lines were out the door for hours on end, the kitchen was backed up and a shift change was happening when it happened.

I had already decided to give my notice once again as my blood was boiling with the stress. Here I was 25 years old, grey hairs showing up, lacking routine for sleep and other components of a regular life; I knew something needed to change. Being the end of the shift, I may have relaxed after leaving the restaurant and got some sleep as was often the case after a rough day. But the time had come to take the next steps and the universe was going to help me out the door. If I wasn't going to listen and take the divinely guided action, it was going to assist me in moving forward.

During the most stressful time of the day, shift change, the owner came into the back to bitch at the staff for something that happened earlier. With the lineup at the door, the backlog of orders and staff changes, this was indeed not the time to come to yell and bitch over something stupid.

My blood started to boil and finally ruptured breaking the surface causing me to speak up and call her out for choosing now to bitch at everyone. A moment later, the words came out the mouth; not mine, but hers, "You're fired. Get the f... out!"

I went into denial for a moment and then chose to go back to the grill to help clear up the orders that had been started already by me and then I would be gone. I was trying to make things easier for the staff taking over, but her ego wasn't having it. Repeating, "Get out now." She clearly wasn't seeing the bigger picture as she was blinded by her own rage of stress, like us all. I packed up and left, leaving the kitchen and staff in disarray. It wasn't my problem any further but I felt bad for them.

She knew how to run a business but when it came to the treatment of staff, she could be mentally abusive when stressed with calling us names, etc... It wasn't abnormal for us to butt heads at times as here you had two powerful souls who had karma, lessons and contracts playing out. Out of the restaurant, she was a whole different person being kind, generous and heart-centered.

We always had a level of respect for each other. Once we could take a breath and relax, we would then talk and I would apologize how something came out. I know from my side, I would never apologize for what was said as it was the truth and she knew it. I would always admit I could have communicated the message better. The next day I went to the restaurant to apologize to her, not hoping to get my job back but to clear the air and move forward. The divine guidance was delivered loud and clear.

During the next few days, I took the time to process what had happened before moving forward with finding new work. I found myself depressed at times, angry, lonely, happy and confused. A whole mix of emotions ran through me as I was processing. I ran into people who I used to work with and learned how my leaving caused aftershocks which would be felt for weeks to come. They all needed time to process what had transpired. Many questioned the events and the environment for themselves at the same time.

The pause caused everyone to come to a place of their own level of appreciation. I learned how loved, appreciated and missed I was by many of those I worked with. This was something in which I did not always feel or was aware of. Too many times we undervalue and don't appreciate what we have until it is gone; this was true in this situations for them and for myself.

As I moved forward I found looking for new employment to be a bit of a challenge. This was because my ex-boss was a big name in town and word got out of her firing me. I had success despite her, as many people knew of her reputation and were willing to step up to offer me a job. Many did so because they knew of my work, but also because they respected that I lasted nine years working for her.

Although I had found work, I can now clearly see upon reflection I was grieving the loss of the relationships I had built up in the former job. I found over the next several weeks reasons not to stick it out with the various opportunities before me.

Having been in an unhealthy relationship with my former boss I wouldn't allow myself to be in a similar situation again. It was a lesson which I have experienced and was ready to move forward without repeating; I could not put myself in another stressful situation or environment. I needed time to process and heal from the unexpected death of the job.

Spirit says too often we all move forward from one place to another without taking the needed time to process. We are better off to take a pause to reflect upon what has happened, to use this time to think about what we have learned through the opportunity and even to heal. We don't do so as we don't recognize that a death has just unfolded and we are indeed grieving.

I have seen this with my clients many times as well. When I bring up that they are going through the bereavement process, they feel lighter and suddenly life makes sense for them. They now understand time is the answer they need in the situation and to figure things out.

For me this time between jobs was a gift, despite the stress of being financially restricted for a period. However, a part of me knew everything was happening for a reason. I soon found myself meeting and hanging out with new friends and before I knew it I was moving to Ottawa. Once the decision to move was made life got magical as Spirit was lining things up and I was finding myself in the flow once again.

The plan was now unfolding and Spirit was smiling down upon me. I was looking up at the night skies, seeing shooting stars and making wishes along the way, more than any other time in life. In fact, I noticed those wishes were very much like me bargaining with Spirit when one is grieving. I would say things such as: If you get me to Ottawa and get me a new job I will be a better person, I promise. I am willing to surrender. This was especially true when my transportation almost fell through at the last minute.

The process continued as I freed myself of many of my possessions and kept only the basics to move; this translated to sixteen boxes and a suitcase. A part of me learned that we don't need more and we can get by with less. Quality over quantity is the key and as I prepared to make the move, this thinking came into effect.

I told my mom a couple weeks before the move which broke her heart; her first born was now leaving the nest and going to explore the world. Deep within she knew it was the right thing for me and was supportive along the way. The ripple effects of me losing my job were continuing to be felt by others. They also would grieve the loss of a relationship in their lives as I moved forward. Sure we would be connected but the energy would be different for all.

Within a month, I was on the road to Ottawa. Upon arriving I had job interviews lined up and felt like I had come home. Within the day I had a place to live, within 48 hours I would start a new job, was volunteering and was getting the lay of the land. I was integrating into society and finding myself meeting new people, feeling grounded and centered. I even was dating in record time. Life truly was great.

It wouldn't be long before I was back in a routine going to work six days a week and then coming home to a partner. Mostly, I was enjoying life but part of me felt I was disconnected; this was especially true when it came to my relationship and eventually the job.

This time I would listen to my inner voice and I took divinely guided action steps. I was choosing to stand in my power and let go what no longer served me. I first let the relationship go as I moved onto the path of my soul purpose. The first steps involved taking courses which were lined up with my interests and passions.

I continued to do so as I discovered my life purpose to be in service for the world. I felt much more relaxed, loving and happier in life. However, I was feeling conflicted still with my passions to be of service and the job at odds with each other. I was moving forward with my purpose and soon the steps were being taken to break free of the job as it was no longer serving me.

Doing so would yield many lessons and opportunities to soulfully evolve, each would hold positive and negative experiences but all gifts along the journey. I talk about these further in The Grand Illusion in my previous book *HALO: Lighting up Heaven on Earth* as I share the many blessings and lessons throughout my life experiences connected to these.

Even though I was the one that had let the job go, I would need time to grieve the journey. I would need time to adjust to the new life for myself. Time would give me an opportunity to reflect on the experience and also to explore the gifts that presented themselves along the way.

With the second job loss after nine years, it allowed me an opportunity to reconnect with my true nature, listen to my intuition, stand in my power, and discover my life path. It would allow me to continue to evolve and discover new pathways along life's journey. Some of which were things I had begun exploring within the first job.

Life has a way of bringing you along the path you are meant to be on. Whether or not, you are aware of it, all roads truly do lead home. Whatever is your highest journey to experience, you will find and it will find you. When you hit a crossroads, you can rest assured the universe will support you along the way, even if you take a wrong turn. Know whatever pathway you may be on, the universe knows how to lead you onto your soul path and will call heaven into action to help you.

Spirit has a plan and everything unfolding in your life is a part of it. Keep your eyes open, listen and follow the heart to discover the sign posts that will guide you along the way. Remember you are never alone; your heavenly support crew is always with you. Let them hold your hand, heal your hearts and help you live your best life possible; the life of your soul awaits you.

Grief happens in various ways and can have long lasting ripple effects on your life. Give yourself permission to ride the waves and do the best to enjoy the journey. Accept that grieving is a part of life's journey and allow yourself to process it however it shows up. This is the real gift and is the one that yields the greatest dividends; often even grander than you may expect.

Use the time between jobs or new careers to follow what truly will make your heart sing. Take inventory of what isn't working for you so you can get clear on what you truly want. This way you can add to what already works for you. As you do so, even if uncertain what that means for a job title or career, you will begin to discover the path that will feed your soul. Let this be the list you use and follow the sign posts to your ultimate calling. Your soul has already been guiding you in your life. Listen to it and discover the gift within career changes.

As you process and move forward, feel free to ask your spiritual support crew for their heavenly help. They truly do want to aid you in loving, laughing and living life to the fullest each day as you follow your heart's calling to create a life of heaven on earth. If you don't ask them for help with this they can only do so much because of free will on the earth, so pick up the phone and call upon heaven now. Big or small jobs, it is their nature to serve you. You are after all the CEO of the company that is called Your Life.

Prayer for those Grieving a Job or Career Loss

Dearest Mother-Father Creator

We come to you to ask for your omnipresent assistance through this time of our career changes in life.

Please help us heal our grieving hearts as we are processing the loss of our jobs and moving forward with the next steps along the journey.

We know this is a great opportunity which will yield many blessings and gifts along the way for us. We understand and know our soul has a plan and everything is unfolding in divine order. We however find ourselves at a crossroads, confused and uncertain which path to take. Guide us in a way we will understand. Let your loving angels take us by the hand and empower us to follow the divine guidance of our soul each day.

We ask for clarity in what our life purpose and mission is so we can take action steps to fulfill it. We know that changes in our careers are often motivated to help us discover our true calling on this earth and this transitional period is no different. It is leading us to the next step on our journeys so therefore please help us relax, let go, and be in the flow during this time.

Help us see the magic within the opportunity to shine our light into the world doing what brings our hearts into harmony with our passions.

Endings are a gift as they are leading us to the new doors of opportunity that await us and we are excited to begin anew today. We know that the wisdom of our heart and soul is one of the greatest gifts; we ask to be able to clearly hear and take action according to this guidance each day.

As humans, we know that we may not always act in accordance with love and light. Therefore, we are now willing to forgive ourselves and those who played a role in our story for the evolution of our soul.

We give thanks for all this and even better. Trusting and having faith in your divine plan for our happiness and joy for this lifetime, we now surrender. And so it is.

Amen

The Pounds of Pain–Crisis of Health

We are a soul with a body while we are on the earth. The body is the temporary vehicle for us to experience and enjoy this realm. When the body breaks down or goes through a crisis, it can be devastating on the human part of us. Suddenly life comes to a halt and we are bed ridden; for days or perhaps weeks and even months. Believe it or not, this is a gift from Spirit.

Often the human part of the equation doesn't take time to appreciate the body, mind, spirit or even the emotions. We may resist or ignore the signs to stop, breathe and listen to the message the soul is giving us. With each passing message ignored, the strength increases until we find ourselves lying in our beds to experience, understand and get the message (aka learn the lesson).

Everything happens by divine design and is set into motion by the bigger part of us. The sooner one understands this the better. Our soul knows how stubborn the human part of us can be. As the creator, we will direct the forces of nature to work in our favor in order to evolve as a soul having a human experience. This includes the body breaking down as needed.

Many times the lessons at play within these moments are to learn to receive, take better care of yourself, relax, listen and follow the wisdom of the soul. Your soul's mission on earth is also a reason why this may be happening to you as you will see in my own grieving health story.

Growing up I was often seen as the chubby or husky kid and garnered names such as Big B, Pork Chop, Chicken and others. I was quite active in my own way with biking, playing, dancing behind the closed doors and just being a kid. But, I had a sweet tooth that led me to the pantry and fridge where I would often indulge in the forbidden foods in excess.

Food was a friend of mine that loved, appreciated and did not judge. I could turn to it and never have a worry it would call me names or undermine my feelings. It offered comfort, support and enveloped me in rich and lavish goodness. I knew it would always be there for me.

As I grew up my love of food provided for me in other ways. I cooked for family, friends, and eventually made a living creating for other people. This for me was not necessarily a good thing as my weight spiraled as I stuff down my pounds of pain through eating. I tried many diets throughout the journey with success, but then something would happen to cause a weight gain once again. Each time I would gain more than I lost.

In time, I would understand the levels of the pain and what the triggers were which turned on the fat program. But there was a missing piece of the puzzle which I am only now understanding. I see it like layers of an onion; there are many levels to why something is unfolding and there may be aspects we won't understand until we work through one level.

Weight is always connected to a part of you that does not feel safe or secure in the world, on a deeper level. For me, growing up with death showing up as part of my life so heavily, it seemed as if I was always grieving. This played a key role in why I wasn't feeling safe or secure and thus gained weight. Add the constant shift of the floor under my feet, the stress and other people's human energies bombarding my auric field and you have the perfect storm for weight gain. Thankfully, this can all be healed and cleared.

As I mentioned I could lose the weight and kept it off for a period but whenever major changes would unfold in my life an earthquake would rock the ground under the human feet. This would cause a shift to unfold in my eating. When my romantic relationship ended I struggled for the next while with my weight. When my mom died and I subsequently my job, that was the final straw that caused a 200 pound weight gain. However, this journey would lead me to the first step in my life purpose: connecting with the afterlife for myself and others.

After a period, I would lose the weight and kept it off once again for a time. During this time, I got certified as a personal fitness trainer so I could be of service to others. But as a side benefit, it would help me with my goal to keep the weight off and in check. I kept up with the gym, yoga and even ran my first half marathon, where I captured a personal best time for me. Everything seemed to be going well at the gym and home. But, the universe would have another plan for me once again that shook me to my core this time.

A month after running the half marathon I ended up in the hospital having gone septic after my gallbladder ruptured. The medical staff were in awe that I had no real symptoms of the rupture.

What had brought me to the hospital was a combination of things though. The latest being bone shivering cold flashes combined with hot flashes the night before going to emergency to be checked out. The only other real symptom was a slight side stitch. But, this didn't bother me as it came and went over several weeks. It was a more uncomfortable nuisance than anything else.

During the admittance to the hospital, other symptoms began but thankfully I was in the right place at the right time after following the guidance of my soul.

A couple days before the Army Run, I had a little acid reflex which was abnormal. This led me to ask my guides what was going on and them showing me a hole in an organ. I figured I may need to have this checked out at some point, if the reflux didn't clear up.

This led me to cancelling my personal training clients and going to the hospital after I had the extreme wavering body temperatures that one fateful night a month later. I found myself in the hospital for ten days.

I found myself over the next several months going to the hospital for constant doctor's visits and blood tests. They had me on blood thinners to help clear up the blood clot they discovered during the hospital stay from the rupture. The pills delayed the surgery to remove the shattered gallbladder. They even led me down a dark path of binge eating as my body didn't seem to take lightly to this medication. I often wanted to run to the bathroom to vomit each time I would attempt to eat any resemblance to healthy foods.

I grieved the life I had lived which was beginning to become a distant memory more each day. I was pissed off and angry that I was gaining weight again and felt powerless at times throughout the process.

In my soul, I knew it was a temporary thing but that didn't matter. I didn't feel comfortable in my own skin and was in denial at first about what was happening. With the weight gain I didn't want to buy new clothes that would fit me better at first. After all, I would get back into my healthy routine right after surgery, right?

While life was on hold, I would continue to be of service in other ways to help people. When I was in communication with my guides I asked, what this was all about. They shared that a part of the reason I was going through this experience was for my life purpose of writing.

Growing up I found myself naturally gravitating towards writing. I often found it easier for me to communicate what was going on within me this way. I always knew I would be writing books and even started one in the library at school one year in my teens, but that was the extent of my book writing. Over the years, I would receive insight and guidance to write but never really sat down and wrote seriously. Sure I would write articles which would be published in magazines and newspapers, but nothing major towards a book.

In this communication, I also received the knowledge that I needed to open up, accept and allow myself to receive the blessings of heaven on earth. I, like many of you, tend to be generous and try to help or give to others all the time. I can find it a challenge to let my good in. This is a lesson I am working on mastering; it has surfaced many times in a variety of ways throughout my life.

I have learned I have to put myself in the flow of energy first so I have more to give to others. After all, if I am not taking care of my needs who will? Spirit has said it is not selfish to do so. This because the aim is to keep the glass overflowing with blessings, seen and unseen. Through being self-first we are able to share to our heart's desire as the glass never runs dry.

I have learned many times we push away our good or self-sabotage as a way to protect ourselves from being hurt somehow. For me, not allowing my good in is a way to protect my inner child. The one that fears the rug will be pulled out from under him when life is going well. This stems from when my earlier years.

Over the years, I have learned that we often hold pain, fear or worry tied to our life experiences in various organs or parts of our body. It is by turning inward to listen to the body and the wisdom of the soul that we can begin to free ourselves to heal and move forward.

For me, the gallbladder and weight issues were also tied to my mom; she had also struggled with both issues. I learned we often mimic or model others who we are closest to or we will go in the complete opposite direction. This all depends on the story playing out with our soul contracts, life lessons and karma.

When I am in service for clients, I will often tune into the body to help them discover what may be going on for their journey. Sometimes the symptoms are cut and dry about what the body is trying to tell them, and sometimes it requires a little more digging to get to the root. Every time we tune in, we learn to love, appreciate and honor the body even more for the gift of being a vehicle for the soul.

The surgery may have happened a few years ago but it is only now that I am discovering the root of my weight journey and how deep it runs. My body needed time to process and grieve the loss of my gallbladder and discover its new normal. This is not something we can rush and will happen in the divine time and way. However, I am now in the process of healing and reclaiming my health and vitality; one step at a time.

My life mission continues with the writing and I have a couple books already underway to be released in the coming year.

I am happy and grateful for the gift of the health challenges as through it I rediscovered the gift of writing. I will continue to be of service in the world as guided by the soul each day.

There may be bumps along the way and I am ok with that as I know I am safe, secure, loved and supported as a soul having a human experience. As long as I hold this perspective, I know that I will stay calm in the eye of the storm and find the gift within the darkness each time.

Prayer for those Grieving the Loss of Health

Dearest Mother-Father God,

We come to you now to ask for your heavenly help to heal, clear and release the pounds of pain we carry within our body, mind, spirit and emotions.

We understand and know we are a soul first having a human experience. With this in mind we ask for the aid of your angels to help keep our mind and hearts centered in this divine truth at all times.

Help us to see past the illusions of the health challenges that may be present at this time. Assist us to look past these illusions to see the truth that we are perfect, whole, healthy and complete, as is all the world.

We ask for your heavenly help in tuning into our body so we may listen and hear the messages of our heart and soul at all times. Help us to trust, have faith, let go, listen and follow the guidance of our soul each day.

Bless us with the healing and enlightenment perfect for our journey so we can be in service in the world as destined soulfully.

Should we be resisting help, please help us so we feel safe, secure, loved and supported to accept this heavenly assistance at all times. Let us relax into the flow of energy for our life purpose, life lessons and receive our heavenly good all the days of our lives, now and forever more.

For all this and even better, we give our thanks. So it shall be, and so it is done.

Amen

CHAPTER 28

Letting Go

Kimberly Hutt

SITTING WITH SPIRIT, REFLECTING on the importance and meaning of a profound dream I was awaked with the other night. I found myself standing on the edge of a very steep and jagged cliff, high in the mountains. This beautiful and terrifying scenery was familiar to me. I hesitated for a brief moment and then spread my arms wide open and fell forward. It was magnificent to witness. I fell with the grace and ease of an Olympic diver. I did flips and somersaults mid-air to plunge through the water's surface with speed and precision. I watched myself surface from that deep dive- refreshed and complete. Judges offering perfect scores as I climbed out of the water. Certainly not bad for someone terrified of heights and water!

Just over a month ago, my family and I began a journey of physical purging and decluttering. Moving from the comfort and familiarity of the farm we had grown to love, temporarily into my Nan's house I knew and loved since childhood and then on to motels and uncertainty as we landed half way across Canada in Nova Scotia.

Positive that I was ready and convinced that this would be an easy transition of leaving behind possessions, familiar surroundings and many friends and loving family. The excitement and adventure was welcomed. By passing truck troubles, lost routes, lack of finances and no commitment to housing or jobs seemed less of a concern as I knew spirit was guiding and had a plan.

Things fell into place quickly and effortlessly as housing, jobs, connections and basic needs were all taken care of within days. Things falling perfectly and precisely into place, just as I had anticipated.

All the packing, purging and relocating our belongings from house to house and cross country seemed to be well worth the effort. Exploring and arranging for the trailering and boarding of our horse and goats aligned quickly as well.

Then reality hit. Unloading the trailers revealed major water infiltration and damage. A massive cleanup of laundering most of our clothes, tossing some pieces of furniture and praying mold would not overcome the cardboard. Staying in motel rooms and eating take out and premade meals from the grocery store caught up. My father in law had travelled with us, bonded more deeply with our family and was about to make the return trip home. Saying those tearful so longs hit hard and fast. Our last connection to home was gone.

We moved into the apartment a few days later, no hydro or amenities for five more days. Cold showers and purchasing ice for the cooler to keep food cold. Knowing we were warm safe and together was what matters and grateful that home is with the family.

All the worries, fears and concerns of whether we had made the right decisions, second guessing choices and doubting the trust of inner knowing that we are where we need to be. Ego was screaming at me. I had made fabulous connections with work, timelines and commitments for book submissions and new adventures for my husband and grown children, but I had energetically and emotionally I began to vibrate differently – lowering frequencies and slipping into grief for all we had left behind and let go of. Our animals were heading our way and we had originally planned to return home for Thanksgiving.

Things started unravelling further when we realized that returning home was not in the works at this time, and the animals ended up delayed and would not be coming now until spring. Disappointed and anxious, I felt bad for my daughter and not having her babies nearby. The light and airy feeling of new adventures slowly shifted to heavy darkness. I was over processing and thinking. I ended up sick with head and chest colds. I remembered this feeling intently as I experienced it several years ago when we sold our house and became home free. I physically was ill and stressed for almost 5 months. I would learn the lesson well and not repeat the process.

I had no idea that grief and loss could be that impactful on all levels of your being – physically, emotionally, mentally and spiritually. I have witnessed this process in so many of my clients and helped them through loss of loved ones, relationships, illnesses and chronic diseases as well as possessions to fire and divorce. These losses in my life were purposely chosen and decided in unison as a family again, I had no idea they would be so impactful on such a deep level.

Out of the darkness and through words of wisdom this week – I heard a beautiful soul say breathe, center, anchor in and ask for assistance from your spirit team.

This past Thanksgiving as we sat down to share our meal as a family of four, it is quite different than a traditional gathering of twenty-four. In our quiet, beautiful little apartment 1600kms away from our extended family and friends, I know that I am abundantly and immeasurably supported, loved and encouraged not only by friend and family but by my own vulnerability and acceptance to grieve the letting go, accept the moment and Souly Reconnect to spirit in all situations.

Kimberly Hutt is one of the co-authors of 365 Life Shifts: Pivotal Moments that Changed Everything and HALO: Lighting up Heaven on Earth

CHAPTER 29

Losing a Loved One to Mental Illness...

Caroline Kimsey

THIS IS A LITTLE of my personal experience of "living" grief; the grief of losing a loved one to mental illness and of the utter desolation, confusion and fear I initially faced.

When my son was fifteen he started to hear voices, could not sleep, seemed to be in torment, culminating with his jumping off my roof. When I began to realize what was happening to him, I cannot describe the pain and anguish I went through. I grieved who he had been, my hopes for him and the relationship we once had as I was left to care for this alternative version of my beloved son; a living grief for me.

During the first year, he became increasingly unwell and was not medicated or diagnosed properly resulting in him threatening my life. Consequently, I had to make extremely hard decisions for a parent to make, including calling the police and not allowing him to live with me anymore. Although this was for both our good, I was left feeling bereft as every instinct in me wanted to protect my son and keep him safe. Watching him go through his inner torment, lose cognitive function and his freedom, whilst trying to care for him, advocate, support and understand what was happening was a strain I nearly buckled under.

I became unwell and consumed with concerns about his care and did not originally accept he would probably not recover. Most of all, I missed him with all my heart. I had brought him and his sister up on my own since they were small and we had a very close bond. There are many challenging things I have endured throughout my life but nothing has torn me apart as this did.

Initially, I turned to friends and family for support, many walked away or criticized. So I looked for support from people who work in mental illness. A psychologist said, "When people are dying of cancer, people show up with casseroles and support. When someone has mental illness, no one shows up for you. However, the mentally ill who are supported, even by just a single loved one, have a greater chance of survival and increased wellness."

This statement gave me a lot of strength to carry on, to be that lifeline and his advocate and not to take it personally! My daughter grieved in her own way and she let me know when I needed to make time just for her so our lives were more balanced.

It has been 6 years now. He has been in and out of the hospital, diagnosed with serious mental Illness; been brutally attacked for no reason and thrown in front of a fast moving bus; placed on the fringes by a society who judge swiftly. This gentle soul, my son.

It has often been a difficult road watching him go through this and learning to understand who he is now, without my old expectations. But I have formed a new bond and respect for my son who endures most of this in a way that inspires me. He does not allow himself to become a victim in his mind, and I do not allow myself to do that either.

I learned as much as possible about mental illnesses which assisted me to understand better what he was going through and communicate more effectively with him. I pushed fear and grief away and listened to my heart and gut. I set clear boundaries I would stick to. I became very patient and carried faith in my heart for all of us. I found support groups and gleaned wonderful advice from those who are going through this as parents or who work in this field.

The gift in all of this for me is I can now say I feel true unconditional love for my children. I look for the blessing in each day, it is always there.

Before I go, I wish to ask you to be kind to yourself. Be there to support your loved ones and make sure you care for yourself. Through it all, you will find a strength and wealth of spirituality and love inside of you that you were not aware of.... for all of you. Lastly, pray every day, give your troubles and worries to God; it helps to lift the burden in your heart. We were never meant to do this journey alone. Things are much clearer and you have more peace in your being when you allow the Divine to support you in every way.

With much Love and Light to you on your path.
Caroline

The Gift Within the Darkness

CHAPTER 30

WE WALK OUR JOURNEY ALONE

Brenda Rachel

We walk our journey on earth alone,
Even though we may bring someone home,
To fill a void or share our space,
Bringing us fullness to an empty place,
Our hearts lightening for a period of time,
Beating in sync like a harmonic chime,
Laughter abounds, quelling our fears,
Planning a future for the coming years,
Our feelings of love growing deeper each day,
Believing that nothing will take this away.
Then something happens, and they are gone.
Days that seemed short start feeling so long.
Now the questions remain,
"How do we thrive?"
"What will keep our broken spirit alive?"
Contemplating life and the path we've taken,
Coming from the choices of our own making,

The Gift Within the Darkness

We understand fully we came here alone
To find our "Soul Love" before going home.
We are all just "ships passing through the night,"
Some close together, some turning left, some right.
We are walking our journey, one by one
Until the sun sets and our day is done.

Dedicated to everyone who has experienced, or is experiencing grief from human or any other kind of loss.

Brenda Rachel is the author of In This Moment: Angels Sweet Reflections and co-author of HALO: Lighting up Heaven on Earth

SECTION TWO

TECHNIQUES TO HEAL AND RECONNECT AFTER DEATH

The Gift Within the Darkness

CHAPTER 31

THE RE-CONNECTION BEGINS

I HOPE THAT THE previous section brought lots of healing insights and answers to you to help you process your loss and grief you are experiencing. It is my hope you found comfort through the stories, healing of your heart and even heard a message from your loved ones through the pages.

In this second section, you will find tools to help you continue to heal and begin the reconnection process. I wanted to share the tools in this section to help you heal and improve your overall quality of life at the same time. These are some of the very tools in my treasure chest as a Medium, which help me to connect with the spiritual realm for my clients.

Using these tools will nurture your relationship with your soul, improve the overall quality of your life and reconnect you with Spirit. It is through regular practice and use of the information within these pages you will receive the greatest benefit. Each is complete in itself, however, when used together can be life changing.

Please be gentle with yourself. Know it may take time to allow your heart to heal so that you too can connect with your spiritual friends and family. Your heavenly loved ones are right by your side encouraging you with messages and signs to confirm they are participating in life alongside you. The more you can relax and allow things to unfold in the perfect way and time, the more likely you are to receive your own divine communication.

In the meantime, there are a world of Mediums available to assist you with connecting with your loved ones. Let the energy of your heart guide you to the perfect Medium for your loved ones to communicate through. The preferred Medium for your loved one may be the next television or radio show or even this book. It may be me or even the next person you meet along your journey. All these and more could be how they choose to deliver their message to you.

You don't need to connect with someone like me in order for Spirit to communicate with you. Let Spirit work it's magic, it knows how best to deliver what you are needing at any given time. You only need to stay open to receiving the messages from Spirit in the divine perfect way and time.

In the meantime, I love and appreciate each of you. Thank you for allowing me to serve you through this book. May you experience the many gifts of heaven on earth each day in all areas of your life.

CHAPTER 32

THE GIFTS OF SPIRITUAL SUPPORT

ONE OF THE GIFTS we have in our life, especially during those darker times, is our Guardian Angels, Spiritual Guides and Departed Loved Ones. I call this our spiritual support crew. Though you could use our team or our spiritual counsel equally.

However, many people coming to me don't understand the difference between the realms of Spirit. So, let's take a moment to explain the basics of how they are different from one another; ultimately, don't get caught up in labels as labels are restrictive and everything is pure continuous energy Guardian Angels

These angels have never lived on the earth during your complete soul evolution. It is these light filled beings which are pure love and are the closest energies to the divine source. They have the purity of intention to serve and bless your life. They will guide and watch over you as guided by your soul contracts.

They will gladly help you further in your life as you reach out and ask for them for their help. Due to the law of free will, they cannot intervene to help you in your life without your expressed permission. The exception being when life's circumstances put you in a situation that could cause you to leave the planet before your time.

All angels are androgynous but because we humans understand things as we have experienced them on earth, they will usually take on the presence as male or female. This can include a name that could lean towards the masculine or feminine nature. The angels tell me many times they take on the role based on your spiritual contract needs and to help balance your energy out. Meaning if you need more feminine energy, you may have a female Guardian Angel. The same is true if you need more masculine energy to support you and your life path.

Despite the depictions in paintings, movies and so forth, angels have no wings or even a halo. What people are perceiving to be wings or the halo is the energy field shining light around them. Angels are just pure energy and therefore pure light. They are here to support us and thus take on the form we are most familiar with to not cause further fear.

The angels are multi-dimensional beings without limitations; angels, therefore they can be in multiple places with multiple people at the same time. We will usually have 2 or 3 Guardian Angels, who are assigned to only us.

Spirit Guides

Spirit Guides have lived on the earth and mastered a particular area of life. They now continue their mission to serve the planet from the spiritual realms. Your main guides will stay with you throughout your earth journey while other guides may come and go as you evolve on the subject of their mastery.

An example would be someone who wants to learn how to draw or paint. They will attract to them, a Master Artist who will now be their guide for this endeavour. This artist will stay with them as long as they have the desire to paint. This guide will direct their new student to any books, courses or physical teachers to help them master their painting skills by inspiring them in divine ways along the earthly journey.

Like your Guardian Angels, your Spirit Guides are centered in divine love and light at all times. However, being that they lived on the earth they underwent a clearing process to release the effects of the ego. This allows them to serve you from a higher vibration and place of divine consciousness.

We usually have 3 or 4 main guides with us, and may have other many supportive guides. Spirit has shared that guides are akin to what we call a family on the earth. The main guides take on a role similar to a mother, father and the children. The supportive guides are like your extended family, friends and associates in life. Together they work for your highest good according to your soul contracts.

Heavenly Loved Ones

These are your family, friends, and those who were connected to you in life who have crossed into the afterlife.

It is definitely possible that your heavenly loved ones can become your spiritual guide once they cross over but they are never truly your Guardian Angels. In truth, though, Spirit doesn't really care what label we give it, as a label is restrictive and love is continuous! The main thing is your intentions to connect with Spirit.

Spirit has told me many times someone's parents will continue to serve them from the higher realms after leaving the planet for as long as we are still living. I can attest to this as my mom is one of my guides and this has been confirmed by multiple mediums which I have encountered since her death.

If one hasn't had a good relationship with their departed parent, often times, the relationship will transform. This is because the loved one has new found perspectives from transitioning back to the non-physical realms and will do their best to be the parent the child always wanted. This does not mean their personality has necessarily shifted, but they are now more heart and soul love centered.

Transition and Grief Healers

When someone is going through transitions in life or grief, we have access to a specialized team of angels and guides to help in the healing our hearts.

When I lost my mom unexpectedly, it was shortly after I learned more about our spiritual support crew. Until then, I was just floating in life with the knowledge, we are never alone, but never truly understanding or connecting. It took my mom's death for me to awaken, which was a part of the divine plan. This can be true for many people who have lost someone close in their life.

Other Team Members

Your team would like to bring to your attention it does not matter what religion or background you have. Every soul in the universe has a crew of angels, guides and other team members available to call upon for aid during your lifetime. Love has no limits or restrictions and neither do the following beings of light.

Archangel Azrael

Azrael is the angel who *brings comfort to those going through bereavement*. I like to think of him as a *loving and supportive grief counselor* (physically, mentally, emotionally and spiritually). As the counselor, he is there when you need a shoulder to cry on or to be heard without judgment.

Archangel Azrael, like all angels, has no gender but many will sense his masculine energy strongly; most often due to the strength and courage (to keep going and living life) he offers us during times of transition.

Archangel Azrael wishes to communicate the following message to you:

Your loved ones are safe and comforted in heaven, having found the peace and relief from their pain or suffering endured during their life. They were not alone at the end of their life and they were surrounded by all their loved ones in heaven, as they made their way home.

Please stay strong. Your loved ones are continuously with you and taking part of the family gatherings, including those important milestones in your life. They want you to live life fully in their memory and follow your heart always, for you deserve the best.

Please let go of the guilt, shame, regrets and other stuff no longer serving you. This will allow the love within you to expand and bless your life. Your loved ones are very happy, healthy and have found what they sought in life. They know it can be tough moving on with your life without them, but this is exactly what you need to do and something they wish for you.

This can be especially hard for a parent grieving a child. We understand it can be tough for you to breathe or want to even get out of bed. You are still a parent, even if you may have physically lost a child. You have the right to continue to go on in the world and your new child is yourself. You need to keep loving and nurturing yourself as you would you have guided your loved one when they were living. Your physical and heavenly loved ones need you to.

The departed will consistently watch over you and their loved ones on the earth but they will not intervene with your life as you wish. They will instead bring your prayers to the creator for the highest outcome of all and stand by you to lend you strength, as you ask for it.

Your loved ones do love you more than heaven itself and want nothing but best for you in life. They apologize to you for leaving you but it was their time. They are sorry for the pain it caused, but, in time you will understand the reasons why they needed to go.

Please honor yourself and where you are emotionally at, here and now. As you do so, you honor your loved ones.

Archangel Michael

Michael is the angel who is the *Great Protector*. Being the *Angel of Truth* he helps us to see past illusions and reveals the truth in situations. He helps to clear energetic ties draining our energy and vitality. This also includes severing cords which are fear based or interfering with universal peace and love. This will help with the healing of our earthly heart.

When we are grieving, it is helpful for us to call upon Michael to clear our energy bodies daily. This empowers the energy of the soul. Michael will never sever the cords of love but will definitely help to release all our fears and illusions. Remember death is an illusion and even though the soul has left the physical body, the spirit energy continues living and evolving. Asking for his help to release all cords of fear and their effects, benefits not only you but your loved ones in heaven as well. This allows for more love to flow in all directions.

Cords can be connected to people, places, experiences and more. It is highly helpful to cut all unhealthy cords regularly with Archangel Michael. This includes cords to old emotions, former relationships including romantic interests or friendships, former jobs, homes, and many other experiences siphoning our energy reserves. When we detach unhealthy cords everyone gets to heal and let go what no longer serves them. Love cords always stay, for love is our very essence and is the foundation of all creation.

Archangel Michael is good at helping us to keep our ego in check and to keep us centered in the divine love of the heart. As the protector he can help shield you, or your belongings, from all lower vibrations or fear-based thinking or experiences, when called upon to do so. Think of Michael as your friendly neighborhood security officer who is always on duty to aid you whenever you call require his assistance.

Michael is your go to angel for anything related with your life purpose. I like to think of him as a wise father figure who points us in the right direction and give us guidance as we take the divinely guided steps. He is always there for us to lend a helping hand. Especially when we are going through the more difficult times and could use the extra strength or courage to keep going.

Michael, like all the angels, can be serious at times when they are on duty, but they also have a lightness about them as you will discover through this next story.

It was a lovely fall day back in 2005 when I was traveling north to teach a workshop. As I was driving, I called on him to show himself in a way that that was easily recognizable to me.

A moment later, out of the blue in the middle of a field all by itself, was this golden colored tree. It was vibrant and perfect in every way. I recognized this as his energy shining through the tree but that wasn't enough for me. So, I asked him again to show himself in another way, and did so a couple more times. This was a gift which helped to make the 8-hour drive go by a little faster. On the second to last time when I called upon him, he decided he would be a little more forward and direct with me. He took this opportunity to remind me when asking to trust, have faith and belief in the answer which follows afterwards. This was something that my wisdom had showed me throughout life already to be true. Still it was so much fun to explore with Michael. This is part of the reason he allowed me to continue for as long as he did up to now.

I was driving in the flow of traffic and noticed I was going a little faster than the speed limit which I usually stick pretty close to, having learned my lesson earlier in life. I, at once adjusted my speed downward, but not before a police car coming in the opposite direction caught me on their radar. Law enforcement is one sign of Archangel Michael's presence.

Driving at the back end of the train of vehicles before me, put me in the perfect position. This position made it easy for the officer to turn his car around to pull me over, which is exactly what he did a moment later.

I immediately knew what was going on, especially when Michael was chuckling in the background. He gave me the reminder that the angels can have a sense of humor.

The police officer approached my vehicle and proceeded to give me the ticket. As he handed it to me I noticed the name on his badge. *Officer Michaels*, it said. I smiled and wished him well, and off I continued on the journey.

I called upon Archangel Michael one last time as I didn't want to push my luck. Though this time when asking him to show himself, I also requested him to not pull me over if he chose to show me himself as a police officer or car again. Your wish is my command, he spoke. Within 2 minutes, a police car went driving by me. I smiled and thanked Michael for playing with me, turned on the music and continued the trip.

Michael is the protector and is always strongly around those on the front lines or who work in the protective fields in any form. One could easily wonder: why those who are surrounded by his energy so strongly, would ever find themselves in positions where they could lose their life while on the front lines?

But truth be told, this happens sometimes because they are fearful themselves or even subconsciously wishing death. Remember what you focus on you will ultimately attract. Of course, they aren't conscious of this as they are just looking for relief from something in life. It could also just be their time and who are they to not answer the call of the divine. Ultimately it comes back to their soul contracts, life lessons and focus of their energy in this lifetime.

Archangel Michael lets us know that he is always a call away and he is often with your loved ones when they cross over. This helps them to feel safe, secure and comfortable transitioning home as he helps ease their fears of crossing over so that they can embrace the truth of the soul. You can relax knowing he is always on the job and your loved ones never cross over alone.

Archangel Raphael

Another angel you can call upon to help you with your grieving heart or the heart of another who is going through a rough time is Archangel Raphael.

Archangel Raphael is the *Angel of Health and Healing*. His main job is to help us to remember our divine perfect health and well-being within our life, including our physical, mental, emotional and spiritual bodies. He is the perfect angel to help you heal the heart as his color is Emerald Green.

When one is going through emotional turmoil, such as we are grieving, he can help you look past what may be unfolding to see the spiritual truth in all matters. He will shine his healing light to help you know everything as healthy, whole, perfect and complete and that all is well and in divine order.

Archangel Raphael can see your pain held within and how it intertwines with life situations and experiences. So when you invite him into your life he goes to work on all aspects of what is weighing on your mind and heart. He will help improve the quality of the health of everything in your life, when called upon. This is his job as the healer.

Raphael, often works in harmony with other angels and masters. Together they will clear away the effects of grief, stress, worries, fears and other emotional baggage we humans carry. This can profoundly influence our health and well-being. When you call upon him, you are giving him permission to come in to help you and your loved ones in these life matters.

Remember, the angels can only help greatly you when you ask. If we are asking for their assistance upon the behalf of others, they can only help according to the divine will or the highest good of all according on the active sacred contracts.

This is one reason sometimes when we call upon our support crew to help a situation it may appear as if our prayers went unanswered. This may feel particularly true if our loved one died after we reached out for heavens help; however this is simply not the case. The angels were by the side of our loved ones before we even finished our prayer. They stayed with them to comfort or aid them as much as they were allowed during this time.

Raphael states:

Your loved ones appreciate you taking time to ask heaven to help them. They want you to know your prayers helped them to let go of the body easier. They were healed of their fears of dying and what was waiting for them beyond the veil.

It was his pleasure to be there for them in a way you could not be. Death is truly a beautiful experience more than you could ever imagine. It is one not to be feared but to be welcomed at the appropriate time. If one has a fear of dying, you can be sure a fear of living life is also present. Now is the time to reclaim your life and therefore be healed.

We love and appreciate you all and will always support you as you request divine assistance.

Archangel Raphael, Michael and Azrael all want you to understand that they can help you heal your fears, both of living life and of death itself. Remember, death comes in its various disguises and isn't just about the physical transition of the body. It shows up in so many unexpected ways throughout your earth journey. Please take time to ask your support crew for the help with all aspects of your life.

Raphael also assists those traveling and looking for healthy relationships in your life, including new friendships and romantic relationships. He will gladly help with the improving the quality of your own relationship with yourself, with everyone else and even your relationship with your life.

Archangel Gabriel

Gabriel is known as the *Communication or Messenger* Angel. This angel can help your grieving heart by helping you to open your divine communication channels and putting you in touch with your loved ones.

I am sure at one point in your life you have glimpsed movement out of your peripheral vision, only to look over to see nothing there. Archangel Gabriel wishes to share with that you aren't losing it, you were seeing Spirit moving by you.

The reason you couldn't see anything when you turned your eyes in their direction, is that on a subconscious level, a part of you is fearful of seeing Spirit.

Often times, Spirit will use outside images to show themselves to you; such as finding a picture of your loved one when you least expect it, or seeing someone who looks just like them. This is done to not cause further fear as they continue to help you release and clear the fears from your consciousness.

Another way your loved ones communicate with you is during your dream/sleeping periods when you are more open to the visitations without fear. Yes, those dreams you had of so and so, are real visitations. Sometimes the dream itself may not make sense to you or may seem dark; this is because you are working stuff out on another level still. Just take a breath, relax and let it go knowing your soul knows what it all means.

Archangel Gabriel will help you clarify the dream communications when and if you are meant to consciously be aware of what it all means. This will happen in a way you will understand at the divine moment. So please trust, have faith and be patient with the process, in the meantime.

The Gift Within the Darkness

Also relax, be patient and compassionate when people are going through the darkness of life's events. They may not hear what you are trying to say or even be able to see the gift within at the time. Their focus is on wanting to communicate with someone in heaven rather than with you. Please try to understand and not be offended by this. Gabriel says to just be there for them as this divine angel supports your communicate efforts.

When you are trying too hard, or are tight, tense, or an emotional experience is affecting you, the channels end up blocked. The best thing you can do for yourself and your spiritual team communicating with you is to just relax and allow it all to unfold in the divine way and time.

Archangel Gabriel is helping you to receive the direct guidance or messages from your soul as you progress through your times of darkness. This divine angel is helping you open up and heal from within your heart and soul. This will help you consciously know the spiritual realm which are always around you and communicating with you.

Pay attention to the world at large for messages that seem to be directed to you. Your loved ones will use all communication channels to speak with you. Your soul will know you are receiving a message. Your job is to pay attention and begin to understand how spirit is communicating with you at all times. Books, television, radio, and even print ads are all ways heaven communicates with you.

You could even walk down the street and see a passing van like the one your favorite aunt used to drive. Or, a bus passes by as the driver looks and smiles at you, looking exactly like her. This is your aunt saying, Hello, I love you and wishing you a pleasant day. This is just but one thing that happened to me after my Aunt Pauline transitioned as I was about to travel to her funeral.

There are so many ways Spirit will communicate with us that one just needs to be open, receptive and pay attention. When you are consciously aware of your inner voice you will know when spirit is delivering a message.

Archangel Gabriel will now do healing work with you should you be receptive and ready to receive. Gabriel asks you to be open to the energy as you read a message from your loved ones. Take a moment to get comfortable and relaxed. Allow yourself to experience whatever unfolds, knowing all is divinely perfect for this moment. Please breathe deeply, in and out, as you read through the following heavenly communication:

> *People are always asking how or why we had to die. To them we say, it matters not how we died, or even why. What matters is that you live and embrace your life fully each day.*
>
> *Tomorrow may never come for many, and so we ask you to appreciate and enjoy every precious moment of this day. This way when you leave the earth to join us, you will be at peace knowing you made the most of your life, each and every moment. Live each day giving your best to everyone, saying and doing everything you would ever want to as if it was your last day on earth.*
>
> *We want you to be happy and not filled with tears when you think about the pain, our struggles or even how we died. None of that matters. What does matter is that you love yourself to live to your fullest potential and happily each day. Make and carry out the changes required to do so now in your life. This will allow you to die happy and knowing you lived from this moment on without further regrets.*
>
> *Let go what isn't servicing you emotionally. For guilt, shame, anger, unforgiveness and regret are just a few of the wasted emotions which do not serve you. You hold the power to make better choices to feel happier each day. Start right now and let the past go.*

When you are thinking about the choices you have before you, take a moment to relax, breathe and ask these two questions:

Will this choice make me feel happy and joyful moving forward? Or will it leave me wondering and filled with regret, guilt or grief about what may have been?

Follow your heart from there on out as you take the divinely guided action steps. We will be with you each step of the way; you can always trust and know this. You never are alone, ever, in any way!

It is time to get yourselves off the couch and stop killing yourself with food or other forms of your unhealthy habits. It is time to nourish yourself with life sustaining foods and activities. We want you to feel good about your bodies and your life. No one else can do it for you; only you can do it for yourself. Remember you have other living people who love and want you to feel good as possible, not just us.

Find your inner motivation to get off the couch and make healthy changes in your life. Do this by finding a reason that is stronger than any possible excuse that you could come up with or anything life can throw at you. Find that why, then write it down on paper and put it somewhere where you will see it daily, and get going with your action steps. This will help you get and stay motivated; it will also help you soar living life to the fullest more each day.

We know you can do this; we want you to feel good about yourself and your life, remember. We will gladly lend you support to be brave, to face living life, to have the courage and strength to keep going on each day. Love yourself to free yourself, here and now.

Right now you may be feeling sadness with the transitions unfolding in life, including our death. It is ok to feel this way; it is also okay to feel not okay with what is happening right now as well. Let the tears out, they are helping to heal your deep loss and pain. One must always honor this to recover and heal fully.

There will come a day when you can think of us and not be sad, but rejoice in the happiness that we are still with you; alive and well, even if we are non-physical in nature. You will see that the transitions are truly a gift from Spirit to you and that they are for your greater good. Once you move past this and can see through the illusions of death, you will understand the true gift death holds.

It's time to take your dreams off the shelf and make them a reality. We want to see you succeed with them in our memory. We feel such pride and joy for you when you focus on being of service in this way, and you follow your heart to live your dreams. Will you let us feel this amazing energy? We truly do get to experience life with you, so let us all rejoice with you as you reclaim your life to live your dreams.

If you aren't sure where to begin, just begin with one simple small step you can do right now, and then take another and another. Before you know it, you will be running and conquering all your dreams! You will feel so good and that will make us truly feel alive in every way, and you will feel us with you at that time. In time, when you look at this whole experience called death, you will see that there truly is a divine plan in it all. You will see it as a gift.

We truly do love you, immensely and that love is what overwhelms you when you think of us often times. We offer it to you to help you heal and move forward with our memory. Honor us by living your life happily, fully and in the gift of the present moment. Thank you for all you have done and continue to each day. It means the world to us.

It is now time for you to stop just surviving and to start thriving! We want that for you and so much happiness. Get out and discover the joys of living life to your fullest potential. That is our greatest wish for you and what would make us feel so happy. We are with you as you begin to pick up the pieces of your shattered life and move forward with us forever in your heart.

We love you so much, more than words could ever speak. Always know this and that we are forever with you all the days of your life.

Ascended Masters

There are so many angels and masters that can truly help you heal and find the light in the darkness of life's most challenging circumstances. You just have to think of a subject and there is an angel or master specializing in this. But, I will focus on a few you can call upon before I offer a prayer to lighten your heavy heart.

Most people have heard of the ascended masters Jesus and Mother Mary. They would like to let everyone of all religions know they are here to help you heal. You need not be of a certain faith or religious order for any master or angel to work with you. Remember they are all another of the Divine's Lightworkers serving the planet and thus come from a place of pure love and light.

Three other ascended masters who are available to those grieving and going through loss are Saint John of God, Lugh and Vywamus. Each is available to aid you through the dark tunnel of cascading waterfall of emotions and transitions which leave you questioning life. It matters not where in the world you live or your background; they are here for you without condition.

Saint John of God

He helps those that need it the most; those whose hearts are weighed down in pain that they are suffering from heart ailments, literally. He often is called upon by those that are suffering from the mental and physical illness that follows a profound period of sorrow.

Many people who feel disillusioned with life or have suffered from a fairly degrading or dreadful life experience will benefit from calling upon him.

When he was living he cared for those that were poor, sick, homeless or needed a helping hand. He wasn't above anyone, taking time from his day to stop and listen to everyone, offering words of kindness, compassion and sincere advice along the way. He would go above and beyond the call of duty to serve and reminds us that service is why you are here on this earth.

When you call upon him, you will know his presence is near you as your mood and spirits will be elevated with his joyful jolliness. He can help those that are suffering from depression, anxiety, and more. He often works alongside Archangel Raphael, who is the master healer and his healing angels.

Lugh

Lugh is like having a powerful magician on your team which can support your transformation and healing experience. It is said he had the ability to assess your inner yearnings, leanings and tendencies. With this knowledge he could pull out of his cupboard a portion that would be perfect for you. Imagine him much like a youthful sun god who brings the light of alchemy to you.

He truly is a master of all trades as no situation is too big for him to handle. His potion closet has all the ingredients he needs and he will create a new concoction with the magical properties to support you and help to resolve the situation. He will gladly aid you with healing from your painful or unexpected life experiences, bringing solutions along the way. Think of the potions much like vitamins that have been infused with energy to support your efforts on the earth each day. They give you a boost of health, faith, confidence, peace and joy as required throughout the day.

Vywamus

Vywamus is a spiritual teacher and healer who continues to serve humanity since his ascension. Many people believe Vywamus is just another aspect of the ascended master Sanat Kumara, perhaps the higher-self aspect. We are all one, therefore, I have no problems with this belief.

Vywamus is the master who helps Lightworkers awaken to their soul power, spiritual gifts and assists with helping them to discover their life purpose. Calling upon him can assist you rapidly heal the physical, mental and emotional levels, and with the spiritual healing of the soul.

He does this by empowering you to face the darkness to allow the light to expand and shine. Just like the Yin-Yang, a little light in the dark is always present, and vice versa. Vywamus helps you to find light in situations and thus expand it doing this and more in a very loving and compassionate way. He will help you take time and understand the lessons contained within life experiences can help your choices in moving forward.

When our loved ones cross into the light, he often helps them through their transitions, he tells me, so *they can heal and be illuminated divinely*.

Call upon him when you are looking for direction in life and you will receive the hope, encouragement and inspiration through his energy.

He will assist you to find the motivation in life and to help you overcome procrastination so you can deal with the tasks that need to be completed. Remember, he helps you on all levels of your being through the healing and enlightenment.

The ascended masters, like the angels, can truly be with everyone at once, for they are without body and boundless. So when you call upon their help and so do others, you all win and receive their help.

Our spiritual support crew, like us in truth, are multidimensional. This is the reason they can be with everyone or everywhere at once. When your loved ones leave their body, they begin to discover this truth for themselves. This is the reason why sometimes you will hear of multiple people receiving a visitation or message from the newly departed at or around the same timeframe. This has happened to me, and I know it has happened for some of you as well.

Placing Your Call to Receive Heavenly Help

There is also no right or wrong way to ask for the aid of your support crew. You only need to pick up the phone and call upon them. The more you begin to work with them, the more you will experience their heavenly presence in your life.

If you are new to this, have trust issues or problems letting go you are better off starting with the little things where can detach from the outcome. Meaning you really don't care one way or the other about what happens at the end of the day. It's not a huge deal.

Examples:

1. You ask for a parking spot by the door of where you are going to. Once you ask, you let the prayer go knowing you will have a spot. It really doesn't matter if it is 2 spots over or 10 as ultimately a spot is assured within a reasonable distance to the door.

2. Or, if you are asking to make someone else's life a little easier in some manner, you can detach to the outcome easier as it doesn't affect you personally. Yes, you want to make their life easier at the end of the day. Ultimately, it's not going to cause you a lack of sleep over whatever happens with their life situations, usually, as it doesn't affect you personally.

Things like these are a great place to start. This is because it can be easier for us to surrender, trust and have faith that our request has been heard and is being worked on. The bigger the issue or the more that we are involved, the harder it can be for us to relax and let go. Detaching ourselves from the outcome is key. The smaller tasks help increase our faith that when we ask, we do receive, benefiting us in all of life.

I often tell my clients is to let go of the steering wheel and give it over to your highest self to drive the car. It sees and knows the bigger picture and how to get you from where you are to where you wish to be; often much easier and quicker than if we were at the controls. So, say your prayers and then let them go with gratitude and a knowingness that your crew is now working on them for you.

Please know there is no reason ever to not ask for divine assistance. Remember every soul has a team and we all deserve to reach up to heaven to ask for support.

Think of them like your managers of a company where you are the CEO. If you aren't assigning them tasks to complete, they are only doing the basics of what your soul employed them for. When you give them more work, they get excited as they love their job and want to make life easier for you.

Many times, we only call upon the heavens when we are going through something weighing on us. But your spiritual support crew reminds you they want to be there for you at all times. They need your permission to help you, however you wish it. So if this applies to the issues of your prayer, ask them to increase your faith and trust in them. Ask them to help you surrender everything over to them. They will help you release the steering wheel that much quicker so they can fully go to town working on your files.

Holding onto the wheel is one reason it can appear as if many of the prayers go unanswered. Every prayer is truly heard and answered by the divine spiritual realm, with many factors playing a role in the answering of each of them. This grasping the wheel tightly and not letting go is but one reason.

If the prayer involves other people, it will involve sacred contracts or if one isn't open to receiving their help, it may seem like it went unanswered. Sometimes, to answer the prayer how you are requesting just isn't in the highest good for all concerned.

Do your level best to always trust that everything is unfolding as meant to be for all concerned. Your prayers are indeed always heard and being answered in a divine way and time. Remember our team is listening to all aspects of our request, not just the physical asking. They listen to our strongest emotions, the guidance of our soul and thoughts as well; it can be much more complicated than at first glance. Divine will is always in play.

My motto is once you have asked to trust, have faith, let go, listen and follow the guidance or the whispers of the soul. This not only will make sure that whatever is meant to be will be. And if you are meant to take action you will be more open to hearing the message of the soul and following the guidance.

You can continue to learn more about the angels and ascended masters available to you through the internet or in books on this subject. I would recommend starting with materials by Diana Cooper, Kyle Gray, Gary Quinn and Doreen Virtue, amongst others.

Prayer for Healing and Enlightenment

Dearest Mother / Father God, Archangels, Ascended Masters and our Spiritual Support Crew,

We come to you now requesting your ever present help to release the heaviness we carry within our body, mind, spirit and emotions.

We call upon you to shine your loving light upon us now to do all clearing.

We ask you to empower our true nature and the gifts of our soul. Touch us now to awaken us to the master you intend us to be on this earth as in heaven.

Please release the burdens of our mind and heart, replacing them with the highest level of your loving light energy. Release our fears, worries and concerns now and help us know universal peace; the peace that comes from the experiencing of divine love.

Release the energy of grief and the pain that lies within, so we can be filled with the light of our soul. We ask for this to be able to move forward with living life fully. Help us know all is well and happening according to the divine plan and highest good of all. Help us look past the darkness to see the light at all times.

Help us know our loved ones in heaven are safe, healthy, happy, and at peace in a loving place with you God. Help us forgive ourselves and our loved ones for the experiences of the past that are holding us back.

Please wrap us in your enveloping love as you offer comfort to those of us who weep the tears of sadness. Keep our minds and hearts centered in your loving light God as you continue to watch over and guide us here on the earth.

Give us the strength, courage and energy required to move forward in our lives and to let what no longer serves us go. We deserve the best in our lives and thus we ask for your heavenly help in releasing the unhealthiness in our lives in loving ways.

We stand before you asking for your heavenly healing energy to bless and completely heal us, our family, friends, and all in the world. We pray on behalf of those souls who are requesting the blessing of health, happiness and your love now God.

We know that with your love anything is possible and we trust in you to always support, bless and provide for us in perfect ways. We now are willing to surrender to your will God, for we know the truth which is that we are one with you, and thus your will is our will.

We are ready to stop the pain, the fighting, resistance, fear and worry at every turn. We are ready to succeed in life and be at peace knowing heaven on earth now and forever more.

Help us hear the voice of our soul and to take action as required, knowing everything will always be provided for as we do.

We know that you will never give us something we cannot handle or complete. Please help us trust in our inner knowing at all times, especially when it comes to the divine high spiritual truths and soulful guidance.

For this and better, we give our thanks. We give thanks for the love and all the blessings in our life each day. We thank you for everything. Amen

Our Animal Guides

In closing this chapter, I want to talk about one other type of guide we have that can help us in our healing of the heart and in our life. And that is our Animal Guides.

We all have animals that are guiding and helping us along our path, whether or not, we are conscious of this fact. Each of the animals we meet have crossed our earthly paths for a reason. Those that we come into contact with more often are usually a sort of guide or teacher for us. Their purpose is much like the other forms of our spiritual crew and that is to teach, heal, support and protect us on the earth. Like our spirit guides, our animal guides serve us for a purpose whether that is for a season or a lifetime.

Pay attention to all the signs that your animal guides are sending you. When you do so, you will begin to know who the main animals are helping you in your life. Some ways they will show themselves to you are through pictures, television, books and of course, in their natural habitat, nature. You may hear their calls when you are outside, or in meditation or on music tracks.

When you see the same animal showing up multiple times, chances are this is a sign they are a guide and giving you a message. To know what the message your animal crew is bringing to you, I encourage you to take time to meditate on the animal itself. Think about their personality and what this is trying to tell you. Think about the colors, where you may have seen them and what the animal means for you. All this and even more will yield information to help you translate their messages.

It has been my experience that our nature friends are connected to the heavens and have much to teach us. I know my cat, Indigo has been a great teacher and healer in my life. Before she came to me I was gifted a drawing of one of my guides which was created by one of my students very quickly in class. When I first saw the picture, it reminded us of an alien, but I put it aside, knowing it may make sense later on. When Indigo went through her first heat cycle, her facial features looked exactly like this drawing. It was then I received confirmation they were one and the same.

A short time afterwards the pieces of the puzzle continued to fall into place. Within a couple years, I was taken on the life review to help me heal and understand things that unfolded in life as spoken about earlier. One part of this review was about a cat I had as a child which had gotten loose and before I knew it, she was gone.

During this review, I was told that Indigo was the same soul of the cat I had named Spicy from my early years. She had come to me as a guide at this time in my life to help heal the heart which never truly got over the pain of losing my childhood animal family member.

At once, I understood why I had gotten so many four legged friends throughout my life and never held on to them. Often giving them away; all because I was looking for the soul of my childhood kitten.

Once I began to put the pieces together, I also understood Indigo further. I understood why she had massive separation anxiety for the first few years of her life after she came home, among other things. She truly was my healer and has taught me so much throughout our time together, and continues to daily.

When we begin to understand the reason things unfold in our lives, such as a pet loss, we are able to heal and move forward. Until Indigo came into my life, a part of me was broken and in pain; I now can see that clearly. Indigo brought a part of my heart back to life with the returning of my power at the same time.

Many times when a trauma unfolds in our lives which deeply affects us on a soul level, we lose a part of us. We may act or react differently to situations after a soul loss. For me, losing my kitten when I was a 6 year old child, profoundly affected the way I interacted with animals and even people for many years. When Indigo's soul came back to me she brought with her, the piece of my soul that was lost in my childhood.

Did I realize that this had happened? No and neither did those in my life. It was very subtle and happened on a subconscious level. The same can happen with all the deaths that can happen in our lives, not just the animal or human ones.

It has been over 12 years since Indigo and I have found each other again. She is a joy in my life, despite that she can be a bit stubborn and annoying at times; the same can be said about me at times, I am sure.

Our animal friends often are just reflecting or revealing parts of our self we may or may not be owning at the time. I know Indigo truly has taught me so much about myself, and the world around me.

Indigo is a special friend and when she transitions, I know that she will continue to be with me helping me. One day, we will reunite for the continuation of the earth journey if it is meant to

The Gift Within the Darkness

be. In the meantime, I will just do my best to love and appreciate our time together now.

I encourage you to pay attention to the animals in your life; they have lots of teach and show you that will bless your life for years to come. The same can be true for the birds, the squirrels, deer and so many more of our wild or domesticated animal friends. The more that you become conscious of what they are sharing with you the more your life will be blessed.

Your animal friends can be your guiding light when you may find yourself in the dark, feeling down or alone in the world. They love you unconditionally and often will take on your energy if you let them to help you. For some, this is why they have come into your life to be a healer for you; this is part of their life purpose. Like many they will often leave a mark on you long after they have been present in your life.

Your loved ones in heaven will often use the animal kingdom to let you know they are with you. When you think of your loved one when a particular nature guide shows up in your life, it is indeed your heavenly friends and family saying, Hello, I love you. I am here.

These are just a few of the many council members on your spiritual support crew. Get to know and work with them more, and you too will discover the many blessings they gift you each day along your earth journey. They truly love and support you more than you could ever imagine.

Your Animals wish you to know they are honored to serve humanity in this way and thank you for allowing them to be in service for you.

There are many websites and books dedicated to this subject which can also be a good place to start with. I highly recommend either Animal Speak by Ted Andrews or Animal Spirit Guides by Steven D. Farmer.

CHAPTER 33

THE GIFTS OF A SACRED RELEASE CEREMONY

THIS CEREMONY IS MOST often used for the mother to energetically give birth to her unborn child due to miscarriages or abortions and the pain associated with the loss. However, anyone (male or female) can use it to release any energy that no longer serves you in any way. This way you can make room for the new to enter your life. I have used it with clients to help them release old emotions, regrets, old beliefs, old jobs, and more.

For this ceremony you will need a stone, branch or something from nature to use. Please take a moment to ask nature if you can use this for your sacred release ceremony. You will intuitively get a yes or no. Please honour whatever answer you get. Most likely you will get an affirmative answer, but on rare occasions people have gotten a no, and had to keep searching. This is most likely due to a resistance within them to letting go. With a little time, patience and effort they eventually are ready to release and viola find the perfect nature piece to use.

Note: You will not be keeping this so don't worry about it looking pretty or anything in particular. It is essentially a coffin for your unborn embryo and like all coffins it will be buried in the ground af-

terwards. *It is ok to feel sad at this thought as you are getting ready to say goodbye to your child until you meet again.*

You may choose to do this ceremony alone or with your partner by your side holding sacred space with you. It is important that you feel comfortable and the energy of the room is filled with one of belief, love and positive energy. If you don't feel that your partner can offer this sort of support for you than you are best to be alone for the ceremony or ask someone else who can support you.

Now that you have your sacred stone, create a sacred environment by having some candles placed throughout the environment, and having relaxing music playing in the background. This is really not required, but I want you to remember this is a sacred birth, so create an environment that feels sacred to you; it matters not what it looks like.

When you are ready to complete the ceremony, please feel free to relax into a comfortable position either sitting or lying down with your nature piece on your belly area.

Next, I want you to place your hands on top of your stone and close your eyes. Take a couple deep breaths, in and out, as you call upon your heavenly support crew. Ask them to aid you with this sacred release of all pain and stuck, stagnant or old energies connected to the loss of your children, from all lifetimes, into the stone.

Breathe deeply, in and out, as you imagine the energy being birthed into the stone now. You may wish to see this is as a dark grey mist. Do this for as long as you feel a need to. Allow yourself to feel whatever emotions you need to; remember this is your sacred space and thus important to honor all aspects of this birthing. Once you feel you are complete with the birth, give your gratitude to your crew and just be for a moment.

When ready to get up you are going to take your stone back out to nature. Here you will hold a burial to allow mother earth to transmute the energies back to nature's source, Spirit. Call upon the full power of love in the universe to envelop and support you with this final step in the sacred ceremony. Be sure to give gratitude in advance for their assistance.

The ideal location for this burial service is off your property. Some have found using the power of water to be very helpful for them and thus throw the stone into a lake or river. Here the energy of the water will cleanse, release and return the energy to Spirit. There really is no wrong or right way to do it. It is your ceremony so allow your soul to guide you with it.

Give your gratitude once again knowing that your ceremony is now complete. Good job. It took courage to let go what no longer was serving you and the pain associated with it.

You are ready to go about your days ahead now with a fresh slate. You may feel lighter right away or it may take a little more time for you to process what has unfolded in this simple but powerful ceremony. But one thing is for sure, you can expect good things to unfold afterwards.

The Gift Within the Darkness

CHAPTER 34

THE GIFTS WITHIN PAST EXPERIENCES

Our past has a profound on our present effect on our future, more than one would expect or even be conscious of. I am not just talking about the events of our current lives before now, but I am speaking about our past lives. Not everyone will believe we have lived or incarnated multiple times and that is okay. But, I would ask you all to keep an open mind and believe in this possibility that which I speak of.

Growing up as a child and well into my adulthood, I had a profound fear of public speaking. This wasn't just the normal run-of-the-mill sort of anxiety we all can have when speaking in front of large groups. This was the kind where you needed a kiddie pool to stand in while presenting to anyone.

Why a kiddie pool, you may wonder? Because as soon as the public eye was on me, my sweat glands would go into overdrive. It was like my body was wringing out the cells of all the nectar normally held within. My clothes would show signs of the moisture. My face needed a towel wiping it dry. My heart would feel like it was in my throat all while I choked on my words.

The Gift Within the Darkness

I am sure everyone could sense the profound fear I had for public speaking. I had no clue where this was coming from but it was definitely uncomfortable for us all.

You may think I am joking, but this was no joke. I did anything to get out of any public speaking in any form growing up. This included even taking a penalty for skipping out on oral book reports when I turned in the written versions instead, playing hooky or physically becoming ill.

As I grew up the fears kept getting more intense in situations and the sweating would no longer happen just in front of groups but whenever the eye was on me. It could be at work, home or anywhere really. When I first began teaching as a Reiki Master, I noticed how my voice would be shaky with fear and the sweat intensified. This was becoming an embarrassing situation as a professional.

One day, when I was teaching a small group, I had a clairvoyant flash of me on stage talking to large crowds and feeling very comfortable doing so. Based on the fears I had, I told spirit that wasn't happening. However, I was open to it perhaps at some point, if I could ever get past this whole fear of public speaking and pouring of sweat.

As I was teaching the classes, I began to slowly get a little more comfortable with being uncomfortable but my anxiety levels and sweat was still at an all-time high. A few short months later, this would all change.

I was guided by my guides to have some energy work done by a past life regressionist as I was guided to my previous lives in a regression. It was during this journey that the lights came on and my life experiences began making sense.

I was taken back to a time in my soul evolution where I had been traveling and sharing my high spiritual truths. I found myself in a coliseum in Ancient Greece and I was about to speak to the masses in attendance. I heard myself telling them I was here to speak the truth, as I knew it. If they didn't agree with what I shared, they had my full permission to do whatever they felt they needed to. The next thing I knew they were literally throwing stones at me and I crawled away bloodied and barely alive.

We continued the regression and I was brought to the end of this particular lifetime. At this time, I found myself hanging on a cross with my then mother at the base crying. I spoke to the masses in attendance once again saying something with conviction, courage and strength. I was very much at peace with whatever was about to happen.

Hanging me out to die a slow painful death wasn't enough for them; they would not let me get away that easy. Instead, they choose to throw stones at me once again; this time killing me in the process. The cross was a commonly used death tool in many cultures, therefore, death by crucifixion wasn't tied to just any particular religious upbringing.

As the regression went on, I was in tears, feeling and experiencing the lifetime as I shared about what was unfolding throughout it. A part of me was very much at peace as I underwent reliving the memories of the past.

Afterwards, once I had time to process everything that unfolded in the session, I could why I had many of my personality traits growing up. With this knowledge and the awareness of the connection to my experiences I was able to heal and finally closed the door to my intense fear of public speaking. This happened very quickly after undergoing the past life regression.

I since have had many opportunities to speak in front of a crowd. I may still get a little nervous, feel warm and have a moment of the sweaty palms and the racing heart but the sweat buckets have been retired. Once I start speaking, everything calms down and I feel so much more at peace (even excited sometimes) while sharing my beliefs and truth. Through understanding of where the fears were coming from I could finally let them go.

The Gifts of Understanding

The deaths we experience in earlier lifetimes do definitely have a profound impact on our lives and the way we live them. Not only have I experienced it myself, but I have seen this in my client sessions as well whenever I guide them into their past lives. Our previous lives don't just have a negative effect on our lives but can also have a positive impact as well.

I once guided a client through meditation into her most recent past life where she discovered she was a young man who had become a priest.

When we spoke afterwards about her regression, she told me it suddenly made total sense why she was always attracted to anything religious.

She told me, she had a collection of crosses and religious artifacts that she had amassed over the years from her travels. Throughout her life she always had a profound sense of faith and was always wanting to serve others in meaningful ways. Both of which were good characteristics that came in handy more than once in her lifetime. After her session, she beamed with her new found understanding excited to share what she had learned about herself with others.

As a healer, I have tuned into my client's past lives to help them understand something they currently experienced. This often will allow them to release any pain they may be having. Once I relayed the information and we worked on clearing the root cause, the symptoms often were lessened or gone completely. Sometimes we have to work through the layers to get to the root, but with each layer of release, you feel better.

I have lived many lives that involved healing or psychic work in some form. Growing up, I had the feeling that there was native energy in our family background somewhere and often saw it in my Grandmother Calhoun's eyes. Over the years, I have learned that this is because of our shamanic roots from our past lives. It doesn't surprise me that in this life I have a similar life purpose.

In many lifetimes, people were often killed for doing any supernatural or paranormal work and were called witches. This was the foundation of the Salem Witch Trials of the 1692-1693 period. Because of this, many people with a natural inclination in these fields often hold back on sharing or acknowledging their interests. It is these people who could have such deep seated fears around their life purpose and nature inclinations that they run in the complete opposite direction in life.

However, eventually, they will face something which will lead them back onto the path of the soul mission. It could show up as a major health crisis or something else. But eventually, they will be led back to the road of their soul evolution and will begin to understand things as they open up to the sacred records held within.

Freeing Herself of the Shackles that Bonded

Let me share with you another example of a past life from one of my clients.

When Marie came to take a class of mine on angels, we got to speaking about what was unfolding in her personal relationship with a roommate of hers. She had deep feelings for this person and would move from house to house with him. She did this despite knowing a relationship was out of the question. He was involved with someone else and had made it known he was not romantically interested in her.

As his relationship developed with his girlfriend, she often felt like a third wheel when they would all do things together. Not everything was always rosy with them all; sometimes there would be conflicts that seemed to affect only her and her roommate's girlfriend. But, mostly, she lived in the attic space she rented from him while they had the run of the rest of the house. She had made peace with this to a degree but was still finding herself longing for the relationship she knew she could never have.

She had toyed with the idea of perhaps undergoing a past life regression or hypnosis in hopes to help her understand things. With the help of her angels, I guided her to look further into her past lives. She wasn't comfortable with the few people who we both knew who could guide her into her past lives but was comfortable with me. She asked if I was willing to guide her through an active meditation to look into them. I agreed and we arranged a time to do so.

The day of the session came and I gently had her lay comfortably on the massage table as we had relaxing music in the background. After taking a few moments to say a prayer and call in her angels to help with this journey, we began the session. She would stay in control and conscious throughout the meditation.

I gently had her become aware of her body while breathing deeply. As she relaxed we had her focus on various colors to bring in healing and extra support of her heavenly support crew. This prepared her for whatever information would be brought to her awareness from the filing cabinet of her subconscious mind. Once relaxed and she was prepared we had her descend into a lifetime which was in the highest good for her journey regarding this man and their relationship. I asked her questions regarding this lifetime and what was going on. As we progressed, I asked questions based on her answers and what I felt intuitively at the same time. We continued to gather information about the town, her name in this lifetime, year and so much more.

Going back a couple of lifetimes, she soon found herself immersed in a life where she was a happily married housewife. She was going to surprise her husband, who worked as a lumberjack in the forest. She prepared a lunch for the two of them and went off happily singing to where he was.

As she approached the area where he was to be working, she heard voices laughing and having a good time. Emotions were surfacing in her as she got closer and closer to where they were coming from. From the sounds and her feelings, she knew she was about to encounter something. She turned the corner and there was her husband and a woman.

When I asked if she recognized the souls and she replied in the affirmative stating that it was her roommate she had been living with and his girlfriend. They were engaged in an intimate affair at the time. The shock of this caused her to drop the lunch basket she had prepared and she ran off crying.

At this time in the meditation, we began some healing work with the angels to help her release the effects from the pain and heartache of the earlier lifetimes. After this was complete we began the journey back to present day.

A few moments later she was back in the room with her eyes open. Still in a state of shock at the information which had come forth, but also ready to move forth as we spoke. After talking with me for a few minutes and feeling more grounded, she returned to her life to continue processing what came forth.

The next time I had come into contact with her she said she had moved out. Things had completely changed in the relationships with her former roommate and his girlfriend. They remain friends as they all live their own lives, even until this day. She finally had found the answers and peace she had sought in the situation which allowed her to move forward.

I truly was happy for her. It took her many years before she could truly open up and talk about the regression again. It had been profoundly healing and enlightening for her; she had been still processing the session long after our time together. This can happen for some depending on what comes forth for sure.

As you can see, everything truly changes when you understand and make the connection between your current life experience and your past lives. This can improve the quality of your relationships, finances, health, and so much more with your newfound understanding.

In truth, every day before today is similar to a past life and has profoundly influenced your future, whether or not you are aware of it. For today comprises the sum of all the days of your soul incarnation, and all the tomorrows will continue to add in the days prior.

However, you need not believe me. I encourage you to look into your own past lives if you have something that has plagued you in this lifetime for a long time. You may just make peace with the past and move forward with a renewed sense of living from the heart. I know I did.

> *A good place to begin is at your local library or bookstore with books on past lives. I recommend books from Brian Weiss as a good starting place; he includes audio meditations to guide you into some of your many lives.*

CHAPTER 35

THE GIFTS OF DIVINE COMMUNICATION

EVERYONE IS INTUITIVE AND receives information from Spirit all the time. Most times this information is delivered in subtle ways and goes unnoticed as we go about our daily business. Often it is only when this wisdom is delivered in powerful ways through our intuitive abilities that we pay attention to it.

In this chapter, we will talk about the various channels of divine communication so you can become more in tune with your natural psychic gifts.

The tools within part two of this book will all help you awaken or strengthen your abilities, especially when all practiced in harmony. The end goal of this section is to help you to receive the healing and enlightenment required for your journey and life forward. It is through the practicing of these tools and techniques that you can be reconnected to the spiritual realms and your heavenly loved ones.

Many of the tools shared within this second section are the very same ones which we professional psychic-mediums will use in our daily client sessions. It needs to be said every psychic-medium has their own gifts and unique but similar ways of connecting with spirit. But the goal here is to connect you to your heavenly gifts.

Our purpose here is not to make you a medium but to help you become conscious of your own potential to communicate with Spirit for your journey. To step into the role of a medium takes time, energy and serious commitment to develop and be able to do so effectively. In fact, this is a lifetime commitment for those of us who are doing this work as we are constantly evolving as souls on the earth.

Our soul is naturally connected to the source of creation and by extension to everything in the universe. There is nothing we are ever separated from as a soul. However, when we come to this planet to evolve as a soul having a human experience we tend to forget this truth; this in turn causes the illusion of separation to occur. Deep within your heart this memory is active and awaits you to reconnect or remember who you are. When someone goes through a spiritual awakening, this is basically what transpires along with a remembering of your life purpose and more.

There are many ways people will begin to awaken to their highest spiritual self. An awakening can happen when someone we are close to dies, a major life event happens, we have a near-death experience (NDE), or even when we are initiated into a healing modality. There are many ways we can awaken; these are a few examples.

A spiritual awakening often begins with people questioning who they are or why they are here and looking for meaning to the physical world. They are beginning to want to gain access to the divine consciousness or understand the universal perspective on the essence of life itself. Whether you are a regular person with a regular life, or a yogi, a monk, a nun, a priest or an atheist, it matters not. A conscious awakening can happen at any time or to anyone without any traditional order to it.

With an awakening comes a natural heightened ability to perceive the etheric forces of Spirit around each of us. Spirit will use one or more of the four main channels of communication to deliver its message to you. One does not need to go through an awakening to begin to develop, understand and strengthen these channels as they are natural to you. The more that you are aware and consciously use these gifts in your daily living the better your life shall be. This is especially true when you are following the divine communication.

True or False?

But how do you know if you are communicating with Spirit or you are making it all up?

That is a question many people struggle with on a regular basis. Let me say that the more you are in tune with your soul the easier this becomes. The more you listen to your natural soulful voice the more that you will begin to recognize the higher vibration, energy and difference between the lower and higher selves. When the information is coming from Spirit, it will be naturally filled with the clearest thought, highest emotion (love) and have a pure positive energy about it. The voice will be quick, to the point and direct. This is true even when the message may be giving us a warning. You will have a feeling of safety, empowerment and truth within the message.

When Spirit is involved, the message will be filled with love and light to guide, bless and support us along our earth journey. Often the message will be repeated in a variety of ways to make sure that you receive it and take action accordingly. Perceive your spiritual support crew as your warm and welcoming cheerleaders who never give up on helping you to improve the quality of your life or evolve as a soul.

Divine communication will lovely guide you to find solutions or even help another as required. Spirits guidance may come in answer to a prayer or even suddenly. There may be an air pressure change or smell of a certain scent when divine communication is flowing forth, which you will be able to sense.

You may receive a gut feeling to make a positive life change or even take certain steps. Spirit will guide you to take the first steps and may further deliver instructions to take after the first step is completed.

Divine communication will feel very natural to you; it has been happening all your life already, after all. It may however take time to get to understand how to work with your abilities. This is especially true even when one was hasn't been utilizing this gift consciously. The voice of Spirit will always ring true somewhere in you even though sometimes it may sound like your own voice. Remember Spirit doesn't want to scare you so it will use the voice you are most familiar with, and will utilize words like we or you in the communications.

When your lower self (ego) is delivering the message it will hold a heavier and denser vibration or energy to it. When information is coming through the ego, it often comes forth with a sense of fear or anxiousness to it. The information may cause you to separate yourself and give you a sense of being alone.

When the ego is involved, it may cause you to take action or to make life changes out of desperation, fear or panic. There will not be a welcoming sensation to it or sense of familiarity. You may even feel somehow disconnected from the source when information is delivered from the lower self.

The ego will cause you to force or make something happen rather than allowing it in a divine way and time. Spirit will never force its will upon us; that is the act of the human mind. Spirit knows of our free will that we enjoy on earth plane and will honor this always. Asking for heavenly help is required so that the spiritual forces can move heaven and earth to aid us in greater ways.

When the lower consciousness is bringing guidance, there may be a discouraging or negative tone to the information. Ego guides you to the worst case scenarios, causing depressing or fearful thoughts. The highest self may show you the worst case scenario but when this happens you will also receive information why this may be unfolding and how to help you through the scenario. The ego often will leave us hanging or will scatter information along the way.

The human consciousness will use terminology that delivers the information in a way that uses the word, I or feels like you're talking to yourself. If the message is muddied, unclear or cryptic the ego may be communicating the information. When the information is coming from Spirit, your heart is receiving the message fully. This is because the ego resides in the mind, not the heart.

When the ego is delivering, the message may be one that causes harm to yourself or another, delivers gossip or speculation. There is no warm cheerleader here. In fact, there is a sensation of a cruel, taunting and cold monster delivering the guidance.

It takes time to begin to be able to discern the information and whether the wisdom is coming from the lower or higher self when first starting out. If you look at your own life experiences, you will begin to understand and recognize the differences moving forward.

Getting Out of the Way

I find that many times our biggest block is ourselves because we begin to overanalyze the information as we are receiving it. The best thing is to settle in and let your heart speak. Through this channel you will begin to be able to take the right action steps in your life more each day.

For many, there is a learning curve to following the heart as you have been living in the head far too long. Be gentle with yourself. Know that mistakes are sure to happen as you begin to connect, recognize and understand the voice of the soul. There is no rush here, you have all the days of your life to master and get it right.

The more you can relax, the more you will be open to the messages of Spirit. This is why often people find themselves receiving insights and inspiration at bedtime, showering or when they are in meditation. This is because you are open to the Spirit world and out of your own way.

The use of these mantra statements can assist you:

- I relax; I let go; I am in the flow.
- I accept; I allow; I am receiving now.

I find that I use them as a focusing mechanism when I am out walking, doing the dishes or whatever I am doing in the present moment. These statements remind me to stay open, receptive and to surrender to the divine within. They remind me to accept and allow the energy to flow wherever destined. They also help keep my mind busy so that I am not over thinking or worrying about something else (which comes from the ego). Feel free to use these or create your own that resonate and help you.

The Gift of Clairvoyance

Everyone has at one point in their life or another had visions. You could have had a vivid dream, a flash of someone, or you could have sworn you saw something move in your peripheral sightline. This happens to us all in varying degrees and is a gift of the soul.

Clairvoyance translates to *clear seeing or the ability to perceive information in the world visually outside of the ordinary*. It basically transcribes to be the ability to see visions, images, mental pictures, dreams, auras, mini movies and the spiritual realm.

When people think of a psychic or medium, they often imagine that this is one of the main gifts they will have. This can certainly be the case for many, however the information from spirit may also come through one of their other communication channels.

In my case, spirit will use all my abilities in the sessions with clients or may focus on one or two of them. My gift of clairvoyance may not be the main way that they are communicating with me at the time. Or it can be the gift that is most utilized in the session. It all depends on many factors including my energy that day.

This is just another reason to make sure that we are doing the best to take care of our body, mind, spirit and emotions. For the better we do the easier it becomes for Spirit to communicate through our channels.

Have you ever had a dream that you woke up that was so vivid, so real like? Chances are the dream held information pertinent to something in your life that you needed to take action upon. Perhaps, it was even a dream visitation with your departed loved one. When your dreams are vivid, something divine is definitely unfolding. Let your soul handle the details as you listen to your intuitive instincts with it.

Maybe you have been so aware, relaxed and open that as you were talking with someone, you saw their true colors shining around them. This is also known as their auric field.

Perhaps, you were walking down the street and saw something that just was just out of this world. Perhaps the vision was of you doing something with someone. Instantly you knew you had to reach out to them only to receive confirmation when you called them your help was needed.

The Gift Within the Darkness

One time I was walking down the street and had a fleeting flash. I saw a group of people including myself doing Reiki or energy work in a park. In this flash, there was complete information about what park, the day of year, reason for it and more all revealed at the same time.

Within two months of this vision, I had gathered a group of people and we had planned the first ever, Reiki in the Park, here in Ottawa. During this day, we gave free mini Reiki energy sessions to people so that they could experience it first hand to help dispel the myths and fears that people have about the unknown. We met many wonderful people as we spoke about Reiki and connected with the community at large.

Many of the practitioners are still connected and sharing in the joy of sharing their light in the world. I only had to trust and follow the guidance and everything flowed for the successful outcome.

Did you swear your saw something move out of the corner of your eye and when you turned your head there was nothing there? You just saw the spiritual realm walking alongside of you, however, a part of you may be in fear about seeing them face on. This is why when you turned to look they faded into the invisible world. Remember Spirit never wants to frighten or cause us further fear.

Rest assured when you feel safe and secure in seeing the heavenly realm, they will begin to get closer and eventually appear right in front of you. The spirit world will detect when you are ready, until then one step at a time. For now, just keep looking forward and be aware consciously of what is happening to the side of you.

These are just some ways that clairvoyance works. When we have fleeting flashes, you are not physically seeing with your eyes. You are seeing through your Third or Spiritual Eye, which is located between your brows just above and between your eyes.

To open and strengthen your clairvoyance, next time you are looking in a mirror at yourself, affirm the following:

- I am naturally clairvoyant.
- It is safe for me to see the spiritual realm.
- t is safe for me to see the truth.
- I see the divine spiritual realm with ease in a divine way and time.
- My gifts bless my life experiences and those I meet each day.

The more you affirm these statements, the more you will believe them. Like all beliefs, when you think and say something often enough, they will become true for you and begin to shape your reality. Besides, in truth, you really are clairvoyant! You may have just forgotten this or closed down this channel for a period for various reasons, none of which matter anymore.

Of course, if you wish some extra support with this or any other channel, you can ask the archangels, ascended masters, or your heavenly support crew. They all love you and are always there for you awaiting your call.

There are a variety of ways that you can work with your gifts to strengthen them. The following exercises to help you in doing just that. Of course, these are just a start and there are many other ways you can practice using your gift of clairvoyance.

Exercise One

Upon waking up in the morning, ask your angels and guides to show you a vision of what (someone in particular) will be wearing today. Or ask who you will be talking with first when you arrive at a particular location.

Now relax for a moment, and write any thoughts you get on the subject in a journal. Letting the information go afterwards.

Then go about your day and when you come home that night take a look at what you wrote earlier to see how accurate it was.

As you practice and strengthen your gift, you will begin to see your accuracy increase. Remember it is like a muscle and you have not been using it consciously on a regular basis. Be gentle as you begin to work with your gifts. Look for the similarities rather than perfection to start with as you familiarize yourself with your abilities.

Exercise Two

When you are waiting for an elevator and there is more than one, take a moment (before pressing the button) to relax and breathe.

Now, ask your guides to show you what elevator will be the one which will open first to take you to your floor of choice. Pay attention to what elevator your eyes fall naturally on, press the button and go stand in front of it.

You may not always get it right, but the more you practice the more you strengthen your channel of clairvoyance.

Clairvoyant information is relayed in one of two ways, through your spiritual eye or through your physical eyes. When it is coming through your third eye, the information will be shared through flashes, visions and often like mini movies playing out. With your physical eyes you may find yourself looking at something in response to a request for information.

Pay attention to both ways as you are developing as the spiritual realm will often use our environments to relay information and guidance to us. The more we are conscious of the many ways they may be sharing with us the better the communications will be.

Exercise Three

If you live with other people or you have company staying with you, this is an exercise that can be fun to explore.

Close your eyes for a moment and imagine another room in your house. For the purpose of this exercise we will use the kitchen.

See yourself walking into the kitchen, opening the doors of the cabinets, fridge or even paying attention to what is on the counter. See what is in your line of sight in the various locations, take a good look around the space in your mind's eye.

Once you have the vision in your consciousness, open your eyes, and go check out the space to see if it matches the information that you received. If so, congratulations, you just had a clairvoyant vision!

If you weren't perfect, did you at least see the kitchen, either fully or parts of it? If so, congratulations, you still had a clairvoyant vision! Remember, we are practicing and looking for similarities to start and accuracy as we continue to progress.

Infinite Possibilities

The possibilities are endless for you to practice your gift of clairvoyance. Anytime you can visualize something you are using this gift. This is something that you can do anywhere at any time, really.

Use an object that is in front of you for this next exercise. Look at the item closely. Study the details, colors, texture and the object from all sides. Once you have the object clearly in your mind put it aside and close your eyes.

Now imagine the item in your mind's eye. Make the object smaller, bigger, turn it around or adjust the clarity.

Hold it in your vision for as long you can and then repeat the exercise again. This is a simple exercise but gives your third eye a nice workout.

Seeing & Reading the Aura

Take a moment to bring one of your hands closer to your face directly in front of your eyes. As you do so, you will probably notice that it becomes slightly invisible. You shall begin to see through and past your hand, as your eyes become unfocused.

Now start to pay attention to just around your fingers and the entire hand. As you do so, you may begin to see a white light hugging the body. This is your auric field you are beginning to see. Once you have it in view, move your hand slowly further away from you and see if you begin to see the energy widen around your fingers or palm.

Next take a moment to look at other items in our home and see if you can see the energy field around them. Perhaps, start with natural items like plants, animals or other items that we perceive in having a life force of their own.

You may find by just staring out the window can yield the ability to see the energy within the window moving. Remember everything has a natural energy that vibrates (including you) , therefore, this is a very real possibility.

When you are outdoors in nature look at the trees, flowers, birds and even the electrical wires. Everything has a natural energy field. When we shift our vision to one which is slightly unfocused it is possible to see energy vibrating in its natural state.

I would highly recommend that you don't use others to practice seeing their energy field without their permission. It can make them feel uncomfortable and besides we want to respect their personal space and honor the divine energy within all. By asking them first, it allows them to also perhaps partake in the exercise by practicing on you as well.

It is fun to do with people as well, so find a partner and let's practice some more.

Ask them to hold on sharing any feedback with you until you are completed the exercise. Now, with your partner sitting and their eyes closed, have them focus on visualizing something.

As they do this, take a moment to expand your auric field to merge with theirs (like two bubbles of light coming together as one).

Now that you are connected as one energy, take a moment to look at the energy field to see what you are picking up on. Describe what you are seeing to them.

Share everything with them as the information may make total sense to them in more ways than one. Or you could be out in left field as you practice the gift. In time, your clairvoyance will become more accurate. For the meantime, just relax and just have fun exploring your gift of clear vision.

Once you are done, have them share with you what they were focusing on and if it made sense to them in any way. You may find you were extremely accurate with what they were visualizing or you may find that it relates to something else in their life.

Once you have completed the exercise, be sure to separate your auric fields. This will make sure that you are both back in your private spaces as two bubbles of light once again.

Sometimes, when you do this exercise, you may even find yourself picking up feelings which is the gift of clairsentience. You may even pick up audio information or have a sense of knowingness with it. However, let's keep things simple and work with one communication channel at a time. In this case, the gift of sight.

You may see colors as well, which could relate to the chakra or energy system or have another meaning all together. So share what this color means to you at the time.

The information coming forth is often symbolic or literal. It is ideal to keep track of the vision symbols in a journal. That way when the symbol comes forth in response to a question that you may ask of your support crew, you will be able to discern it much more readily. We will talk more about this in the chapter on signs and symbols.

I see what you mean is a statement that is often used by people who have a natural clairvoyant tendency in life. They are often found in the creative or visual art fields, as designers, architects, painters, sculptors and in many other fields. Anything that allows them to use their visual abilities is a natural fit for them.

The Gift of Clairsentience

Have you ever walked into a room and at once felt uncomfortable or even better yet, comfortable? Have you walked by an area, where there is no scent normally, only to smell something such as flowers or the perfume of someone that deceased wore? This is your gift of clairsentience in action.

Clairsentience translated means *clear feeling or the ability to sense what is unseen to the human eye and is non-physical in nature.* People that are clairsentients are creative souls with huge hearts. They sense deeply and often are moody because of their ability to perceive and pick up on the energy that surrounds them.

If you find yourself using the words, I feel often, then more than likely you are naturally a clairsentient channel. Clairsentients make great mediums with their ability to pick up and sense the spiritual realm. Those with this channel open also can make great musicians, writers, healers and more.

People who are highly sensitive often have this channel wide open and therefore are overwhelmed by the intense energies in the world. We call people who have an above average sentient channel, an empath or empathic, due to the fact they feel deeply.

For some clairsentients this gift can be challenging for them as the emotions of others and life itself can trigger many sensations at once. Spirit wants you to know there are ways to help you manage this channel so that you can thrive doing things you love without being overwhelmed.

I personally find it challenging in certain circumstances where there are large crowds of people. The same is true when I pick up something is about to happen in the world. The following exercise has helped me immensely and I hope it does you as well.

There are three chakras that can be helpful to empaths to adjust your sensitivity to the outside world: the sacral, solar plexus and the heart chakras. Imagine each of your energy centers like volume controls on a stereo. If you want to feel more, you turn the volume up. If you want to feel or sense less you lower the volume. Another way to adjust is imagine each as a balloon where you deflate to lower your abilities or inflate to heighten your abilities.

We need not make it more complicated than that. Spirit always says: *Simplicity is best*.

You need not be an empath to be affected by the energy around us. We are all sentient beings naturally to some degree. Therefore, we are all susceptible to receiving or picking up on the information that is being relayed in the world. This is one of the reasons it is best to surround yourself with uplifting or positive people and energy as it helps to strengthen your energy fields lovingly.

How many times have you felt low in energy or even sad, down, angry or extremely vulnerable, however, you could not figure out why for the life of you? Chances are it is because you are picking up energy through your psychic clairsentient channel from someone else. Instead of asking: What's wrong with you? Ask: Whose energy does this belong to?

If you pick up on someone else's name then breathe the energy out asking that it is transmuted back to love and return it to the sender. Their energy belongs with them as does yours belong with you. Energy can go both ways so make sure to breathe your energy back to you at the same time.

Sometimes there may be negative cords attached to us from those that have left the physical world and those cords are affecting us in our daily life. Take this time to cut the negative or fear based cords so that the love cords, which will always remain, can be strengthened. You will feel better by doing so, as will your loved ones in heaven.

It is a good idea to take a moment to ask for heavenly help to clear you of other people's energies each night at bedtime.

Guidance from Above

Remember, your spiritual support crew is always sharing guidance with you through your psychic abilities including the gift of clairsentience. So, why not be more conscious when you are sensing something by asking questions, such as: What is this sensation or information about? Why am I receiving this information? Or another question that may be pertinent at the time.

Questions just help you to get clearer and connect you deeper to your own personal guidance system through your divine communication channels. By asking your support crew questions or giving them feedback it assists them in communicating clearer with you.

Everything is energy. Therefore it is possible to sense energy and the information it contains from around the world; the location does not matter.

Often when we think of someone, a part of our energy goes out to be with them. This in turn may cause them to pick up on us at the time. Due to this same psychic connection we are also able to receive information from them at the same time. This is why we sometimes feel a certain way and is also another important reason to take time to clear ourselves each day.

That tightness in your muscles, tension on your head, nausea or even butterflies in your stomach is all energy that contains information for us. However, many times we are not paying attention or taking the time to tune into it to discover what it is trying to tell us. We just assume it is because of something that we have going on in our life, not that it may also be about someone else.

Take time daily to check in with your body to see what it is trying to tell you through your feelings.

When you begin to pay attention, you just may be amazed. Don't wait for something negative to happen before you begin to be conscious. Let today be the day that you awaken to the power and energy within your senses. Only you hold the ability to do so. When you begin to transcribe the energy that spirit shares, one will often find the quality of everyday life improves. After all, your heavenly friends and family want you to live the best life possible.

Let's Tune In Now

Take a moment to close your eyes and just become aware of your body. Then ask the following questions, making note of the answers:

- How do the clothes that you are wearing feel?
- How does the chair you are sitting in feel?
- Is the room temperature comfortable for you? Or is it too hot or cold?
- What smells are you picking up on?
- Are you tasting anything out of the ordinary?

When you answered these questions, you were connecting to your gift of clairsentience. Do you want to know how I could know this when I am not there with you? It is simply because you were asking how something felt. That's how! Nothing mystical about that.

Wait a minute! You were asking about the way something felt, but how do the last two questions, regarding smelling and tasting, fit in? I bet you were wondering that? Am I correct?

This is simply because within the gift of clairsentience is two other gifts or lessor known abilities. The gift of *clairambience is the ability to receive information through the sense of taste*, whereas the gift of *clairalience is the ability to receive information through your sense of smell*.

These are why many people will suddenly taste or smell something out of the ordinary. So next time you get a whiff of something or an odd taste, remember to ask Spirit for further information. You just may be picking up on a heavenly loved one who is trying to share a message with you.

As you may now be aware, the way you position the questions make all the difference in the way the information is delivered to you.

If the questions would have involved how something sounded or looked like, then you would have been working with your gift of clairaudience or clairvoyance. So be mindful of the way you ask your questions to the spiritual world. When you ask clearer questions, you get clearer results.

The same is true in life, the clearer we communicate the better our chances for a successful conversation or better results we receive.

Exercise One

Close your eyes and take a moment to imagine someone. Think about a conversation that you had with them. How did you feel? Was the exchange uplifting or empowering for you? Or was the conversation draining or disempowering in some way?

Now think about a song and the lyrics in it? How does it make you feel? Does it uplift you? Do you find yourself sad, down or some other emotion as you listen to it?

One last scenario:

Consider for a moment a television show such as the news? Does this show uplift or empower you? Or does it make you feel fearful, sad, angry or frustrated? Perhaps, you have a different emotion?

Whatever you are sensing is okay. Just get the information and then let it go, breathing in love to shift your vibration upwards once again.

Remember everything is energy and therefore you are affected by everything whether you are aware of it or not. Be mindful what you watch, listen or share in the world as you will be expanding the same energy and attracting that same energy to you.

Exercise Two

You can do this exercise alone or with someone else.

If you are doing by yourself:

Bring your hands together for a moment like you are holding a ball in them.

Feel the energy there being held between your hands for a moment. Now slowly move your hands apart until they are separated about a foot. Close your eyes and tune into the sensations between your hands. After a moment slowly move them together.

Pay attention to what you are noticing in each stage of the exercise: What are you sensing? Heat? Tingles in the palms? Pressure? Something else?

It matters not what you felt, but if you were feeling something then you were working with your clairsentient channel. Good job!

With a Partner:

Have your partner either sit or lay down and get comfortable. Have them close their eyes and focus on something that invokes a certain emotion or even simply just focus on the emotion itself.

Give them a moment. Now I want you to imagine yourself blending your energy field with them for this exercise. When you are ready, begin to scan your hands about 6 inches above their body as you describe what you are feeling or sensing as you do so.

You can also sit in a chair to tune into their energy (if this feels better for you) and get a sense of what they are feeling at the time. Share with them as you are picking up the information until you don't sense anything more being received.

Once you are done sharing with them what you picked up, have them give you feedback. Let your partner share what they were focusing on and if the information you were picking up made any sense to them. This will help you to discern and understand further what you were picking up for future reference should you receive similar information again from Spirit.

You can do this over and over again, each time with them choosing to focus on something different so that they feel a different emotion for you to practice sensing.

If they wish to join in the fun, exchange roles and begin again. Once you are done, it is important that you separate your energy fields so that you are in your own private space once again.

Now is also the time to ask your spiritual support crew to clear both of your energy fields of what no longer serves. Also ask your angels and guides to fill you up with the highest love and light.

In the beginning, you may get scattered information and none of it makes sense in the moment. As you gain confidence in your gifts and abilities, you will see the accuracy increase and also receive feedback to confirm what you are sharing. Sometimes, only time reveals how accurate or how the information makes sense.

Exercise Three

This is an excellent exercise to check in with your body each day.

Close your eyes and begin to focus on your feet. How do they feel? Are they tight or tense? If so, ask what information your soul is trying to tell you through your feet now? Ask for further information to be shared if you need further clarity. When you are ready to move forward begin to imagine that your feet are now relaxing and filling with loving light.

Continue to move up your body, section by section. Taking time to check in to see what you are sensing and if your soul is trying to share something with you. Once you are with your check in make sure to relax and fill each section with the loving light.

When you reach the head or face area pay attention to each little area. Is your mouth relaxed and open or is it tense and shut? What about your teeth? Are the top and bottoms clenching together? What are you feeling or tasting on your tongue?

Ask what your soul is trying to share with you through the various sensations and information you receive? Then fill with loving light as you relax further.

Do the same for the rest of your facial muscles including the nose, eyes, forehead, ears, the crown of head, etc... you get the idea.

Imagine doing that all the way from toes to crown each day, how relaxed would you be by the time you are finished?

When we are relaxed, we are more open to receiving information from the divine realm.

When you do this relaxation exercise as you lay down for bedtime, you may find yourself relaxing into a deep sleep as your body unwinds from your day. Certainly a wonderful way to end your days and prepare for a dream visitation with your loved ones, perhaps.

Always be Aware

The main thing when doing any exercise is to stay open and do not censor or judge anything; just be aware. If you are driving down the roadway, you would pay attention to the information and take appropriate action. You would not normally be judging at the same time; though your ego would try to argue with the signs or ignore them, perhaps.

When we are expanding our awareness, we are training ourselves to be present and aware of the information and energy that lies within. This allows us to take suitable action as needed. Remember God is one and the same as you; therefore the feelings and sensations are messages from the divine source within. Now why would you ignore your divine guidance system when it allow you to start to live the amazing life you are destined for?

Start to pay attention to how you feel each day. When you are down, think or do things that uplift you. When we have better feelings, we are lined up with who we are as our true nature, love. The better our vibration, the better we are at manifesting and attracting what we wish more of in our lives. Not only that, the easier it is for your loved ones to connect with you. After all, life is supposed to be fun. So have fun, laugh, sing, dance and live blissful all the days of your life.

If something is causing you to feel worried, or you don't feel right, pay attention to those messages as well. In life, you probably have had such a sensation about something but went ahead and did it anyways, only to regret it later on. Correct? Let us learn from these events. This way the next time you receive such guidance you will surely take the divinely guided steps. Hopefully this will yield a more joyful and loving experience moving forward.

Be conscious of what sensations you are experiencing wherever you are. This way you will find yourself more empowered to choose better feeling thoughts and experiences. Become the conscious creator you have always been as a soul. You hold the power.

The Gift of Clairaudience

Clairaudience is *the ability to clearly hear or perceive information that is outside the ordinary realm of hearing.* This is the channel that is connected to your ability to listen to the spiritual realm.

Your team wants to keep you being at peace; therefore, they will use the most loving and gentle way to communicate with you. This is the reason why when you first start to hear the voice of Spirit they will use your own voice, within. It is much like when you are having a communication within your own head trying to figure out a decision. However, when you pay attention closely, you can discern something different about the energy coming through.

When your guides detect you are ready, you will start to receive the information through voices other than you own (either female or male). This will be their voice and they will then choose if the voice is delivered from within or outside of your ear. This will happen within you are not fearful and are very comfortable with hearing the voice of spirit.

It is always best to surrender to the power of the soul to decide or figure out the details on what is the best way for spirit to communicate the information with you. The soul knows what is in your highest good and which way to best deliver the information. So, leave the details to the expert.

The Gift Within the Darkness

Your job is to get out of the way and to stay open to receiving the information however it is presented to you. Why would you want to put limitations on Spirit just because you think one way is superior to another way? Your soul will use all your senses if you are open and willing to allow it to do so.

An example: Have you ever been walking down the street and out of the blue you hear a conversation that someone else is having? Has it ever seemed to answer a question or give some insight into something in your life that has been on your mind? If so, you have been communicated to by your guides physically. They just used the outside world to talk with you.

This happens all the time through radio, television, books and so much more. We as humans are not always consciously paying attention to the many ways spirit speaks to us and this is something we should do more of.

The Gift of Music

Have you ever had a song repeating in your head, or perhaps kept hearing it on the radio? Perhaps, the song title kept showing up in a variety of other ways in your life? If you have answered yes, then you have been spoken to by the spiritual realm through this song.

Take the time to pay attention to the lyrics or the story (meaning) of the song. By doing so you can be sure you will discover the message spirit is sharing with you. Often this divine wisdom will assist you in your life with providing insights or solutions to a problem or information about something to come. This is often another way your heavenly loved ones will communicate they love and are with you.

Your spiritual support crew will also use the voice of others to deliver the message. The more conscious and present we are in the moment, the more likely we will hear what is being shared with us when this happens. This allows us to take appropriate action. When spirit is communicating with us it does so on all levels of our being and will always be with complete information.

Example:

We could hear a song on the radio that someone who died used to listen to it all the time. We immediately sense they are with us and sharing a message. Perhaps the lyrics share the information: Everything is going to be okay. We, at once, know exactly where this message fits in our life. We don't overanalyze or question the information further. The message was completely delivered with the divine communication.

Music has always been a big part of my life and therefore my heavenly loved ones will often use songs to deliver their messages.

For instance, every time I hear the song, Gloria by Laura Branigan, I know my mom is with me. Gloria was my mom's name and when the album came out, she would replay the entire album over and over again. So this song is her way of letting me know she is with me. However, there may be a line or two from the lyrics which also jumps out at me which is giving me further information that she is trying to tell me.

She and my other loved ones will communicate through other songs, television shows and in other ways. Each time their presence will be felt and the message will be received.

The Gift of Being Present

Spirit will also use other audio communication forms to deliver their messages and therefore it is best to stay present, open and aware at all times. When we are doing so we are more likely to be conscious of the divine communication.

Being present also helps us to be more aware of what is actually being communicated in each conversation that we hold throughout the day. Spirit says that many times we are not always present or hearing what is being said. Therefore, this can cause confusion or misunderstandings to happen.

One thing that is for certain when spirit is communicating they will make sure that you truly understand and get what they are saying. This may even mean they deliver the messages over and over in a variety of ways until you do. They love you that much.

Let us practice being aware and present in all that we do each day. You will be amazed how this will help you in your life as you do so. It is also an act of love when we do so. Both for others and ourselves.

Exercise Time

Grab a pen and paper, or open up a fresh computer document to type in.

We encourage you to practice both ways so that you can get familiar and find which works best in the long run. We often tend to go to our comfort zones and this can be a good thing at times. However, keeping in the theme of being open and letting spirit be free to communicate in the best way possible, explore both options.

I like to do this exercise after being in a meditative space for a few minutes as I find it helps me to be open and relaxed for the process. I also find it helpful to say a prayer to help ensure that only the love and light of spirit is communicating through me at all times. Fear will stop divine communication in its track; where love open us up to the flow of energy. Feel free to use the prayer below or use/create another one that you like.

Dearest Mother/Father God,

We come to you to ask you to envelop us in your divine love and light now. We ask that you and the Archangel Michael watch over this divine communication that we are about to have. This way we feel safe in the knowledge that only love is present and communicating through the words as they flow freely through us now. Please keep our mind and heart centered in divine love and light at all times. For this and even better, we give our thanks. Amen

Now you are ready to begin. Write or type at the op of the page:

Dear God and my divine spiritual support crew: What message do you have for me today?

Close your eyes and mentally repeat the question to God and your divine spiritual support crew.

Next begin to write down everything that you hear, see, feel, sense, smell, taste or think of. Even if you think you are making it up or imagining it, write it down. Your job is not to edit or try to analyze it at this time. It is to be open, relax and write the words of spirit.

You can ask other questions and receive answers for as long as you wish. You can direct your questions to a certain person such as one of your guides, or even your heavenly loved ones. Either way, you are practicing the gift of divine communication.

This exercise will help open and strengthen all your natural gifts of divine communication. The exercise is especially helpful with your clairaudience as you begin to just write what you hear. It matters not whether the voice comes from within or outside of your head.

In time, you will become proficient and be able to sense the difference in tone, feel and energy as different members of your spiritual support crew share with you. You will discover the way that spirit speaks will be different from your normal communication style which is a sure sign that you are not making this up.

The more practice that you get with this exercise the stronger your auditory muscle gets. Like anyone who is studying a new language the more practice that you get the more fluent you become in spirit speak.

What's the Buzz?

As you become more accustomed to divine communication in this form, you may also become conscious of when you are receiving messages in your everyday world. You may even discover if you hear the voice of spirt through your left, right or both ears.

When we are opening up to hearing the heavenly audio messages, we may begin to have a buzzing or itchiness in one or both of our ears. This is often associated with the higher frequency or vibration of the spiritual realm as they communicate with us. It is much like the old way of connecting to other computers with the modems. You would ring up a certain number and the computers would exchange information through the various tones and vibrations to establish the connection. When we receive a download of information on many levels at once it is very much the same idea.

Spirit is speaking to you in a new language that you are not humanly familiar with. You may need to give them feedback so that they can adjust the language speed for you or even the communication style. By sharing with them how the information is coming in or sounding like to you, you are helping them correspond with you in a better way you are sure to understand.

Like any conversation, if you don't let the other party know what is working or not, how will they ever be able to adjust the way they interact with you? They will only assume that you received the information, which in this case is true. Ultimately, your soul has acknowledged the message within your heart level as you received it, so no worries. Though it is always nice to be at peace when hearing and not annoyed throughout the process, don't you think? Why not take the time to give feedback to your guides so that they can help you understand them?

You can always have a divine communication with your heavenly crew anytime. You don't need to go into an exercise to do so. The more familiar you get with your natural communication gifts and with your spiritual crew the easier it will be do anytime, anywhere. Just take the time to listen to the response you receive after you begin your conversation.

As you continue to open and practice communicating with your team, you will find that a level of trust and faith in the information given begins to unfold. This is especially true when the guidance is filled with a sense of empowerment or is uplifting and repetitive in nature.

Remember you are an equal to the spirit world, not above or below them. Their guidance is like a best friend who has your best interest when giving you guidance. It will always be supportive, consistent, mature, strong, powerful and familiar. It will always come in complete with any further inspired action steps that you would be best served taking. These are always a good way to recognize when the communication is coming from your support crew.

The Gift of Claircognizance

Claircognizance is *the ability to clearly know information that is outside the normal mind of thought.* It is a superconscious state of knowingness where one has no earlier connection to the information which comes to their conscious awareness; you just know it. The information flows to you through thoughts, inspired ideas and you have a 100% certainty about the information.

For many, this is one of the trickiest channels as our minds will often get in the way and cause us to overanalyze the information. However, when we get out of our way while trusting and following the insights, we gain proof how accurate the information is.

During your dream states all your channels of divine communication are open. This is because we are relaxed, open and

The Gift Within the Darkness

receptive not to mention because our overactive mind is now out of the way.

I am sure if you took a moment to think back on your life, you can remember a time when you just strongly knew something, without necessarily knowing how you did. At one point in all of our lives this has happened. This is an example of claircognizance in action.

Have you ever felt like the top of your head was on fire or like there was a vortex circling it? If so, chances you have experienced this channel at work receiving information to assist you in your daily living. The top of the head is where this energy center is most active and located.

Are you the type of person that needs to think about something before making a decision? Do you find yourself using the words, I know what you mean? This comes from a profound and deep connection where you are accessing the knowledge from within the heart and soul. This is the type of knowingness I speak of here. Chances are you are aligned in this communication channel when this is the case.

Have you ever just knew facts, had some insight into something, or were inspired in some way? If you answered yes to any of these, then your claircognizant channel was at play.

Perhaps, you just knew what to do in a situation or how to fix something or even just had an awareness where a situation was going? Once again this is your clear knowing channel at work! You truly can be a bit of a Know-it-All at times.

You will find people who are claircognizant in jobs that use their intellect. This includes jobs that involve teaching, writing, research or doing something technical.

Those that are inclined towards their natural gift of claircognizance may also be very skeptical when it comes to things that they can't touch or prove physically. They often need some sort of tangible or undeniable proof to believe in the unseen.

You Are a Mind Freak

Let me elaborate a little here. You are not actually a mind freak but you can definitely cause a stir with a couple of your natural powers. Once you comprehend and grasp how this part of your natural gifts work, you can freak anyone out so use this gift wisely to not cause fears to take hold.

The *ability to communicate with your mind is known as* telepathy and is an aspect of claircognizance. Have you ever thought of someone and then heard from them shortly afterwards? Then you have telepathically picked up on their energy as they thought of you. Of course, this also goes the other way. They think of you and you call them. When they answer they say: I was just thinking of you.

I know a few people that I have been known to freak out a few times when I called them or said something they just thought of. Perhaps, you do as well. I find that the closer two people are the easier it is to receive information in this format. This is why couples often finish each other sentences or know what the other is thinking.

Twins are very psychically connected through their gift of claircognizance and clairsentience. This is why they often will know or feel how the other is doing or what they are experiencing in their life moments. The gift of telepathy is also very strong in twins. It only makes sense seeing they would have a very deep and close relationship with each other. After all, it is one that goes back to the womb. The only other bond that can be this close is that of a mother with her child.

We are all born aware and conscious of our natural gifts of intuition along with how the channels work. When we are an infant, we will use our natural communication channels to interact with our parents in the best way we know how.

The Gift Within the Darkness

As youngsters, we will just keep trying a different channel until we find the one that connects with our parents the best. When this happens that we know our conveyed message has been heard as they are now responding to us. It usually doesn't take long for us to connect once we start to voice ourselves. As we evolve on the earth, the bond with our parents grow and so does our parents sixth sense when it comes to us.

The *gift of being able to move objects with thought* is known as *telekinesis* and is another aspect of claircognizance. This is not as common in the everyday world as not all claircognizant channels are able to use all parts of their gifts. However, with time, practice and a little nurturing patience, everything is possible.

Claircognizant Suddenly Receive

Claircognizant channels will often receive sudden information in a variety of ways. They may have a profound knowingness of their connection with the divine and all of life. With this comes a heightened sense of this divine truth that they sense in the heart of their soul, not just as a concept.

When they meet someone for the first time, they often will have great insights into this person's character and the future course of the relationship.

There gifts can also give them foresight into world events to come and beyond the human mind. They may not have proof in the moment, but in time, they will see how profoundly accurate the information is.

The natural tendency to know or have great insight help claircognizants to get to the truth in a seemly complex situation. Their cognizant channels helps them to focus on the core issues often bringing healing and enlightenment in simple but powerful ways.

Claircognizants tend to know how to build or fix something without having the instructions to go along with it. They appear to have a familiarity to the object and this guides them to know what do to when they have never encountered this before perhaps in this life.

People who are naturally inclined as a claircognizant are divinely inspired with ideas or concepts that seem to come out of left field. They may even know facts with clear accuracy without prior knowledge or memory of ever seeing, hearing, learning, reading or knowing anything on the subject.

Clearing Your Mind and Space

To make room for you to receive claircognizant impressions from the spirit world, you must first learn to clear the closets of the mind.

Let's compare your conscious mind to a computer hard-drive for a moment. When the drive is filled with useless programs, or information that you no longer use, it slows the computer down. This is because everything is filed back in the recesses of the filing cabinets in case the program or information should ever be required. However, when you defragment your hard-drive of the useless bits of information, the drive begins to work more efficiently with the computer assessing information quicker.

Now if you take it a step further and you clear the drive of the old programs, you free up space. Think of these old programs as your beliefs that you have taken on throughout life. Some serve you well and others not so much. However, through the superconscious highway of the universe, you can access immense information once you install a new program. But first we need to free the mind of the old energies. Meditation is just but one way that can assist you with this.

Remember a belief is just a thought that you think or say over and over in your mind and voice in the world as truth. However, you hold the power to change your thoughts and beliefs at any given moment.

Sometimes the root of them is entwined so deeply that we need the help of a professional to release and clear the root, layer by layer. In these cases, the help of an energy worker, therapist or even hypnotist can help you shift the energy of the mind. The longer you have held onto this belief the stronger the hold or effect on you.

The mind holds great power to influence our lives in so many ways. When we begin to shift the energy within, our life can also begin to shift. Wouldn't you agree that you deserve to be free of the old news that keeps playing in your mind? In my opinion you certainly do as you are worthy of greatness in your life.

Repeat the following with me:

I am willing to release the need to control. I am willing to relax my mind now. I am willing to let go of the old and worn out limiting beliefs which no longer serve me. I am willing to open up to the infinite potential of the superconscious mind and to my spiritual support crew now.

Just using the words, *I am willing* ___ and filling in the blanks helps the spiritual realm help to reprogram your mind. It does so with programs that are in your highest good based on the words which follow, *I AM*.

When you do begin to shift consciousness, you open up to the world of possibilities the spiritual dimensions hold for you.

Take time to make space in the mind for the new energy to flow. This helps you to relax and open up to spirit communication in a deeper and more meaningful way for your life. This is something I am sure you would agree you would like to have more of on a daily basis. If so, say yes to the energy of the gift of claircognizance now and take a moment to relax into the energy.

Balance is Key

Take time to nourish yourself with life sustaining activities which bring balance and harmony to you and your life. Doing so is greatly encouraged to help your natural divine communication abilities.

Drink lots of water, nourish the body with healthy and whole foods. Cut out things that are draining your energy and vitality. Love yourself to free yourself; love yourself to nurture yourself.

Maintaining a healthy and balanced lifestyle assists you with your increasing your intuitive awareness with your gifts and abilities. Take time to show yourself divine love by taking care of your soul's vehicle on earth. This sends a clear message into the universe that we are also respecting our divine communication gifts. This is turn heightens them.

Take a moment to close your eyes and ask yourself:

- Where could I use more balance in your life?
- What steps can I take today and in the coming months to balance my world?

When we take a moment to tune in and ask these sorts of questions we are also setting the intention with the higher self to make it so. Ask for your heavenly support crew to assist you with bringing balance into your life. By doing so, everyone wins in life.

Some other ways that you can increase your health and balance include going for a walk in nature or making time to get to the gym. Make sure you get adequate sleep each night as it will help you maintain a more positive outlook in life. Make a conscious effort to spend time with those that uplift, recharge and support you in being your true self each day.

Part of balance includes ignoring what others think of you. It is your opinion that matters most. If you can honestly say you are feeling good about yourself then that's all that matters.

Also stop putting your perceptions of what you think others think of you on them. You may be totally off base until you open up and have an honest conversation to see how they perceive you. You may find that they hold you in much higher regard then you even do of yourself. This is more often than not the case.

Mind your Vibrations; Let Others Mind their Own.

You always have the power to choose how to feel about others and most importantly about yourself. Spirit wants you to soar so choose something that lets the heart open and be free to share in the love. Love is after all the most important emotion and ultimately the only one that is real. Love is the energy of spirit and therefore what ultimately flows in all divine communications.

Exercise One

Find a quiet and meditative space where you will not be disturbed for the next five to ten minutes.

Sit comfortably with your eyes closed and breathe deeply. When you do so you are literally breathing in divine inspiration and energy. Take three or four breaths and give yourself permission to relax your mind and body. Ask your angels to help you with this task, if required.

Now take a moment to feel your mind linking with the mind of divine consciousness; imagining your mind and the superconscious mind becoming one.

Now ask a question that you would like to know the answer to or receive guidance about. The clearer and more precise the question, the better. This will assist you in receiving clear and precise answers.

Some questions to start with are:

- What is my life purpose? How can I serve the world?
- What steps would be best for me to take to improve the quality of my health? My finances? My relationships? My career? My happiness?
- What divinely inspired ideas have I received recently that I should spend time focusing on?
- What would my guides and angels like me to know at this time?
- What life lessons am I to master in this life? What steps should I be taking to master this life lesson?

Take the time to relax and just be open to whatever flows into your mind and heart after asking these questions. Ask for further clarity as needed with follow up questions. You may wish to write down the information you get so that you can reference it over the coming days and weeks.

Exercise Two

This exercise will require a partner. It doesn't matter if you know them or have never met them. You will be opening up to the spiritual realm to receive information about your partner in this exercise.

Take a moment to center yourself. Taking a few deep breaths as you call forth your angels and guides to watch over you and help you with this exercise.

Next, take a moment to blend your energy with your partner. Think of two bubbles of consciousness becoming one. Then begin with asking the following questions:

- What knowledge about _____ would you like me to know?
- What is a challenge that _____ is experiencing in their life? What knowledge would you like me to share with them on this subject? What is their solution to resolving this challenge?

- What is one of _____ greatest fears? How can they overcome and release this fear now?
- How can I best serve _____ and help them at this time?

Share the information with your partner as you receive it. Have them hold back on giving you feedback until you have shared all that you received on each question. This way you are more likely to be coming from spirit without ego interruption.

Once you have completed the exercise, it is important to remember to pull your energy back in so that you both are in your own private space and bubble of consciousness once again.

Also, ask your angels to do any clearing of any residue energy that you may have picked up from this person. Take a moment to ask the angels to bless this person with healing and enlightenment for their highest good. Give thanks once you are done.

You can now switch roles if they would like to join in in practicing their gift of receiving information as well.

Remember the point of the exercise is to be of service and to do the best you can. So take the pressure off your shoulders about being accurate or right-on with the information. With time and nurturing you may find this to be the case but at the start you may only get a few things that make any sense.

In Closing

Divine communication is an amazing gift that you have the potential to develop and use in your daily life.

Continue to practice, learn and understand how to work with your divine spiritual support crew. By doing so you will see the benefit of having a meaningful and close personal relationship with them. Not only that, you will have a better understanding how they have been working with you throughout your entire life. Moving forward you can count on the fact they will continue to deliver divine information to best serve you and your life.

It is an exciting time to be you. How exciting to begin to realize your natural gifts and to know what a powerful soul you are having this human experience.

Even more exciting, is knowing as you practice and work with the materials shared throughout this book your loved ones will be by your side cheering you on. They truly look forward to one day having a direct communication with you without being only in your dreams states or through a medium.

Your loved ones are so excited for you to know what they now understand and know. As you continue to awaken as a soul having a human experience, you will awaken to this knowledge and more. I hope that you are feeling the healing and enlightenment unfolding in your journey with grief as you step into the power of your soul.

Know that your loved ones are safe, alive and well. After all, they are indeed in heaven with all of the divine creation by their side. They want you to know that indeed there is a God and the Divine's love flows freely to you now to heal your heart.

Imagine the possibilities of where you are going as you realize your full potential while utilizing your gifts and abilities daily. There has never been a more exciting time for you to awaken.

As you continue to develop a deeper connection with all that you are, your natural gifts and level of trust and faith in your spiritual support crew will expand. Continue to listen to their guidance and take suitable action steps. This will yield you living your best life possible each day moving forth.

You may miss your family and friends who have left the physical world but through the practical guidance within this book you can reconnect with them once again.

Remember be gentle on yourself as you heal and open up to your gifts as like anyone who is learning a new skill you may make mistakes on occasion. Thankfully, every time you do it helps you better discern that much better the next time around.

Make the commitment to continue to practice trusting, having faith, listening and following the guidance of your soul and your heavenly support crew. Make a conscious effort to get to know them so you can call upon them for help as required through life. Always know they are supporting you in more ways than you are conscious of in every given moment. In life, make it your motto to expect the best and know the best will appear with heavens assistance.

I have said it before and will say it again, practice the techniques offered throughout this chapter and throughout the book. In doing so, you will continue to open up to the innate psychic gifts and abilities, along with the infinite potential of your soul. Read, take classes and learn as much as you can. Most of all, keep connecting with your spiritual support crew and expanding your awareness! Make the time as you are worth all this and even more.

I love you and appreciate you as does the entire realm of heaven.

CHAPTER 36

THE GIFTS WITHIN SIGNS AND SYMBOLS

ALL AROUND YOU ARE ways Spirit is communicating with you. It could be the picture you see which tells a story of getting out into nature and relaxing at the beach. Or it could be the birds chirping on the balcony giving you permission to relax into the music of your heart. We don't recognize just how many different divine communications unfold in our lives each day.

Your loved ones are always communicating with you in subtle ways you may or may not be picking up on. The more that you know and believe you are receiving divine communications, they more you will begin to be conscious of when this unfolds in your life.

Spirit often uses symbols to communicate with us, not just verbal or written forms of words to deliver the message. They aren't here to tell us what to do but they will lovingly guide us along the journey and help us connect with our own intuition. These symbols may come to us externally or internally through our senses. The first step is recognizing that Spirit is indeed communicating with us and then looking for the many ways it does so.

When Spirit is guiding us externally the signs will be things like animals, birds, sounds, sights, and the written or verbal communications. It can even be through the many thousands of expressions of life we encounter each day. Many times, when a sign is shown to you a part of you will recognize or know it as such. Start beginning to trust in this part of you and the information that comes forth with the sign. Your life will be better for it.

An few examples:

You see a red cardinal and you instantly know this is a sign from your loved one who had an affinity for this bird and collected items with it on them. The same can be said if the sign was a dog, car, song or anything else.

You may remember the story of how little Bella sends her mother rainbows from heaven as her sign after she transitioned to spirit.

Another sign from your loved one could be seeing someone who reminds you of them so much that you could swear that it was them. What is happening here is that they are using the energy field of the person you have encountered to show they are still with you, alive and well.

This happened to me the day after my aunt had died when I was getting ready to leave to travel to her funeral. I happened to look at the driver of a vehicle that was driving by and looking back at me was someone that looked exactly like my Aunt Pauline. Not only that but this person was driving a vehicle that was the make and color of a vehicle she owed at one point in life. I could have easily chalked it up to a pure fluke. But, I knew it was her soul communicating she was all right and was going places freely as she used to do. Had I not been open to Spirit and recognized this sign it could have easily been missed.

Brian D. Calhoun

A Sign from Heaven

Signs will come in many ways and this next story of me asking for one that I would not miss to confirm something I knew would work out for me.

At the time, I had been going through financial challenges and had gotten an eviction notice early that morning. A part of me was at peace with receiving this piece of paper. But, another part of me was nervous and fearful of what could happen. I figured I couldn't control what was a potential situation that could unfold but I could go for a walk and just let nature help me.

While out for my walk I had asked for one of my favorite signs to be given if everything would work out, a feather. I asked that this would be shown over and over in a variety of ways until I said: *Thank you, I received the message.*

I had been walking for about 30 minutes at the time and was on the way home when I came across it. Not more than 5 minutes away from my home was my sign. This reassured me that yes it all was going to be okay and I could relax into my soul energy again.

Heaven made sure I wouldn't miss the sign. It made sure the sign would so big there wouldn't be any questioning this was the sign in answer to my prayer.

The sign delivered was not one little white feather but literally hundreds if not thousands of perfect little white feathers; all in a single location.

Yes, one could think that this was a busted pillow that had not been cleaned up, but I knew it was heaven giving me the sign. The thing was I had just walked by this very spot on my way out for the walk and the feathers were not there. It was especially weird due to the fact of the way they were arranged at the time; all perfectly laid in a pile where the breeze hadn't gotten to them yet. Just another way I knew this was Spirits sign.

With every external sign, you will always receive an internal recognition. A sense which gets activated at the time, such as me having the feeling and knowing when it came to my feather sign. Goosebumps or a feeling of being enveloped in a nice warm bath where your muscles relax can also be a sign. The signs aren't always recognizable immediately outside of ourselves and may be more subtle, if at all noticeable to the naked eye.

Sometimes the signs are more literal to you. Such as in the case of a red light or stop sign. As someone who comes across this sign you know to stop and wait until you get the green light or clear pathways to move forward.

But, sometimes Spirit will use these symbols to also relay another message to you, such as when you are contemplating a decision to move forward with quitting your job. The symbols could be read as stop and do not take action yet or the time is not right to decide. Use this time to pause, breathe and wait for the green light to move ahead. In the meantime, get clear on what it is you truly wish for in your next job.

Spirit could still be setting things into motion for you to move forward with your plans. This way you can have more ease and grace moving forth. Often, the events of the day or week led up to the moment when the ego or human reaction is spurring you to quit. If this the case your plan to quit may not work as you wish it to be as with my next story.

Shifting Gears

I had been working in the restaurant industry for over 18 years and had enjoyed it, mostly. Like every job, there are ups and downs, but the people and creativity kept me going. I loved to be of service and to see the smiles on people's faces as they received their food. It was always a pleasure to hear about how they enjoyed their meals. It brought joy to my soul.

My path had been changing with the introduction of Reiki into life, my mom's death, connecting to the spiritual realm and living a new path. I began to undertake the role of professional teacher and energy healer. With this my hours at the restaurant were decreasing as my spiritual journey time was shifting up. What once was a 6 days a week job had become 4 days with increasing periods of time off to focus on my other endeavors.

My finances had been improving as spirit was helping to make the transition very easy for me. Every time I dropped a day at the restaurant (to follow my new found passion) I made even more spiritually than what I lost by dropping the traditional work day. I also found myself increasingly happy and more relaxed. However, this would soon change as I entered a darker period of work at the restaurant after my mom's death.

Something had shifted and I couldn't figure it out. All I knew was I dreaded going into the restaurant, increasingly. There were personal conflicts happening with my boss's wife and a couple coworkers with my vibrations shifting at the same time. This was weird as I was just doing my regular normal job. I would come in saying hello to all but would be ignored increasingly. Still I would focus on doing my job even though it began taking a toll on me.

After a period of time, I found myself increasingly frustrated when I would come back from my days off and embracing my spiritual endeavours. The job at the restaurant was no longer enjoyable or allowed my heart to sing. The people I would connect with normally in the afternoons and who I would have beautiful conversations regarding many creative, spiritual and holistic endeavors were no longer in sight.

In hindsight, this makes total sense now having learned more about the law of cause and effect within the law of attraction. I had been in a darker heavier space at work. Therefore, how could I expect to connect with the Lightworkers while on the

The Gift Within the Darkness

job? After all, whatever you give time, energy and focus to (both in mind and heart) and holds the strongest energy, you will ultimately create. I can now see how I was the source of the heavier energy that was playing out in this restaurant job. At the time though, I was in denial.

I went about my days as per usual. After coming back from my days off, this one day I walked into work to take over the kitchen from my boss and lost it. He left the restaurant when I came in as per his usual routine but left a mess for me to clean up; something else that wasn't necessarily unusual. I was his employee who he was paying but this was not the norm. Thirty seconds to wipe the counter literally would have made it so much better.

I had a certain standard of cleanliness and regularly would come in to clean and organize everything to my liking, especially after my days off. However, this one small thing got under my skin that particular day. That was it, I called upon spiritual realm and told them to *"get me the f..k out of there. I am done."*

Within a couple weeks, I had a clairvoyant dream where I saw myself giving my notice to my bosses and saw the date on the calendar by my workstation. I woke up, got ready and went in for work.

After being at work for a short time, I found myself in the exact location where I had seen myself giving my notice. The boss was by me, and everything was as I saw in the dream. I had problems calling out the orders to my boss this day. It seemed like every time I had to clear my throat before speaking.

It took me a short time to realize the connection. Once I did though, I mentally told Spirit I would give my notice after the weekend for a date a week later than I saw in the dream. After I said this, the problems with my throat cleared up and no more clearing was needed. The message had been received and acknowledged by me.

The very next week an article was to come out in a local newspaper which was written about me and Reiki in the Park. However, the following Sunday came and no article was published. I was perplexed about the reason but had faith in the end result after the reporter contacted me to let me know the publication date had been moved.

Anyways, I gave my notice and on my second last day at work the article came out. Spirit had a plan to help me out of my job while helping with the financial part of the equation moving forward. This article was a part of the plan to allow me to be in service full-time for Spirit.

I began the journey with teaching my Angel Lights Practitioner course. This was a condensed weekend version of a 16 week program I had been teaching to empower people with their natural intuitive and healing abilities. The courses would propel them forward on their service pathways.

I soon found myself with more time on my hands than before when I was working at the restaurant alongside my spiritual endeavors. This was not a good thing as it gave me too much time to think about all the time I was not busy making money. This led me down the financial road of darkness. I had to borrow to pay the bills but my fears soon took over as I began the cycle of financial destruction.

The signs were clear I should get another job to help support me but my ego wasn't having it. In truth, I was enjoying the relaxed space of not being in the restaurant industry. I was definitely being stubborn and resistant, sure signs of the ego in play.

Looking back, I can see that I was also grieving the life I knew as my career at the time. I hadn't truly come to terms that I may need to reach out for external support to help me take care of my expenses. I was in denial of the seriousness of the situation. Death and the process of grieving a loss can show up in so many ways for sure. This was just another way it touched my life.

The Gift Within the Darkness

Spirit loved me so much it was persistent about me taking the step to get a job and would not stop until I was willing to so. At times, I was pissed off at Spirit during the process and even tried to bargain my way out of the situation. It was in my darkest hours when I finally saw the light which was always present.

After a lengthy period, I took my services outside the home and into a public location. This would help me to do continue my light work. As I continued to listening to the guidance that Spirit was giving me, the journey was lighting up once again. I was finally moving on to accepting the situation.

This allowed me to breathe a sigh of relief knowing there were an increase of clients and students filling my schedule. I found doors of opportunity to be in service in other locations began to open up for me. Life was improving as long as I followed the signs and symbols of Spirit.

However, Spirit still wanted me working for a time period so I ended up with a part-time job which took care of paying the rent each month. Most importantly, this helped me to get out of the head and get grounded once again so I was not always living in the Spirit realms. It allowed me to connect with people and to be of service in another manner. The job wasn't foreign as I had been doing readings, classes and such out of this location for a period; it offered me an opportunity to focus on other endeavors. Not to mention it was in my wheel house of my interests, which was a true win-win for all.

Many times, I would introduce the store to newcomers as it was a living breathing entity. I would also let them know about the services which were offered in the back of the shop. I never once let the new customers know I was one of the practitioners who worked in the back. In fact, some of the other staff, if they were on site, would often jump in and let the customers know I was the one doing the readings. These staff members were a sign from spirit that I was truly being actively supported by others.

Of course, there were always people that came shopping that knew who I was having had sessions with me. I would still focus on helping them find the perfect crystals, essential oils or other product they sought. It was my way of keeping balance and staying grounded at the same time; something which Spirit had given me a sign to implement more in my life. This because I was living in the spiritual space too much.

We may be a soul, first and foremost, having a human experience but we must remember to keep things in balance. The energy of Spirit is very enticing and many who are on the path will often spend a little too much time focused in this realm and neglect their earthly journey.

Eventually, it was time to move on from the job and I took the action steps to follow the signs appropriately. This continued to allow me to focus fully on doing what made my heart sing in a place which is filled with love. I moved forth in a relaxed manner knowing all is and always will be taken care of by Spirit. As long as I stay aware and connected to my true nature things I am in the flow.

To this day, I can still find myself sometimes living in my head too much and Spirit will need to remind me to get out of it and do something else. It may do so by sending me clients who need this reminder as well. In fact, Spirit often jokes, if they could fix one problem with the world, it would be just to get rid of the minds of everyone. We all live in our heads way too much and this would allow us to live from the heart more often.

I could continue to share other stories where Spirit showed me signs, but the time has come to turn the attention to your own signs and symbols. Spirit assures me they send you them daily in your life and that every single day information is presented to you to guide you along the way. Spirit says, many times you miss then because you may not be watching for them or may not even know how to interpret them.

The Gift Within the Darkness

Exercise Time

I would like you to take a few minutes to think about what reoccurring things which keep appearing in your life that might be a sign.

Next, pull out your journal and write each of these symbols down. As you write each of them down, take a moment to analyze what this particular symbol means to you at this time and write that down. Make the effort to pay attention to the colors, texture, your feelings, knowledge and all the various aspects of this symbol. This exercise isn't about what the symbols mean to other people; the exercise is about what they mean to you.

You don't need to be at home to do this exercise; it can be done anywhere you are at and at any time. If you are standing in the grocery line, take a look around you at the various things going on and think about what each thing means in the experience at the time to you.

Let's give you an example now of a sign which could show up in your life. One that could have couple multiple interpretations for the same message.

You are standing in line and the cashier is having problems putting something through for someone or they are having bank card issues.

- The message contained within this could be to just relax, breathe and take a break for a moment. You always have a choice in how to react in each moment. You can let this situation frustrate you or you can choose say a little prayer to help resolve the root of the situation playing out.
- If you are seeing people all around you having conversations with people and laughing. This sign could be for you to strike up a conversation with the person next to you and enjoy a few laughs.

- This message could also mean to take some time to relax and enjoy life more with your friends and family. This is especially true if you have been working so much and have neglected them some.

Take time each day to get more familiar with the many ways spirit is communicating with you. The more you understand the signs and symbols, the more you will live a life in the flow of everything as you follow your divine guidance.

Using Tools

For some people using Tarot, Angel Cards, or other Oracle Decks can help them to receive messages from Spirit.

Those who are experienced with the decks know to understand the full message one must go into the symbols, colors, and all aspects of the card. The message on the card, if there is one, is just one part of the entire divine communication.

As someone who has worked with many oracle decks and has taught others about them, when I find myself using them I just let the card tell the story. This way it helps to keep the ego out of the way as I let the cards dictate the story that is unfolding before your eyes.

My spiritual support crew will guide me through the cards meaning through my intuitive senses. They will also guide me to ask the appropriate questions about what I am picking up through the card at the same time. The same is true for anyone who is reading cards. They are just a tool to help us turn within for the guidance further.

And just because you get the same card over and over, doesn't mean the message is the same. You need to look deeper within to see what Spirit is trying to say to you through this card. You may discover something new within the card every time. This happens to me all the time still, even after many years.

Using cards is a wonderful way to begin to develop your own abilities to help you in your daily life and get to know your signs and symbols further along the way. I know for me working with the cards and even reading crystals or stones helped me when I first started.

Tools have been used through the centuries by many and they can potentially help you should you choose this as an option on your learning pathways. A gift of using tools is that those you are reading get to see the imagery that you are interpreting, and can allow for a fuller experience.

There are many books on tarot, crystals, and other sacred tools along with information to help you interpret your own signs and symbols. The possibilities are endless.

I am excited for you to get to open up the door to you being able to reconnect and receive messages from your heavenly loved ones in this way. If I can be a conduit for the spirit world and many others can do it, so can you! You just need to believe in yourself and your abilities.

CHAPTER 37

THE GIFTS WITHIN MEDITATION

THROUGHOUT THE MANY AGES of mankind, one of the main paths for spiritual enlightenment has been meditation. Questions have been asked, such as, what is it? How do you do it? How to shut the mind off? Why should we meditate? And so many others.

Let me tell you this: *You meditate every single day already.* Yes, you read that right and I will talk about how you are doing so shortly. But, first let's talk about what meditation is and isn't, so we are all on the same wavelength.

Meditation is a practice of getting out of one's own way to enter a state of divine union with the highest self or universal energy consciousness. It is through this altered state of mind that one opens up the infinite wisdom that lies within the heart and soul. In this space answers, healing and insights are often brought to your conscious awareness.

Many people think meditation is about shutting off the mind and going silent. This can indeed be the case for some people, but for most, it seems like an impossibility as their mind is constantly active. For these people there are more beneficial ways to help keep the mind quiet as you enter an altered space.

Meditation can heighten your intuitive channels and the ability to sense Spirit around. The path to connecting with Spirit is as varied as there are people on the planet. There is no one set path for all of us.

For some meditation is going for a walk and just breathing in the fresh air, while enjoying the sights along the way. For others going to the gym, yoga, running or doing another form of a more intense body movement allows their mind to get out of the way. Yet, for others, the simple daily things such as listening to music, watching television, cleaning, or just staring into space brings them into the altered conscious state of mind.

Meditation can be thought of as surrendering to the magical place within the spaces between the fabrics of life. It is this place where the suspension of the mind becomes possible and the connection to Spirit can be accessed. It is a place where we transcend time, space and the physical world to enter a stage of the divine union with our highest self, God.

Ultimately, meditation is all this and even more. Meditation is essentially learning to tune out the background noise of everything so we can open up to the higher state of being present. Though this awareness we become more receptive, accepting and at one with our true nature, therefore, the gifts of our soul.

Meditation isn't about stopping our thoughts all together; for some this is accomplished with a daily practice of tuning in. But for most people this isn't a realistic endeavor. When one goes within, it is more about just observing and acknowledging our thoughts rather than giving them more energy.

Put another way, meditation can be like watching clouds in the sky. One knows of them and may even see images that have taking shape in the sky. As this happens they surrender to the flow, become the observer and let the clouds float on by without given them much more energy.

In between, watching those clouds, sometimes there will be a precious jewel of wisdom which gives us clarity or insight on something held within our mind or heart. It is in the space between the clouds where the answers to life's questions are found and your soul is nourished. Meditation will help to heal the grieving heart by opening it up to the soul life force energy.

When entering the state of reflection it is important to do so without expectations. It is best when one opens up the mind and heart to just allow whatever is meant to unfold to happen.

Everyone meditates daily however we often are not aware of the many ways this sacred union with our soul unfolds. We are essentially in a meditative state each day whenever we lose track of time and are focused on a certain task at hand. This could be seen as a form of quiet contemplation as we are really not thinking about anything in particular while accomplishing our daily tasks. I am sure you can think of a few ways you meditate without really ever thinking of it as meditation.

What are your favorite ways to meditate? For me, there are many ways but a few of them are:

- I love connecting to nature. The act of just being present, appreciating the moments, being aware, allowing and at one with the world brings such peace;
- Music is also very meditative for me. When I am allowing the soul song to flow, it brings me into harmony with the softness of the divine.
- Being present with my cat, Indigo as I listen to the sound of her purr as I pet her is healing and enlightening to me.
- Painting, writing or cooking are also all divine connections for me.
- A nice warm bubble bath with candles and soft music in the background is a regular routine here at my home. Not

only does it clean the body but helps clear the etheric bodies, especially when we use sea salt and essential oils.

There are as many ways to meditate as there is breath. The important thing is to allow yourself to flow with the perfect way, here and now, for you.

Mastering the art of meditation is a key to connecting with Spirit. When one is in this relaxed, open and receptive space, we become more aware of the presence of the surrounding energies.

When one is tight, tense or in emotional pain it can be nearly impossible to be aware of the love, which is around us at all times. This is one reason that signs are often missed by those going through transitions and loss when they all they long to hear from their departed loved one. When we are in the heavier states, it is nearly impossible to feel heavens hands on our shoulders as they say to us:

I am here with you. I have found peace and the relief I often sought in life now. Please let go of the burdens you hold, give them over to me, I love and want to help you heal. I want you to be happy.

Meditation can help open us to feeling our loved ones and hearing the messages they offer. Other perks of meditation include feeling more positive, energized, supported, and connected to the divine. With this daily routine of tuning inwardly comes solutions, insights, healing and so many other benefits.

The Divine doesn't really care if you are sitting in some pretzel-like position with your legs crossed unnaturally, fingers held a certain way (mudras), or whatever else you can think of. The Divine just asks that you get comfortable and relax into your breath. You can use guided meditations or just turn into your heartbeat as you slowly breathe deeply, in and out.

If you choose to get into a quiet space to breathe and be present, then that is what is perfect in that moment for you. If your mind is active, just be present with it, and say, thank you for sharing, and then turn back to your breathing. It is as simple as that, eventually the space between will lengthen.

I personally love to mix up my meditation styles to keep things fresh as I can get bored and restless when I don't. One day I may do a slow walking meditation, noticing every step I take as the foot hits the ground; another day, I may dance and tune into the rhythm of the movement; another day I may sit and listen to a guided meditation; or another still may even involve chanting an affirmation or mantra for a length of time. The point is to take time every day to nurture your soul connection.

Meditation can help you move into new wavelengths and vibrations which hold many benefits. Studies have shown that throughout our conscious daily lives we have more active brain wave patterns (Gamma State). It is when we are in deep sleep we hit the slowest brain wave patterns (Delta State). Each state has its own purpose and reason.

Let's talk about these in brief to give you a better understanding of what unfolds when you are conscious throughout the day within your brainwave states. With this awareness, you will understand how meditation could help you and your life.

The Gamma State (31 — 100Hz)

Here is where we are hyperactive and in the active learning mode which helps us to retain information.

Have you ever noticed how when you are taking a class or perhaps at an event, the facilitators have people clapping, or jumping up and down, or dancing around? The reason is that this helps to increase the likelihood of the attendees permanently assimilating the information that is being presented. It helps also to shift the energy of the room as needed. However, over stimulation can lead to anxiety for some.

Gamma waves are associated with higher states of conscious perception typically. This is the frequency where in a relatively small amount of time, large amounts of information are processed.

Benefits of high amounts of gamma activity include having high levels of intelligence, better self-control, increased intuitive abilities and have greater feelings of natural happiness. In this state we are also generally more compassionate beings.

The Beta State (16 — 30Hz)

Most of our days are spent in this space. It is the state of the working or thinking mindset where we are attentive, focused, alert, and engaged in decision making or problem solving. This state is where we are working on goal-oriented tasks or reflecting actively on a particular issue. This includes trying to figure out the funeral details after our loved one dies or our next steps for work, etc...

Depression and anxiety have been linked to the Beta state due being in-a-rut or rut-like thinking cycle. Insomnia can be a cause of the abundance of Beta brainwave activity. This is the state that handles the flight or fight response.

It is rare that when we enter a meditation space that our brainwaves function in either the gamma or beta states. However, there are active forms of meditation when this has rarely unfolded.

The Alpha State (8 — 15Hz)

Here our brain waves slow down and we start leaving the thinking mind. We feel calmer, peaceful, centered and grounded in this space. We enter the alpha state when we are daydreaming or begin to consciously practice meditation or mindfulness.

Think of the feeling one often has after taking a walk in the woods, gardening or doing light housework. It is the feeling we often have after a yoga class, or after any activity which helps us to relax the body and mind. I am sure you have a better sense of being in the Alpha state if you have ever had this feeling now.

The Alpha state is when we are reflective, lucid and yet in a slightly diffused awareness. The right and left hemispheres of the brain are balanced or in-sync with each other. We are more able to remember our dreams and meditative states.

With regular practice of entering the Alpha space, people have found that they have reduced their stress, anxiety, or even the state of depression. They have lower blood pressure and reduced their chronic pain. They also have experienced an increase in motivation, happiness and energy overall. Who wouldn't want to experience these side effects?

The Theta State (4 — 7Hz)

Here is where we truly begin meditation; this is the point where our mind shifts from being verbal to being more visual in nature.

Being in the deeper Theta state of awareness allows us to strengthen our intuition and become in touch with the wholeness of our being. When we are in Theta it can help us to solve the more complicated problems that life can throw at us. We move out of the head and into the heart when we practice getting to this space regularly.

When we are relaxing for sleep we will enter Theta regularly. It is very much like that drowsy space that comes before the final curtain call of sleep each night. This is a part of the reason many of us tend to find our intuitive abilities more active at this time. It is also why we may have our greatest brainstorms, insights or answers come forth during this time.

Benefits include increased inner peace and emotional stability. One who is in deep relaxation will have improved memory, feel more inspired and have a deeper spiritual connection and heightened intuition. Another benefit is being able to fall asleep quicker and have a more restful sleep; reduced mental fatigue. All these benefits and more allow for quicker healing to take place. Many of the benefits from the alpha state are also experienced in the theta state.

The Delta State (.1 to 3 Hz)

These are the slowest brain waves. We normally enter this stage during our deepest part of dreamless sleep. These waves are very helpful to the body to help with the healing and repairing of itself.

Tibetan Monks, who have been meditating for decades have reached this space during their alert and wakened state. Have you ever noticed how those that have practiced meditation for decades, such as monks, have a higher level of empathy, understanding and compassion for others? Entering this state has been one of the main reasons for this.

For the average person, the Delta stage is the final state during sleep when we move out of the body, mind and emotion and into a true space of Spirit. The Delta is where the deepest relaxation, healing and connection to sprit and the subconscious mind can take place.

One would benefit experiencing the various states of brainwave active to truly know how the state of mind affects the overall state of being. My purpose in sharing this information was to reveal some basics of what is happening in your mind throughout your day. By knowing this, you will also understand what is happening when you begin an active meditation practice regularly.

Over the years many people have found that they could tune into these brain wave states through meditation music. I too have found there are many wonderful composers out there that have utilized the latest technologies to support our meditation space. You could spend hundreds of dollars or hours researching to try to find the best meditation music, if you wanted. But, I have found that the best music is one that brings you a calm, relaxed and peaceful place. For me, I find nature sounds mixed with gentle instrumental music works best.

Remember you are already meditating in your life and so you probably have music in your collection already that will work. Or you could just open up the window to let nature's harmony be your inspiration. I am sure you have ideas already which are a great place to start.

In fact, I encourage you to begin to practice noticing your breathing throughout your daily routines. Make a conscious effort to take a few deep breaths, in and out, as you tune in during whatever you are doing. This will help you in being open and inspired throughout the day. It will also connect you deeper to your soul. We all would benefit from doing this more in life, wouldn't you agree?

Breathing is a natural thing we do while alive and yet many of us do not breathe deeply enough. Breathing can be healing for us. It opens us up to the inspiration that comes from Spirit which can help us in our daily lives in a variety of ways.

When I am with clients, Spirit will often remind them to breathe and breathe in deep. For some have literally stopped breathing, for a moment or two and this reminder causes them to take a breath. Make today the day you bring in the power of your breath into your life and start a daily conscious meditation practice.

Now who is ready to meditate? Below you will find a very short meditation which you can do anywhere and whenever you have a few minutes.

Breathing Meditation

This meditation can be as short as 5 minutes or as long as 1 hour. This can be the perfect meditation whenever you have a few minutes of time; such as when you are at work on a break.

The Gift Within the Darkness

Sit comfortably with your hands on your thighs or even on your heart. Take a moment to breathe in deeply and relax into the chair closing your eyes as you do so.

Now I would like you to focus on the top of your head. Imagine the beautiful sun shining down upon you and filling you with its light. Imagine this light pushing out all the heaviness and darkness out of your complete being with every breath you take. As you breathe outwardly, imagine letting go all which no longer serves you through the soles of your feet and breathe in more light.

Cycle through each of the colors of the rainbow with each breathe in and out: Breathing in red, orange, yellow, green, blues, indigo, purple and finally the brightest white heavenly light. Feeling yourself calmer, more focused and connected as you breathe with all of heaven meditating by your side.

Let go of all the day's events. Letting go all your worries, your fears and everything that has weighed you down.

Now allow yourself to breathe in divine light, wisdom, guidance, insight and healing. Allowing yourself to breathe in safety, security, support and the knowledge that all is well and taken care of. With every breath know everything is unfolding as according to the divine plan and know everything will work out somehow in a beautiful way.

Visualizing the beautiful light cycling through you from above your head and throughout your body all the way down into mother earth.

Now visualize the earth's light cycling back up through the soles of the feet, through your body to the heavens above.

Continue for as long as you wish to and then close the meditation with a moment of gratitude for all the divine blessings in your life. Open your eyes when you are ready to continue onward with your day.

CHAPTER 38

THE GIFTS WITHIN MOURNING PAGES

MEDITATION IS ABOUT TUNING within to connect with your heart and soul. As you now have discovered there are many ways do to so.

When we are grieving or going through a transition, we tend to want to turn away or resist the part of ourselves wanting to be heard. Our emotions and how we are really feeling needs to be listened to. We need to dive below the superficial surface so that we connect to the deeper feelings. These deeper emotions can be scary for many to open up to. This is because if we give ourselves permission to go there, we could turn on the water works and never shut the valve off again.

I know all too well what that feels like, having experienced many transitions and grief in my life. I, too wanted to run and hide and at my mother's funeral, I did just that. I hid how I was feeling away from those also hurting and didn't even let myself truly cry. I found an out of the way bathroom, locked the door and stared into my eyes, to regain my composure. When that didn't work, I went outside to get away from everyone. I could only do this for so long before having to return to the funeral.

However, after the funeral, I could turn to my old friend, food to stuff my emotions down.

It took many years for me to understand I had been not facing the truth of my emotions and how I felt within about many things. This wasn't just about my mom's death. It was also my father leaving, moving homes, changing schools, friendships ending and so many other deaths.

If you are like me, you may do the same thing and not even realize it. The following tool is a technique that my guides inspired me to use regularly and I have given to clients over the years. Mourning pages helps us to heal, process what is lurking under the surface and connect to the soul level.

The Process

Every day, I would like you to carve out much needed self-care time into your schedule. Make this an appointment that is unbreakable. After all, you owe it to yourself. It need not be long, it can be as little as 10 minutes or as long as 30 minutes. The most important thing is that you follow through with your scheduled appointment.

Grab a pen and paper (or a journal); no computers for this exercise. The act of writing via the hand helps you to get in touch deeper and be present in the experience. Computers will often leave us not fully present or connected to the energy.

If you wish, set a timer so that you know when your allotted time is up. Though don't let this stop you from continue to write once you get in the zone if you have the extra time available.

Now I will make this as simple as possible. You are now to just start writing whatever you are feeling! If you are feeling nothing, write: I am feeling nothing. If you are feeling confused, write: I am confused. And you keep writing whatever you are feeling in the moments as the pen moves across the pages.

You may feel one way as you begin and end up feeling something else as the pen continues to share what is going on within you. You are connecting with the truth of your emotions under the surface, which is the point of this exercise. You are allowing yourself to just feel and write; no thinking or overanalyzing here.

You can use this exercise to help you get in touch with your feelings about anything; not just the loss of your loved ones. It can aid you in revealing how you feel about your job, home, yourself and so much more.

After losing my mom, I went through a couple years of eating myself to death. I ran away from living life to the fullest, hiding out in my apartment away from the wold. By the time I connected with the heart, I felt hate for myself which led me to some of my darkest moments. But, this exercise was a gift in the darkness that helped me to connect to my heart and start the process of healing and learning to connect with Spirit.

Through writing about how I felt about everything, a shift began. Some days the writing was light and other days I was writing like a madman that was pissed with the world. And you know what I was in those moments. Not because of a situation or anyone. But, because I was mad at myself for not letting myself feel and know myself on a deeper level; for not allowing myself to feel and live my truth.

However, as I opened the floodgates, I felt lighter and lighter, and this translated into weight loss as well. Within the year I had shed 200lbs of pain and found myself once again. I felt happier and alive. But was I done?

Not at all, there were other levels that needed to be gotten to, and this was where the mourning pages came in. Writing was always something that came natural to me in life, so it made sense that Spirit would have me process my feelings at a core level in this way. It is through these pages, I began to get connected to

Spirit and found myself opening my mediumship abilities along the way.

I will say there were challenging days to sit there and write my feelings out. Other days I did everything but sit and write. However, in the end that only added to my emotions of guilt or anger towards myself. This was because of not having the integrity to follow through with my commitment to heal and understand what was going on within myself. No one else could do it for me; but here I was not doing it for myself.

I had to find a reason which was stronger than any excuse I could come up with to keep my commitment. Once I did, I then put sticky notes to remind me of why I had started and why I was doing the mourning pages to keep me focused in prominent locations where I would see them.

I encourage you to do the same as it will only help your goal of healing your heart and regaining your life! Remember your loved ones want you to be happy and engaged in living life to the fullest in their memory. This will make them so happy when you are doing so. But only you can make the choice.

Through completing this exercise daily, I moved from the deep levels of grief I was feeling to a place of happiness once again. Mourning pages changed my life for the better and I know they will help you too.

As you take time to write your mourning pages, you will discover precious diamonds throughout the words. These diamonds are words and wisdom shared from the spiritual realm as you move through your feelings to the center of your heart.

Mourning pages can truly be a form of meditation that brings you into a deeper connection with your spiritual support crew and departed loved ones. I know that this is just one tool that helped open up my relationship with Spirit and continues to bless many others along the way.

CHAPTER 39

THE GIFTS WITHIN YOUR ENERGY CENTERS

THE WORD CHAKRA IS Sanskrit which means wheel or disk. When it comes to yoga, energy work, meditation and mediumship the term refers to the main energy centers of the body. These each have a profound impact on our body, mind, spirit and emotions, but also in our life.

It is important for us to know about the seven main chakras as we will work with them as a part of the reconnection process. There are many more chakras but for our purposes we will stick with the basics. I know many people will be familiar with these energy centers, but I wanted to talk about them briefly for those who are not aware of them. Also, I will share a little on how grief may affect each of them.

The chakra system is connected to the energy of the rainbow with each chakra having its own vibration and color. However, I wish to point out that just because we are focused on each of the centers separately, in truth, there is no beginning or end to them. Just like life and the rainbow, one vibration flows into the next, even if we don't fully see or understand how.

As you read through the following information put yourself into the energy of the chakra by breathing in and out the color associated with it. This will help to bring in the healing, clearing and balancing required for your energy center.

Root Chakra

The first main energy center is located at the base of the spine and is called the *Base or Root Chakra*. Represented by the color Red, it is connected with the energy of *Safety, Security and Stability*.

This chakra relates to the physical or material level of life; this is also where we store our fears, worries and concerns. This is the energy center involving trust, courage, strength, acceptance and the ability to focus, feel grounded and centered. Many of our beliefs we learned growing up or took on from our parents, society or foundational life experiences are held here.

When this center is out of balance, blocked or disconnected in any way, you will notice that you will often have lower back issues. This can happen when our reoccurring thoughts are in fear or worry around the topics of money, finances, career and more. The death of someone, or something important, can have a major impact on our lives and leave us literally fighting for survival on an energetic level. By reconnecting to our traditions and ancestors, this can be empowering for us to both heal and recognize death as a powerful tool to help make the grief experience less isolating.

Some affirmations you could use to aid this chakra in maintaining or returning to balance are:

- I am safe, secure, loved and supported, at all times and in all ways.
- I am prosperous and abundant, in known and unknown ways.
- I am connected and supported by the universe always.

- I am grounded, centered and rooted in my true nature.
- I nurture my body's needs and requirements.
- All is well, taken care of and happening exactly as it is meant to according to divine will.

Sacral Chakra

The next energy center is known as the Sacral Chakra and its color is orange. This chakra is located between your naval and genitals. It is connected to your *creativity, sexuality, relationships, desires, and emotions.*

This energy center is also affected when we are hard on ourselves, suffer from shame, guilt, blame, grief or another old emotion tied to the past. We store all these emotions and beliefs in this center.

When this chakra is out of alignment, we can have lower to middle back problems. When we feel unsupported in our relationships and are constantly thinking such thoughts, it will manifest in the body, sooner or later.

Uterine and bladder issues, sexual problems, impotence, weight issues, lack of flexibility, sciatica, and problems with our intestines are a sure sign this center needs work.

Death represents a change in the relationship, not the end. Many times we can have unfinished business with our loved ones which need healing. This can be accomplished through prayer, meditations, journaling, or even consulting a medium.

Whatever your choice, it is important to find a way to process your emotions related to your loved ones and redefine this relationship. The longer one puts aside dealing with the emotions or unfinished business, the longer one is stuck in the stages of grief. The tools in this section of the book can all help you heal.

Affirmations to help balance this chakra are:

- I am a creative soul who is well supported.

- I am creative and allow my creativity to be expressed.
- I am in the flow of the universe energy of life.
- My relationships are now loving, supportive, healthy and balanced.
- I am nourished, nurturing and blessed.
- I am balanced.

Solar Plexus Chakra

The third chakra is known as the *Solar Plexus or Power Center* and is located above the naval just below the ribcage. The color associated here is yellow and this center is tied into the emotional energy system. This is where *our power and intuitive gifts are centered*. Connected here is an etheric cord from the body to the soul (much like the umbilical cord of a baby).

When we were in our mother's womb our soul comes and goes freely, through this silver cord, between the physical body and spiritual level. This is why many mothers feel their baby moving as the soul is often getting adjusted to the physical body slowly. But, once the soul is born and the umbilical cord is severed, a part of us now realizes that we are tied also tethered to the earth. When the baby realizes what has transpired it begins to kick and scream not happy they aren't as free as they were as the soul. Babies are connected and very much aware of who we are as Spirit.

When this chakra is aligned and in balance, we are very much able to stand fully in our power with a fair amount of ease. We have a healthy digestive system, are self-confident, have strong willpower, understanding and radiant joy, energy and vitality.

Blocks with this chakra can cause a fear of rejection, oversensitivity to criticism, the need to exert power over others and one to be hot tempered. Even blame, judgemental behaviors or a fear of change can cause this energy center to become out of balance or blocked. Feelings of a lack of recognition, low self-esteem, addictions, nervousness, anxiety and stomach, food or digestion issues may arise when this center is out of balance.

This chakra is where we learn self-empowerment and is where our self-respect and integrity lies. This is where we define our core self with others and with the relationship with ourselves.

Mourning the loss of our loved ones or our experiences, leaves us also mourning the loss of the relationship we had with the deceased. In the early stages of our grieving process, we tend to define our new roles as widow, widower or orphan or one of the several other labels. This is natural, but if we hold on to this new label for too long, we can lose a part of our identity and self. This is one reason it is important after losing a loved one to take inventory regarding one's sense of purpose and goals. This can be as simple as returning to our lives and remember what we enjoy about it, such as what television shows or foods we like. Remember your loved ones want you to be happy and move on with life, not get stuck in grief.

Your affirmations to support this chakra center are:

- I love and accept myself fully.
- I lovingly stand in my Divine power and truth at all times.
- It is safe for me to be powerful.
- I now breathe in my full power & energy as a divine creator of the universe.
- My true nature shines and radiates through me always.

Heart Chakra

In the center of your chest is your *Heart Chakra*. This chakra is the center about *love, compassion, forgiveness, understanding, harmony, generosity and acceptance.* This chakra is also the center of both the upper and lower chakras. Therefore this center helps you to be in balance with the heaven and earth energies flowing through you.

The color normally associated in the rainbow is green, but I like to think of it as a nice watermelon blend of greens and pink. After all, we do associate pink with love and love is the energy of the heart.

This is the highest of the emotional chakras. The sacral chakra being the lowest and the solar plexus being the middle emotional chakra. To fully be in the center of the heart, the energy must be able to travel freely to the upper and lower centers through the heart. It is when this is happening we can truly live and come from the heart.

When this chakra is imbalanced or blocked one can suffer from heart issues, possessiveness, be jealous, filled with resentments or anger and have unbalanced relationships. Just to name a few examples.

One cannot fully love themselves if their heart is filled with any old emotions or blocked in any way from experiences of the past. One must first forgive and let the old, worn out and what no longer serves go in order to move forward. It is then the heart can be filled with the soul love which has the power to heal and perform miracles in our lives. We cannot love, accept and honor another fully, until we can fully love, accept and honor ourselves.

People who have had heart attacks usually suffered or had a blocked heart chakra which needed to be opened. Those that have died due to heart failure or heart attacks usually have completed their life lessons and mission. They are now moving to the next level to continue to evolve as a soul.

Losing someone or something to death and holding onto the old emotions does not serve us in any way, shape or form. If you had issues with the loved one when they died, it is important to find a way to forgive them to set yourself free. Forgiveness is never about the other person or the act that unfolded, it about healing the part of ourselves that is in pain. Why not take the time to allow yourself to process your grief by loving so much to forgive where required today? If not today, at least become willing to let unforgiveness go today.

Love is always the answer and the healer on our journeys. Grief is always caused by the love we have for the departed; therefore, grief can be healed by love.

It is also possible to have a heart that is so wide open it leaves us vulnerable to attracting relationships which are not healthy. This could include relationships which take advantage of our kindness and drain our energies at the same time.

Those with hearts too wide opened tend to want to help fix or heal others. This is often because their soul purpose is that of a healer. This can also lead to being resentful of always being the giver in relationships and not being appreciated for their generosity.

Remember the heart chakra is the center of balance. Therefore, if we tend to give out more than we allow ourselves to receive, we can also get into trouble financially. It is equally important to give back to ourselves and allow ourselves to receive the gifts that the universe wishes to give us. Otherwise, eventually we will find ourselves laying on our back learning to receive in another way. Today, make a concentrated effort to make sure you are giving to yourself as freely as you give to others at all times. Remember balance is key in everything.

The affirmations for this chakra would be:

- I am a channel for divine love and light.
- My heart is aligned and balanced with heaven and earth. All is well and flows with ease.
- I fill my body with love and I am loved.
- I forgive everyone, including myself knowing we are all worthy of being loved.
- I love and accept myself fully.
- I am surrounded by love and light at all times.

When you want to feel more, focus on your sacral, solar plexus and heart centers to open and expand them wider. Remember these chakras work in harmony and are the center of your emotions. If you want to feel less adjust them smaller.

Throat Chakra

Next up is our *Throat Chakra* and the color associated with it is sky blue. As you can imagine, this is the *center of expression and communication*; this can be through writing, speaking, painting and many other forms of self-expression. This chakra is deeply connected with the lesser known or spoken about chakras of the ears and is also responsible for our ability to communicate with spirit.

This chakra is connected to listening, wisdom, truth, freedom, independence, inspiration, choice, and our ability to create our life on path and purpose with the soul. Manifestation begins in the mind and gets expressed through this chakra.

We all have the right to speak our truth and to be heard, however, it is also important we only express what is it that both empowers and is aligned with what we truly wish.

Example: If you want today to be a warm and sunny day, then ask for that, rather than saying, I hope it doesn't rain today. Words are very powerful and the universe hears everything you are expressing in body, mind, soul and emotion. Let's make sure everything is lining up with what you truly desire.

Blocks with this chakra can lead to people having problems such as ear infections, weariness, thyroid issues, disorders of the throat, and neck or cervical spine problems. This also includes laryngitis and hypothalamus or esophagus problems.

As you can see, blocks will make it difficult to communicate. This is because we are feeling suppressed by our swallowed emotions and feelings. The voice may seem weak when the feelings are unclear, garbled and need to be expressed. Go out into nature and release at the top of your lungs.

It is important to maintain integrity between what you are thinking and feeling. This is because the throat plays an important part in transmitting the information between the head and the heart. One must make sure their heart and head are going in the same direction to keep the information highway of the throat clear.

When we are going through grief, our throat chakra can sometimes end up being underactive. This is especially the case when we are compromising the way we are feeling by holding in our emotions or desires within. When we are grieving, sometimes, we don't even know what our own truths are and often expect others to anticipate our moods or desires.

It is important that we don't get caught up in the trap of becoming a victim of our loss. By expressing gratitude for the gifts the departed brought into our lives we can become aware when we may be sliding into victimhood. Reacting to the loss and playing the victim does not come from a place of truth. It may garner sympathy or attention, but it will definitely not help us heal. Gratitude in itself does not mean we are glad the person is dead, but, rather that we are grateful for the influence they had in the experiences of life. When we are grateful it allows us to move into the opportunities for growth and grace presented by the loss.

The way we express what we are feeling through this experience is important, but, this must be done in a way which is filled with truth and integrity. We can do so through speaking with the person's highest self when we have something which needs to be said to them. Or we can find another way to get what we are holding in off your chest in a verbal, written or emotionally honest way. It is in expressing our truth that we can keep processing and moving forward without getting stuck in our grief.

Holding onto the way we feel is not doing anyone any good, especially ourselves. It does not allow ourselves to be open and honest with ourselves or the world.

When we are grieving, we don't always take the time to check in on how we are feeling. We are reacting most of the time due to past experiences with death or even the day before events. It is important to check in when we are processing and express whatever we need to, no matter how small. Healing can happen in very subtle ways.

> Iyanla Vanzant once said: *"When you stand and share your story in an empowering way, your story will heal you and your story will heal someone else."*

I agree with her as through the sharing of your story you can begin to get in touch with your truth and therefore heal. It can sometimes be scary to start this process as we all have fears of being judged or ridiculed. But, I can tell you this, it is freeing to let yourself express your story. Writing this book was scary for me but I can tell you it truly brought forth insights and healing I didn't even know I was needing. So get out your journal and begin speaking your emotions.

The affirmations for the throat chakra are:

- It is safe for me to express myself in all ways.
- I communicate my truth clearly, easily and effectively at all times.
- I am in touch with my truth within my heart and soul.
- I now allow my truth to be freely expressed with gratitude.
- I allow my divine communication channels to be fully opened.
- I am able to communicate the messages of my soul and spirit.
- I easily manifest my highest good.

When you want to hear the voice of Spirit louder, focus on expanding your throat and ear chakras fully. This will increase your sensitivity to all communications. Therefore, you may find it overpowering to leave them fully open at all times so you may need to turn down the volume of these centers at times.

Third Eye Chakra

The next chakra is located between your two physical eyes and is known as the *Third Eye*. This is the chakra of *vision, insight and wisdom*; it is also the chakra most people want to develop so they have the ability to see the future or spiritual realms. The rainbow color associated to this energy center is royal indigo blue.

Our spiritual eye seeks to see and know the truth of all things. It helps us with our ability to see across time and space, but also to look at the world from all aspects of self. A healthy third eye will give us the ability to see the bigger picture. This helps us come from a higher place when dealing with the physical world. This insight gives us the ability to see a part of us in all of creation as a reflection of the inner self. It is this which allows us to accept it as our own, heal, bless and love all as appropriate.

Our spiritual eyes or clairvoyance is fully opened during our dream state as we are not fearful of seeing the truth or spirit. This is why people have very vivid dreams and have visitations with spirit in them. Dreams are when most people grieving can connect with their loved ones. The emotions are not in the way to block the awareness of the heavenly realms in the dream state.

Our sleeping state is also a time when we can leave our physical body to travel to spirit. It is here we learn, teach, heal and prepare for the next phases of the journey. Upon returning to the physical plane, we will often end up having déjà vu experiences as we follow the path of the soul. This is because you have as your soul essence traveled to the future and lived it already.

Having remembrances of having been somewhere, met or done something before is a sure sign you are on the right path. Keep listening and following the guidance of your soul.

Imbalances or blocks in this chakra can cause us to become delusional, unimaginative or be indifferent. We can have poor memories, be spaced out, have poor concentration, not be able to see and not be able to see the bigger picture. We may have problems accessing insights or wisdom from Spirit, have headaches, eye problems, and pituitary or pineal gland problems. All of these and even neurological problems can all be connected to an energetic block in this energy center.

Even though someone may be going through grief at the time, it is through our third eye we can begin to experience a sense of peace. This is true even if our grieving is not complete. Wisdom is not emotional, and this chakra is a part of the accumulation of knowledge and experience. Remember the emotions related to our life experiences are processed in the lower chakras.

Through our gift of our intuitive abilities we can tune-in to process messages and signs from the departed loved ones. We first must be willing to expand our understanding beyond our personal physical experiences. We do this by examining and releasing the beliefs that no longer serve our highest good and/or are blocking or limiting us in some manner.

When we can honestly look at where our beliefs have played a role in our lives, we can recognize what may not be working or serving us further. It is here we can set our self-free. We can see what has helped to shape us, in both a positive or negative way, to be the person we have become in life. Once we have this information, we can make necessary changes to support our happiness, joy and life path ahead. We must remember to forgive, as and wherever required, as we move continue to forward with grace.

Affirmations to support this chakra center are:

- I look and see through the eyes of love.
- I am able to clearly see, across time and space, what is real and true.
- I am in tune with my highest self and the bigger picture.
- I follow the path that is clearly laid out in front of me.
- I am a gifted clairvoyant who follows my intuition to create my life on path and purpose.
- I see the signs and messages of spirit with ease.

When you want to see Spirit clearer, focus on expanding your third eye center. This will increase your sensitivity to see spirits energy when you are ready. Like all other centers you can adjust the sensitivity of this chakra at will in either direction.

Crown Chakra

The last chakra is located at the top of your head and is called the *Crown Chakra*. This is your spiritual chakra and is *our direct connection with God, Universe, Source, Divine or whatever name you wish to give the highest self*. The color associated within the rainbow to this chakra is purple.

Much like our root chakra connects us to the earth, our crown connects us to our spiritual essence. This chakra plays an important role in connecting us to the energy of all that is. We must have clear, balanced and opened chakras from the top of our head to the bottom of our feet as this allows us to maximize the energy flowing through us and into our lives.

This chakra is where we are inspired by the Divine because of the strong connection to the power greater than ourselves. This chakra is connected with universal consciousness, enlightenment, faith, spirituality, bliss, divine wisdom, integration or unity with the omnipresent being of love. This center can help us live more in the present and in harmony with the divine will, both spiritually and physically.

The Gift Within the Darkness

I often speak with clients of a funnel being located above our heads. When we are not as open as we can be to receiving or are blocked, the energy will flow much slower as it works its way through the funnel.

Can you imagine trying to pour bread dough through a funnel? You need to have a funnel that is much wider at the bottom for it to be able to make it through. The same with your heavenly good; if the funnel isn't as open as it could be it slows the manifestation energy down in our lives.

So it is imperative to be open to receiving and allowing source energy to flow freely through us. If not, this chakra could become blocked or out of alignment. When this happens confusion, depression, senility, fear of success or lack of inspiration could take hold.

When this chakra is not allowing the energy to flow freely through them in either direction, it could lead to a disconnection from source energy. Spiritual addictions or over-intellectualizing can even occur.

When the crown center is blocked or disconnected from source one could manifest migraines, brain tumors, have amnesia or develop mental health issues. Nervousness and muscular system disorders can also be symptoms this chakra needs healing support.

After the death of a loved one, we often struggle with expressing our grief in a variety of manners as you learned throughout this book. Death can have a profound impact on this chakra as you can imagine. However, prayer and meditation are very supportive in aiding this chakra in returning to a balanced and open state after loss.

Remember, the gift in the darkness is not denying the sadness or pain, but to acknowledge it and keep moving forward. Walk through the shadows of the dark knowing there is a reason for it all. The reason we may not fully understand or know yet, but it is to serve us and the bigger picture in a meaningful way. In time, we will understand this once we get through the difficult period and can see the light once again that has always been shining.

One gift of loss is the unexpected finding of our life purpose and reason for being on the earth. We begin to transcend the physical. This is done by shifting from the perspective that we are a human being having a spiritual experience to the true perspective that we are a soul having a human experience. We also begin to understand we made a choice to be here to serve the planet in a meaningful way, each day. This is done through sharing and expanding the energy of love.

Those who are courageous to face their darkness and the pain of grief can process and often find their pain is transformative. It is these people that will often have a deeper understanding of their life purpose. The energy of processing and moving past their grief allows their relationship with the Divine to be more authentic.

One begins to find meaning and greater compassion through their suffering. This leads them to see and experience gratitude for the gifts contained within. With this comes a greater feeling of happiness, lightness and joy in their everyday experiences. The fear of death and dying no longer becomes them as they have risen above the pain and into the light of the gift. The crown chakra awakening assists us with all this.

Affirmations for this chakra are:

- I am now conscious, aware and understand my life purpose.
- I take steps to joyfully move forward to achieve all I am meant to along the path of my life mission.
- I am deeply connected to my highest self.
- I trust, have faith, let go, listen and follow the guidance of my soul.

- I am wise, learn and know through my connection with my soul.
- I am in total happiness, in harmony and one with the Divine. All is well.

Chakra Healing

It is highly recommended to take time each day to work with your chakra system. This will be helpful for your own healing and the improvement of your life. Don't wait until you're your system or life is out of balance to begin your journey.

Start simple and perhaps check in with one chakra each day and by the end of the week you will have completed one cycle. When you can dedicate a little more time, then you can add another chakra and another until you are doing a quick check in each day.

Start with doing a check in each morning or evening with your energy centers so you can do any clearing or balancing as required. It really doesn't take long once you get into a routine. Just take a moment to visualize one chakra and then see yourself using a polishing cloth to clear and balance it. Keep it short and simple.

If you notice a darker area or it looks ragged or something weird, take a few moments to go deeper into the area. Ask questions to get more clarity and information about this abnormality. Let me give you a couple to start you out:

- • ____ Chakra, what are you trying to tell me?
- • What do you need to balance your energy?
- • What emotions or pain are you holding here?
- • How can I serve you?

Awareness is often the first step along the path of healing and enlightenment. Allow yourself to have an open and honest conversation with your energy centers. They hold great power and blessings which can aid you in your life journey.

You must follow through with whatever guidance you are receiving to help balance them. You can't just read a book and expect to be an expert on the subject, you need to put in the work and master it! The same can be true with the chakra balancing. In order to yield great benefits from it in your life, you must work with the system regularly.

Remember grief can be held in any area of the body. It is not just held within the main chakras that we have spoken of and are working with here. It therefore is important to scan your whole body to see where things are being stored, especially when it comes to holding the old pain or emotions and grief. This is important for your journey on the earth and to allowing yourself to be free to be happy in every cell of your being. When you can clear out the old, it allows room for more love to flow. Remember, *love is the basis of who we are.*

Once you have checked-in with each of the chakras, dust busting and polishing them take a moment to visualize them all in harmony and the same size, from head to toe. This will aid you in bringing them into balance with each other.

One area in particular many people hold energy that isn't their own is in the areas of the upper shoulders and neck. I know for myself, I have this problem during or after sessions at times. Like everyone, I sometimes neglect my energy needs due to life demands. But thankfully this is improving as I master my energy and do a check-in daily. Make your self-care a non-negotiable appointment with yourself. You deserve it as much as the next person.

When we take on other's energy and responsibilities, it can lead to our neck and shoulders feeling tense, sore and like the world is weighing us down. This is something that often happens unconsciously when we worry about others or what they are going through. It can even happen when we are jumping in to try to help them with their problems. Remember this is their job, not yours. You can be there to support them, but you need not own their crap. You have enough of your own, don't you think?

Let's take a few moments here and now to breathe out the energy of others. Now, as you breathe in, call your own personal energy and power back from the world now. Continue doing this for a moment or two.

Some people can have problems letting go of the energy knowing it is being returned to someone who is having a hard time. In this case, ask that it is transmuted back to love and returned to source with blessings of loving light. In this way, you are being of service for you both. After all, you owe it to yourself, and to them.

Make it a habit to do this nightly as you lay down ready for sleep. Sending love and light at the same time to all the world and to yourself. Especially during times that are troubling and dark such as when one is grieving.

Awareness is Key

As I have said before, awareness is the first step. Therefore, becoming aware of your chakra system is a great aid in helping you to recognize how your daily emotions and experiences are affecting you.

Everything is vibration and frequency. Your chakras are no different and is one of the reasons for the connection to the rainbow. Everything whether color, music or even the totality of you is vibration and frequency.

If you want harmony in your life, you must begin with bringing balancing back within you. Only you hold the power. However, you don't need to do it alone and if you need assistance with this there are people, like myself, who can help align, balance and even connect you to your soul and the heavenly realms. This can assist you with healing, enlightenment and moving forward in your life.

When we look within our energy systems to be aware of our emotions and connections, we begin to feel more empowered. This helps us to gain a better understanding of our life and the energies which have affected it. After all, who wants a death from when you were in your mother's womb still affecting you forty some years later? Isn't it time to take charge and heal your emotions of grief from that period? Is it not time for you to be happy and free to live a fearless life? I think so and so do your heavenly friends and family. You are worthy of such a life, I promise you.

A simple event may have not affected you directly, but it definitely has a profound effect on your energy systems in other ways. It often does so by triggering old energy you have stored within in relationship to some life experience including loss. You certainly don't need grief in its various disguises causing you to live a life in fear or darkness in any way.

Take time each day to look for and find the gifts in all your experiences. This will help your soul light you up from within. It is through this you will be healed and blessed with freedom in heavenly ways.

> *Grief is like a vice grip holding you stuck in a way that no longer serves you. The gift within grieving is not salvaging what is left of someone but to find a new meaning to the relationship with your loved one who has transitioned. Allow yourself to move forward with meaning and with a sense of purpose in love and light.*

Old emotions have a way of reinventing themselves and disguising themselves in our lives, as you have learned throughout this book. They are complex and ever changing as anyone who has every suffered a loss can attest. You just never know when it may come up to the surface by some trigger in life. Do your daily check-ins with your energy bodies. This way you will be in much more control to keep them from raging through your life like a fire caught up in the wind.

Yoga, Exercise, Prayer, Meditation and Energy work, such as Reiki, can all lend a helping hand in assisting you to be empowered, balanced, and connected. They are all powerful alternatives to help connect to your soul energies and heal your grieving heart. In turn, they can help you with your own personal goals for living life.

Find what works for you and know it is a strength to reach out for support when you need it the most along the pathways of life. You were not put on this earth to do it alone; you were born unto a world with many who can understand and get where you are at. After all, we are more similar and alike than one knows at first glance. Everyone's private stories have all been touched by death and the grief that follows at some point. Make today the day that you reach out and connect with others.

As you clear and work with your energy centers and the techniques within this book, I truly know that you too can have a meaningful and deep connection with your heavenly support system.

With enough time, energy and focus on getting to know yourself as an energy system you will access and learn through the universal library that is the divine soul. You will therefore have a deeper connection and understanding of who you are, why you are here and your intuitive guidance system.

Continue to make time for your self-care and to dedicate a few minutes each day to checking-in, clearing, balancing and running the energy through your chakra system. You and your life will be better for it.

If you wish to continue to learn about chakras, the internet, local library and bookstores are a great resource to start with.

CHAPTER 40

THE RE-CONNECTION PROCESS

It is a good idea to practice the previous chapters as a way to prepare yourself for this process. The more you heal and are familiar with the techniques the better your chances of reconnecting with your loved ones.

PUT ASIDE 30 MINUTES or more where you won't be disturbed for this reconnection process. Shut off your phones and find yourself a comfortable location where you can sit upright with your feet flat on the floor.

Let us now call upon your angels, guides, and heavenly loved ones. We call upon and ask Archangel Michael to watch over you and to keep you safe throughout this reconnection process with your loved ones.

Close your eyes and imagine your feet sinking deep into the ground; like strong roots of a tree. Take three very deep breaths, in and out. Allowing yourself to come back to center after each breath.

The Gift Within the Darkness

Next as you breathe in, feel yourself pulling the energy of the earth up into your legs and up into your body. Affirming: *I am grounded and centered in my soul.*

As you breathe out, let go of all the energy of the day, the week, the month and all the years since the incarnation of your soul. Keeping what is real and true; which is the divine love, divine light, the wisdom, energy and wholeness of your soul. Do this for the next moment or two.

Now, imagine that deep in the center of the earth there is a beautiful white liquid light and allow yourself to breathe in this nurturing energy. Breathe this healing energy up your legs to the base of your spine. Allow it to fill your ruby red root chakra.

Feel this chakra being healed, cleared and balanced as you breathe deeply and affirm: *I am safe, secure and supported.*

Doing so for the next moment.

Allow yourself to breathe, in and out, as the energy continues to move up your body to your sacral chakra.

Allow this beautiful light energy to purify, heal and balance your orange energy center. Let your natural creativity awaken and flourish as you continue to breathe and affirm: *I am naturally creative.*

As this divine energy fills your chakras with this liquid white light begin to feel yourself connecting to the energy of your soul.

Now allow yourself to breathe in the golden color of yellow as the energy continues to move up and into your solar plexus. Feel this energy center being empowered, healed and balanced with soulful energy.

Continuing to breathe deeply, in and out, as you affirm: *I am powerful soul.*

Imagine the energy expanding and filling your body as you breathe, in and out.

Now see and feel the liquid light moving into your heart center. Let it fill your green heart chakra with vibrant pulsating light. Feel your heart being healed, balanced, opened and connected to the energy of your soul.

Feel the presence of divine love and light enveloping you now. Embrace this loving energy as you invite love in while breathing and affirm: *I am love. I love. I am loved.*

Take a moment to breathe and allow yourself to be blessed with love for a few moments.

Now, the energy continues to expand and now moves into your throat chakra.

Feel this light expanding and filling your sky blue center to awaken your divine communication gifts.

Give yourself permission to open up and embrace the energy of your intuitive gifts with conscious breathe, in and out. Feel your throat chakra being healed, balanced and opened.

Begin to sense the energy around you as all your chakras continue to open and expand. Breathe in and affirm: *I am a clear channel and express my divine truth.*

Now, become aware of your third eye as the light continues to expand and move up your body. Breathe in and out as the light fills this indigo colored chakra. Allowing your energy center to be healed, balanced and opened. Giving yourself permission to see the divine spiritual realm.

Feel your third eye expanding and connecting to Spirit as you breathe and affirm: *It is safe for me to see. I am a gifted clairvoyant.*

Feel your entire body expanding with every breath you take, in and out. Begin to feel your entire energy body expand and beginning to embrace Spirit now. Allow the liquid light to continue to fill your being from deep within the earth all the way to the top of your crown.

The Gift Within the Darkness

See and feel the light filling your purple crown chakra to heal, balance and awaken you to the wisdom of your Soul. Affirm: I am wise. I am connected. I am awakened fully. I am one with all of creation now.

Feel yourself connected and one with all of creation for the next moment or two. Just relaxing, breathing and allowing yourself be one with the universe as you do so.

When you are ready to move forward, take a deep breath and invite one of your heavenly loved ones to come closer to you now. Feel both your energy fields blending as one. In this space, you are now ready to have an open communication with them.

Now is your opportunity to say anything you need to get off your chest with them. You are in a safe environment without judgment here. Take the time to ask questions and let your soul receive the answers. Be mindful of everything you see, hear, feel and think as your loved ones will use all your abilities to communicate with you.

Let yourself feel whatever you feel and if you need to cry, let it out. This can be a very healing process for you.

Note: You may think you are making things up at first. You may pass things off as wishful thinking or your imagination running wild. You may even be blocked at first with expectations or your mind overanalyzing everything.

Just relax and sit with your loved ones. Nothing needs to be said physically for your soul to receive the healing and information you need energetically. When you are ready on all levels of your being, you will have a very open and real divine communication.

Now ask your loved ones if they have a message for someone else who could benefit from hearing from them. Let them share this information with you, including who it is for, when or how best to deliver it to this person.

Relax and allow the energy to be shared through your soul connection. You need not try too hard or force something to happen. Your soul is now receiving and you will be conscious of what you need to be at the divine moment and time.

Now it is your turn to receive once again. Ask your loved one if they have a message you need to hear which would serve your highest good.

Let yourself receive without judgment, questioning or over-analyzing what you are receiving. Just relax into the knowledge the soul understands it all. The message will be of your highest good for this moment and your life.

Now feel your loved one sending from their heart to yours, love and light. This energy will help you heal and reclaim your life. Feel these soul energies of yours returning to you and filling your heart. Feel yourself releasing all that no longer serves you as you breathe in and out.

When you are ready to come back and proceed with your day ahead, take a moment to give gratitude to your heavenly support team including your loved ones.

Know that your loved ones will remain ever present with you. Feel yourself and your heavenly loved ones energy field separating. See both of you in your private sacred space as this happens. Now take a moment to feel yourself pulling your energy back from Spirit as you begin to prepare to come back to the awareness of the room around you.

Feel yourself pulling the energy down through each of the chakras as you adjust each of them back to their natural size. Feeling all the excess energy pushing down through your feet into mother earth.

Let go of everything that isn't your personal energy, returning it to the earth to be transmuted back to love.

Know as you do this, you will remain connected to your soul and to your spiritual support crew. Your loved ones will continue to walk by your side as you continue to process and move forward in life.

Let us give thanks to your angels, guides and loved ones for everything you have received through this reconnection process. Let us give thanks for the continued healing and improvement of everything in your life, as you continue process on a heart and soul level now.

***Note:** I recommend doing this meditation whenever you feel you wish to have a divine communication with one or more of your heavenly loved ones.*

The audio version of this meditation can be found on the author's upcoming meditation CD entitled: Meditations for a Grieving Heart. (Early Fall 2018)

Continue to explore and learn while connecting through this meditation with your angels, guides and even your higher self. This meditation is a great opportunity to explore and learn more about your true nature as a soul having a human experience.

CHAPTER 41

IN CONCLUSION

KNOW THAT AS YOU continue forward on your journey, your grief will subside, little by little. It won't ever truly go away and often will come in waves. But it will lessen to the point where you will have more good days than sad, I promise you.

Take to heart the most powerful messages your loved ones offered you throughout this book. Know anytime you need to hear from your loved ones you can open up the book to any page and receive a message perfect for you right then. Let this be a reference book where your heavenly support crew can continue to bless you with gifts for as long as you need it so.

It is my hope and prayer by reading this book you found healing and enlightenment to help your grieving heart. I pray that you feel lighter each day and soon you see the gifts within your version of darkness.

I can assure you that by implementing the provided information, energy and techniques into your daily routine the quality of your life will improve divinely. As you continue to work through your grief your loved ones will continue to be right by your side.

In time, as the energy lifts within your heart and mind, you shall begin to feel and connect with them more regularly. You too can have daily conversations with heaven and receive the direct guidance that is sure to light up your own personal heaven on earth. Use and practice the tools regularly contained within this book to help make it so.

Remember your heavenly family and friends are always watching over and participating in your life. Make each day a reason for them to celebrate with you by living your life fully in their honor and memory. This truly will make their heart sing with joy and happiness. I know it won't be easy at times but know they want this more than you want it for yourself. Let's make them proud, one day at a time.

From my heart and soul to yours, I love and appreciate the opportunity to be of service for you. Thank you for allowing me in your home, hearts and life.

Call to Action

Join us today on the Author's Official Facebook Author page to stay informed about upcoming events, book signings and any other book news.

While you are on the page, you will be well supported by others that understand what you are experiencing yourself. Be sure you take time to interact and connect with those who contributed their stories within this book and myself while there.

Remember, you are never alone on this journey. Death and the grief that accompanies it touches everyone at some point in our lives.

Let today be the day that you take time to reach out to share your story and ask for help when you need it most. Whether through the Facebook page or a local Bereavement Support group it is a gift of love to connect.

You never need to go it alone. We are all here for you. After all, we are in this together.

About the Author

Brian D. Calhoun is an international Psychic-Medium, Reiki master, energy worker, inspirational teacher and coach who was raised in the city with the literal heart of gold: Timmins, Ontario. He has dedicated his life to bringing messages of love and light to people around the world for over 18 years. He now lives in Ottawa, with his cat, Indigo.

His skill at what he does, has meant that he is regularly called upon to contribute to articles, magazines and books on various subjects. He has also released guided meditation CD's and appeared on radio and television.

Brian also has a flourishing writing career and is an International Bestselling co-author of several books including: Guided by the Light: Following Your Angelic Guides; 365 Life Shifts: Pivotal Moments that Changed Everything and HALO: Lighting up Heaven on Earth.

His upcoming works include: Meditations for the Grieving Heart Audio CD (Early 2018), Heavenly Guidance for Daily Living (2018), and The Cottage Cheese Effect (2019)

Brian's aim in life is to help as many people as possible around the world, to live a connected and heavenly life where all their hopes, aspirations and dreams are realized daily. To him, everyone has their own spiritual beliefs, and he asks all to trust in the higher power that is the highest level of God of their own understanding, while keeping an open mind and heart.

He hopes to one day have his own world-renowned Spiritual Retreat Centre where people would go to relax, learn, heal and connect with many International Teachers, Healers and more.

When he has time to himself, Brian enjoys many of the creative arts, cooking, meditating, walking, spending time in nature and keeping active. He also loves adventure and travel, has swam with wild dolphins in Hawaii, and he is passionate about being involved in community matters, volunteering for various groups whenever he can.

Be sure to follow Brian D. Calhoun to see what is writing about next through his social media accounts and on his website at:

www.BrianDCalhoun.com

Facebook & Twitter: @BrianDCalhoun

Instagram: @BrianDCalhoun_Author

www.ingramcontent.com/pod-product-compliance
Lightning Source LLC
Chambersburg PA
CBHW030901080526
44589CB00010B/94